LIVES OF
CRIME

LIVES OF

The Melbourne gangland murders and other tales of true crime

CRIME

Gary Tippet & Ian Munro

 HarperCollins*Publishers*

HarperCollins*Publishers*

First published in Australia in 2008
by HarperCollins*Publishers* Australia Pty Limited
ABN 36 009 913 517
www.harpercollins.com.au

HarperCollins*Publishers*
25 Ryde Road, Pymble, Sydney, NSW 2073, Australia
31 View Road, Glenfield, Auckland 10, New Zealand
77–85 Fulham Palace Road, London, W6 8JB, United Kingdom
2 Bloor Street East, 20th floor, Toronto, Ontario M4W 1A8, Canada
10 East 53rd Street, New York NY 10022, USA

National Library of Australia Cataloguing-in-Publication data:

Tippet, Gary.
  Lives of crime.
  ISBN 978 0 7322 8609 5.
  1. Criminals - Australia - Case studies. 2. Crime -
  Australia - Case studies. I. Munro, Ian W. II. Title.
364.994

Map on cover courtesy of Ausway Group
Cover design by Michael Donohue
Internal design by HarperCollins Design Studio
Typeset in 11/15.5 Giovanni Book by Kirby Jones
Printed and bound in Australia by Griffin Press

79gsm Bulky Paperback White used by HarperCollins*Publishers* is a natural, recyclable
product made from wood grown in a combination of sustainable plantation and
regrowth forests. It also contains up to a 20% portion of recycled fibre. The
manufacturing processes conform to the environmental regulations in Tasmania, the
place of manufacture.

5 4 3 2   08 09 10 11

CONTENTS

THE DEAD DUCK LIVES

O ut of nowhere, he produced the gun.

There was the conversation. Then, there was the gun.

From somewhere inside that tight T-shirt, or those three-quarter track pants, came the gun. A six-shot revolver, like the ones kids use to play cowboys.

A .38 calibre. Not an ugly little snub nose. Not a cannon-like Magnum. But full of lethal menace all the same.

The big man made a lunge for the gun at the end of the tattooed arm and the world exploded.

It was the loudest noise he had ever heard, and something burned the air alongside his left ear.

Dominic Gatto was still grabbing for the gun, wrapping both his paws around the little man's gun hand.

'I had hold of his hand with both my hands and just pushed it towards him,' Gatto said later. 'I have got to be honest; I thought I was a dead duck.'

As he forced the revolver back against the little man, Gatto felt himself toppling forward. He was trying to hold the little man's trigger finger in place, trying to force it to squeeze out another shot.

He did not fall, but pressed the gun towards the little man

and the world exploded once more. And again, and again and again, showering the pair of them with burned cordite.

Andrew Veniamin, alleged hitman and all-round Melbourne western suburbs bad boy, lay on his back, a lake of blood forming behind his head and soaking his shirt.

A scorch mark on his chest told of the closeness of one shot that either sheared his carotid artery, or severed his spinal cord, its ultimate path unclear.

Despite the severed carotid, there was not much blood spray on the walls, just the growing spill behind his prone body. A third bullet had entered his head above the right ear, bounced off the interior of his skull and drilled through his brain. But all that became known later.

Gatto eased the gun from Veniamin's grip and walked out of the passageway, through the kitchen towards the restaurant area of La Porcella, an unremarkable faux Italian restaurant in inner-city Carlton, which he treated as his office.

He had the revolver, a Smith & Wesson, in his right hand. With his free hand, he tested his left ear.

He told his mates that Veniamin had said he had killed his close friend and gangster Graham Kinniburgh three months earlier, and now he had tried to kill Gatto too.

'Can you believe it? He killed Graham and he told me he was going to kill me,' someone remembered Gatto saying, before asking if his ear was bleeding.

Gatto slipped a little Sterling .25 calibre pistol, his own gun bought from the now-deceased drug king pin Lewis Moran, out of his right trouser pocket and palmed it to a friend, telling him to look after it. (Pity that Lewis sold it. There was a night in March 2004 when two gunmen came charging through the front doors of the Brunswick Club on busy Sydney Road – Lewis' preferred drinking hole – that he could have used some hardware of any calibre at all.)

Anyway, there would be no mention of this little gun for nine months, until it became clear that Gatto's story of self-defence was not believed, and that he would be tried for murder.

There were two Dominic Gattos who appeared during the Supreme Court trial for the killing of Andrew Veniamin in May 2005, 14 months after Veniamin died.

To begin there was the tall and trim Gatto, capped with a helmet of greying hair, and eased into a well-cut business suit. When the jury was absent, this Gatto conducted audiences with the retinue of family and associates that arranged themselves behind him each day.

His wife, his brother John and his wife, sometimes his children – young adults – were there, while above, in the public gallery were the usual court watchers and non-family Gatto supporters. These included building industry workers in their union windcheaters and non-industry types in dark shirts and gold jewellery.

Once the talking was done Gatto would turn back to the court, draw himself to his full height, fill his chest and run his thumbs around his belt line to prepare for the next court session.

And sometimes, when the jury was present, this Gatto could not suppress himself. So when the prosecutor held aloft the six-shot revolver that killed Veniamin, and assured the jurors not to be afraid, the gun had been rendered harmless, this Gatto smirked and lowered his head too late to hide his amusement. And as the prosecutor related the story of how Veniamin was shot, this Gatto turned to smile encouragingly at his family. Despite 14 months in custody, he had the air of a man at ease, and enjoying himself.

This Gatto speaks in aphorisms, such as 'you don't know what's in a man's heart'. Interviewed at the restaurant two months before the shooting, he said this to police while referring to Veniamin.

The cops were investigating three underworld shootings, including the murder of Gatto's best friend, Graham Kinniburgh, known as 'The Munster' for his resemblance to the 1960s American TV character Herman Munster.

Kinniburgh was gunned down outside his home in the comfortable, leafy suburb of Kew soon after midnight on 13 December 2003. It looked like a professional hit, although The Munster managed to fire a shot before his attacker finished him off.

Another expression this Gatto relied on was 'you never get into trouble minding your own business'. This was to explain why he lied to police, telling them he knew and had heard nothing about who was responsible for the murders of Kinniburgh and two others.

Another was 'keep your friends close, and your enemies closer'.

If this last saying sounds familiar it may be because it was previously delivered by Al Pacino in his *Godfather Part II* role as Michael Corleone, a character ruthless with enemies. Yet when Gatto said those same words, it sounded as if he had made the expression his own. He was trying to justify having stayed in contact with Veniamin long after he had ceased to trust him.

In the witness box Gatto was charismatic and persuasive, but also aggressive when crossed and revealing of a lifestyle where carrying a gun is as routine as donning a business suit.

The other Dominic Gatto was in the court only briefly, captured on a security videotape at Crown Casino. This Gatto appeared drinking and talking at a bar, a bear of a man, dressed in a vast short-sleeved shirt that shrouded him like a curtain.

This Gatto, 30 kilograms heavier than the man who faced the jury, was the one that confronted the diminutive 168-centimetre Veniamin at the moment of his death.

This Gatto was captured on camera during their casino 'peace conference', called days after Kinniburgh's murder. Veniamin had to stretch to put his heavily tattooed arm around Gatto, and to offer him the obligatory kiss of greeting and farewell.

This Gatto made another appearance, on another videotape. During this second recording, at the homicide squad's office, he is seen distractedly inspecting his fingernails during police questioning while a few kilometres away, in a passageway at the rear of Carlton's La Porcella restaurant, investigators picked their way around Veniamin's still-cooling body.

They had been friends, Gatto and Veniamin. And Gatto's mates were friendly with him, too. Steve Kaya had known the dead man most of his life. Faruk Orman said he had retreated from his friendship with Veniamin in the 18 months before his death because he was crazier and even more out of control than when Orman was close to him:

'Like, he was always unpredictable, you know, but he just got a lot worse.'

Orman and Kaya, who knew Veniamin from his days growing up around Sunshine in Melbourne's western suburbs, and the late Ron Bongetti – like Kinniburgh, a father figure to Gatto – were there the day Gatto shot Veniamin dead.

While there were two Gattos, there really was only one Andrew Veniamin.

According to prosecutor Geoff Horgan, SC, the 28-year-old from Sunshine was 'not a particularly nice man'.

While the defence agreed, they offered a more graphic description of a murderous, psychopathic thug. This was despite Kaya describing Veniamin as a friend and a nice type of lad. He had known Veniamin through Veniamin's parents who, as with Kaya himself, originated from Cyprus.

Kaya, like Veniamin, is a mere 168 centimetres tall, but lightly framed where Veniamin had the sort of muscularity that can only be found in a gym. And unlike Veniamin, Kaya, who identifies as a company director, dresses formally in dark blue pinstripes.

Kaya related how he had to talk Veniamin out of a shooting rampage at the St Kilda Road police complex after a police raid on his mother's house turned up one of his revolvers which police seized.

And it was Kaya who negotiated a payment to Veniamin so that he would abandon his bid to kill a man who beat up his brother in a Melbourne nightclub. The man bought his life with $20,000.

Kaya knew plenty about Veniamin. Everyone in Sunshine knew something. Sure, murder was one of his first resorts, and Veniamin liked .38 calibre revolvers because they don't jam.

Police believe that even before Faruk Orman decided he was too crazy to be around, Veniamin had murdered a prominent Mafia figure Frank Benvenuto at his Beaumaris home in May 2000, and drug dealer Dino Dibra outside his West Sunshine home five months later. Two other killings, of his former friend Paul Kallipolitis, whose body was found in his West Sunshine home in October 2002, and Nik Radev – a drug dealer and standover thug, killed in Coburg on 15 April 2003 – came in what Orman assessed as Veniamin's crazy time: the last 18 months of his life.

Senior Constable Boris Buick, an investigator for the Purana Taskforce – an operation set up to investigate Melbourne's gangland killings – identified three stages in Veniamin's criminal life: 'Phase one he was part of the Sunshine crew, where he and others, Paul Kallipolitis, Dino Dibra, were running amok, out of control. In these Sunshine days Veniamin, with Dibra, were raiding "crop houses", used for growing hydroponic crops of marijuana and committing frequent acts of violence.'

Veniamin graduated to hanging around Gatto's group briefly, but soon found more action further north of Melbourne with amphetamines dealer Carl Williams.

'Then there was the phase where he moved into the Gatto group … and away from the Sunshine group,' said Senior Constable Buick. 'And it was during this phase that he came to the interest of the Purana Taskforce. And as the Purana Taskforce began to look at him it became obvious to us that he was moving, or had moved into the Williams camp, and out of the Gatto camp. And it was at this time that we began to target him fervently.'

Veniamin looked fit and toned, but was not as healthy as his appearance suggested. He was often in pain, and had recently been hospitalised after repeated bouts of pancreatitis. He had a brother, Stephen, who had done time in prison, but it was Andrew police identified as 'a shooter'. Police intelligence reports suggested Andrew Veniamin had an undefined psychiatric illness and was inclined to snap into violence, particularly in the company of peers and associates.

The defence compounded this impression when it produced as a witness Pasquale Zaffina, whose misfortune had been to lose a girlfriend to Veniamin.

They had arranged a meeting in a park to settle the matter with their fists, or so Zaffina thought. But Veniamin, dressed in a T-shirt and track pants similar to those in which he died, produced a revolver from behind his back and, in a struggle, Zaffina was shot three times.

From Gatto's perspective, this showed Veniamin's ability to hide a weapon in the sort of clothes he wore at La Porcella, but there was nothing in Zaffina's account that suggested Veniamin turned his back, potentially displaying the hidden weapon to his victim before reaching for the gun. Whereas at La Porcella he reputedly led Gatto out to the passageway.

The fervent targeting of Andrew Veniamin included listening devices bugging his telephone calls and a tracking device installed in his car. The phone bugs showed that even as he moved closer to Carl Williams, Veniamin maintained his relationship with Gatto.

In conversations beginning in July 2003, and continuing to the day of the shooting, they were 'buddy' and 'mate' and 'champ' to one another in calls overheard on Veniamin's phone. They had little to say, but they made it as amiable as possible. What is also clear, through the self-conscious bonhomie, is Gatto's seniority to the fawning, eager-to-please Veniamin.

In the days before the shooting, the mood between them had openly changed, with Gatto asking of Veniamin: 'Hey, what's happened to you? ... You given me the arse? ... I haven't heard from you for a month.' The reason for the change was the murder of Gatto's good friend and old style crook, Graham 'The Munster' Kinniburgh.

Gatto called the Crown Casino peace conference to 'clear the air' with Veniamin and Williams. The phone contact diminished after that. Gatto was worried that he might be the next victim of the underworld shootings and said he rang Veniamin 'just so I could keep tabs on him'. There was a brief call on 23 March 2004 when Gatto summoned Veniamin to La Porcella.

He arrived in his trademark track pants and T-shirt. According to Gatto's defence, somewhere in there was a .38 calibre revolver. According to the prosecution, police surveillance on Veniamin was so rigorous he could not afford to be carrying a firearm in his car or his clothing. If so, then he had minimal time to arm himself – the phone call that beckoned him to La Porcella came just on two o'clock, and he arrived there six minutes later.

According to the prosecution everything that happens is at Gatto's instigation: Veniamin's visit, the private chat, the walk out to the private, narrow passageway.

On Gatto's account, however, after 20 minutes or so Veniamin kicked him underneath the table and gestured that he wanted to speak privately. Once in the passageway, Veniamin complained that he was hearing rumours Gatto still blamed him for Kinniburgh's death.

Gatto reminded him of two of his mates he had killed – Dibra and Kallipolitis – and told him not to come around any more. 'I was looking at him in the eyes and his face went all funny and he sort of stepped back and he said – he said, "We had to kill Graham",' Gatto related.

'I didn't see where he pulled the gun from, but he stepped back. He had a gun. I just lunged at him. I had hold of his hand with both my hands and … he had his hands on the trigger and I just forced his hands, squeezed his hands to force him to pull the trigger.'

Prosecutor Geoff Horgan, SC, rejected Gatto's account. 'If Veniamin had wanted to kill him, he could not have missed. Confined space, huge man, he doesn't see the gun drawn, all Veniamin's got to do is pull the trigger. As simple as that,' Horgan said.

The central issue was who carried the .38 into La Porcella. No-one claimed Veniamin went there with the intent to kill Gatto. If that is right, then why would he be carrying a gun at all, given that he was under surveillance?

Could Veniamin have disguised it in his light clothing? Would the Carlton Crew have allowed him to?

Senior Constable Buick said Veniamin's track pants were fitted with a drawstring. If left untied it would have been impossible to retain a .38 revolver and still walk around. If the drawstring was tied it would have made it difficult to retrieve the revolver quickly. It might have been a significant detail, but no note was made of the state of the drawstring when Veniamin was undressed at the morgue.

As unpredictably violent as Veniamin was, not only did Gatto's mates say they did not see the bulge of a gun when he arrived at the restaurant, they said they were not looking for one. Really? A man they believed had killed at least six, maybe eight people; is violent, moody, unpredictable; juiced-up on drugs; and who they believed had killed Gatto's best friend? This very man they suspect might have Gatto in his sights walks into view and they don't look for a gun? They dropped their guard that much?

If so, it can only be that they thought coming armed onto Gatto's turf was too much even for Veniamin. As it happened, the defence did not claim Veniamin arrived intending to kill Gatto, but that he 'snapped' during a confrontation.

Other mates came into play. Brian 'Mickey' Finn (an emaciated septuagenarian and La Porcella regular) said Gatto handed him a .25 calibre pistol for safekeeping after the shooting. The subtext to this is that if Gatto had a .25 pistol then the .38 revolver was Veniamin's. But Finn did not come forward for nine months, and then only because he thought it would 'look good for Gatto' if he did so.

Another man, kebab shop owner Halil Sertli, said Veniamin had stored a cache of weapons at his shop which he had retrieved shortly before a police raid 11 days before the shooting.

Subtext: Veniamin still had access to a .38 revolver. But Sertli did not come forward for 12 months and then only at the urging of Faruk Orman.

If human testimony was sometimes problematic, the scientific evidence was inconclusive. Gatto said the struggle continued until the last shot was fired. But the dead man had no defensive wounds.

The neck wounds came from point-blank range, or close to it. The gun was an arm's length away when Veniamin was shot in the head – an awkward prospect if Veniamin still gripped the gun.

Pathologist Malcolm Dodd said the severing of the spinal cord would mean almost instant collapse. Dodd, however, agreed that Veniamin might have been able to remain briefly upright and to have fought on if the head and carotid artery wounds were suffered first, but in that case more blood would have been expected on the passageway walls. And the lack of blood on the lower legs and feet also suggested immediate collapse.

The non-crippling neck wound would have caused immediate difficulty breathing, choking, and possibly suffocating Veniamin with his own blood.

The prosecution argument ran that heavy deposits of gun-shot residue on Gatto's lower trouser legs and damage to the floor suggested a shot – which actually missed – fired downwards at the dying man. Patches of saturated blood below the knees of his pants suggested he had knelt near the body to fire a shot into the wall for appearances sake.

But the webbing of Veniamin's right hand – between thumb and forefinger – was coated in residue in the classic shooter's position, and residue was also found on the inside band of his boxer shorts. This might have suggested a recently-fired gun had been carried there, but for the fact that it seems the boxer shorts could have been contaminated with residue when his body was undressed at the morgue.

The residue on his hand might suggest he was holding the pistol, but it may also have been deposited if he had been trying to wrest the gun from Gatto when he was shot.

Veniamin's DNA – some of which resulted from blood spatter, but some of which may not have been from blood – was around the trigger of the revolver. Gatto's DNA was all over his .25 calibre pistol, but not at all on the revolver which he admitted handling.

It remained unclear in what order Veniamin suffered his injuries.

It was a case that seemed to lack for certainties, but there is this: even now, with police assurances that Veniamin could not have killed Kinniburgh because he was at that time on the other side of town, Gatto remains convinced of his malevolence and is unapologetic.

'I'm not convinced that he didn't do it,' Gatto said later, 'but I'm certainly sure of one thing, that he was part of it.' Besides, Gatto believes, if anyone else had done the job on Veniamin, they'd have been given a key to the city.

The police argued that Gatto's story does not ring true: more likely that he would draw Veniamin to his home turf, than that Veniamin would go in trying to hide a one-kilogram weapon in those light clothes.

But then, there is one more truism that Mick Gatto might adopt: 'history is written by the victors'.

'TIL DEATH US DO PART

On the barest telling of the events – and it's not the facts that are in dispute here – the killing of Frank Osland was just one more sordid domestic murder.

What happened in Bendigo on the night of Wednesday 30 July 1991, was this: about 4.45 pm Frank Osland arrived home from his job at the Waterfall Quarries in Axedale, 20 kilometres to the east, foul-tempered and belligerent as usual. In the words of his wife Heather: 'He was in a real shit-o again.'

Heather made a curry for dinner and, some time between six and seven, they and Heather's son David Albion sat down in the kitchen to eat. Frank was served first. That was another given in the Osland household: no-one touched their food until Frank was good and ready.

What was different this night was that Heather had crushed six or seven Prothiaden antidepressant capsules and mixed them into Frank's curry. He only ate half before pushing his plate away. The meal was shit, he said, and went outside to his shed.

He was back in 10, maybe 15 minutes, stumbling up the kitchen steps. He sat at the table and began to nod off, his head sinking into his hands. Abruptly, he stood up, pushed back his chair and stomped off into his bedroom.

A look passed between Heather and David. The young man went out to the shed and found a length of metal pipe. When they looked inside the bedroom, Frank seemed to be asleep. 'I'll do it, David,' said Heather.

'No, Mum,' he answered, 'you're not strong enough.'

David lifted the pipe and brought it down on his stepfather's skull with all his force. Frank's eyes opened and he said 'Fuck'. It was the last word he ever spoke.

David hit him again and they held him down until the body stopped twitching. There was so much blood, David said later, that he had to put his whole palm into the wound to staunch the flow until his mother could slide a plastic bag over Frank's head.

Later they put the body into the back of Heather's Laser and drove to a clearing in the bush near Maiden Gully, about eight kilometres west of town. Earlier that day they had spent hours there digging a grave, waist-deep and coffin-shaped. Now, in the rain, they pushed Frank in, face-down, and covered him up.

In the early hours next morning, David drove his stepfather's Holden station wagon 150 kilometres to a truck stop in Campbellfield, on the northern outskirts of Melbourne, and dumped it. His mother, who had followed in her car, drove him home. Two days later Heather went to the police and reported her husband as a missing person.

They did what they did, Heather said later, just to get rid of 'all the shit out of our life'. The shit being Frank.

Years later, after his dust and bones had been recovered from his shallow grave, others spoke in kinder – although not much kinder – terms of Frank Osland. At Heather and David's murder trial in the Bendigo Supreme Court in September 1996, prosecutor Bill Morgan-Payler told the jury: 'It certainly seems not to have been a perfect marriage. Frank Osland seems not to have been the ideal spouse.

'What's new, says the Crown?'

Frank and Heather's marriage was not the same as any other. And yet it was too similar to too many.

It began in Karratha in the dust and dry heat of north-west Western Australia in 1977. Heather Albion, separated mother of four from Adelaide, had gone to the blistered company town for a holiday with a girlfriend. Outside the supermarket one afternoon she bumped into Frank Osland, a mine worker for Hamersley Iron.

Heather had grown up, comfortably middle class, in Bendigo where her father was a grocer and her mother was a knitting mill overlocker and, for a time, president of her local lawn bowls club. She'd gone to Camp Hill Primary and Bendigo High before completing a secretarial course, and attended Methodist, Presbyterian and Anglican churches. She had met Frank Osland in 1970, when he worked with her then husband Alan. Now, their friendship rekindled into holiday romance, and Heather soon returned to Adelaide, sold her business, packed the kids, Sharon, Erica, Paul and David, aged between seven and 12, into her car and headed back to Karratha and Frank.

She thought she loved him, she told Justice John Hedigan at her trial: he didn't drink, gamble or follow the horses, he just worked hard. He was ambitious and keen on gardening.

'I thought he'd be someone special to look up to, a good father figure for the children …

'After a couple of weeks he showed his true colours.'

Frank was a big man, 16 stone in Heather's measure, while she was only five foot three. He stood over her, laying down the law about what she and the kids could and couldn't do. It was a long list. He said she wasn't allowed out of the house and took her car keys and removed the distributor cap from her car to keep her there. Nor could the kids have friends around. His was the first plate on the table and no-one ate until he was ready, even if the food went cold. She had to wash with Solvol because he didn't like the perfume smell of soap. She couldn't have a shower unless he'd had one first, couldn't wear shorts or make-up, always had to wear a bra.

'He said I'd just be slutting around like his mother.'

Heather said he regularly beat her and, sometimes, the children. Once he dragged her youngest daughter, Erica, into the house by her ears and when Heather intervened he turned on her. 'He threw me onto the bed and started punching the shit out of me,' she said, '… in my stomach, in my ribs, in my head.' There was some form of violence – slapping, poking or pinching – every few days and sometimes he'd drag her into the bedroom and begin punching.

'Then he'd decide he was going to do his other bits and pieces on me … he always liked anal sex.' She said she'd beg him to stop, but he wouldn't: 'I think it made him more powerful.'

All the while there were constant threats. She said he would tower over her like a big gorilla, 'point his finger about three inches from my nose and threaten me. He'd kill me, he'd kill my children, he'd chop me up … I've heard it 101 times how he was going to kill me and the kids.'

Once, when she left him after they moved to Bendigo in 1980, he said he could get to the children. 'He said he'd chop them up and send them back to me in the mail and if I loved them enough I'd be able to stick them back together again.'

Heather believed him. In Karratha, she said, he 'belted shit' out of his Staffordshire terrier, Adam. 'I locked myself in the bathroom,' said Heather. 'I'd never seen such violence in my life before, especially cruelty to an animal.' The dog had to be put down.

On another occasion he killed a neighbour's cat with a piece of pipe when she and the children took refuge at their house, saying he'd do the same to the neighbours. Heather's youngest son, Paul, told how he ripped the heads off the children's budgerigars.

Erica said the kids were terrified of him. He used to give them what became known as the Osland glare. 'Out of 10, I'd give him an eight on scariness,' she said later.

Once, as the family tried to leave, he pointed a rifle at Heather's head, saying if she walked out the door she'd be killing them all. That night a policeman found the rifle fully loaded with the safety catch off.

'Some of it sounds too bad, too horrible, too horrifying to be true,' Heather's barrister, Felicity Hampel, told the jury at the opening of her murder trial. 'Some of you will think … why did she put up with it for so long? Some of it will make you think: why didn't she leave him?

'She did. Time and time and time again. But every time she left he'd follow her and she would go back because she was terrified for herself and terrified for her children.'

In fact, Heather left Frank Osland at least eight times. Once she threatened to seek restraining orders against him, but changed her mind when he told her that a bullet goes further than an intervention order.

At one stage, while she was living away from him in a unit, he kept threatening to bomb her car or burn down her flat. 'I was always frightened to turn the ignition on … thinking I was going to explode.'

Yet, on 24 November 1984, they married. Heather had holidayed in the United States and when she flew home, Frank was waiting at the airport. He'd sent her flowers while she was in America. 'He said he missed me while I was away and then he promised he'd change. It had taken him the whole nine weeks to realise that.

'He always reckoned his jealousy and moods were because I was still an Albion, I didn't belong to him.'

Heather accepted his proposal and for the few months before the wedding she was happy. But when she arrived at the church he looked her up and down. She was wearing a cream, lace-top frock and a hat with little pearls hanging down over her face. He didn't like the hat and said she looked like shit.

The violence resumed and for the next seven years Heather would wear black eyes and choke marks under caked-on make-up. She left, or was thrown out, a number of times, but she would always return. She said she knew she couldn't get away.

'She would go back because she didn't know any other sort of life, because she was totally subjected and subjugated to him,' said Ms Hampel.

Heather Osland, she said, had been diagnosed as suffering from battered-woman syndrome. It was on this rarely used defence that her plea of not guilty hung: despite the lack of any immediate threat but 'goaded beyond endurance by a life of hell', she believed she had no option but to kill Frank in self-defence.

What exactly is a battered woman? Forensic psychologist Dr Kenneth Byrne told the court it was 'a woman who has been forced, usually by a man, to comply with his wishes without regard to her rights by physical abuse and sometimes by psychological abuse'.

Dr Byrne said such physical abuse could range from pinching, pushing or pulling hair 'at one end of the spectrum' to severe beatings and brutal assaults at the other.

He said there were nine types of psychological abuse used: social isolation, by controlling the woman's movements or contacts; exhaustion, by depriving her of sleep or food; threats of death or sometimes torture; control of the way women perceive reality; interfering with their ability to think clearly, through abuse, violence or isolation; holding out false hope; humiliation; forcing her to use drugs or alcohol; and repeated sexual abuse.

Typical characteristics of such relationships are that the battered woman is initially surprised by the abuse; the assaults are unpredictable; overwhelming jealousy; bizarre sexual behaviour; and that the woman conceals the abuse, typically believing it is her fault.

They also include the use of weapons to instil terror; the woman's belief in the omnipotence of the man; and, finally, her belief, in her heart, that he could and would kill her.

Battering men, Dr Byrne said, suffered low self-esteem covered up with bravado. They confused sex with aggression, believed women were inferior, and deserved to be beaten, and had a Jekyll-and-Hyde personality.

As a result, battered women develop both 'learnt hopelessness', where they became submissive and learnt to put up with their lot, and 'learnt hopefulness', where they believed their men would one day change for the better.

It was a bland and clinical explanation, conveying little of the horror that Heather Osland testified her husband had subjected her to. Nevertheless, Dr Byrne testified that Frank Osland seemed 'at the extreme end of the severe battering male ... [with] a degree of callousness and a degree of brutality which is, in my view, quite extreme'. Heather, he added, fitted the profile of a battered woman 'like a glove'.

But, in the end, the defence was to little avail. While the jury was to accept the evidence that Heather was a battered woman, other aspects of her behaviour, before and after the killing, were to weigh more heavily against her.

Just a couple of hours after Heather and David arrived home from dumping the station wagon, three workmates from Frank's car pool had arrived at the door to collect him. Heather said she couldn't find him, that he must already have gone to another quarry he would sometimes be called to.

Two days later, when he still hadn't turned up, she reported him to Bendigo police as a missing person and his car was listed as a 'wanted vehicle'. About the same time she collected his outstanding pay. When his car was recovered in September, she collected it and traded it in on a new car for herself. In April 1992, she held a clearing sale and made $6634 from his tools and equipment. About February 1994 she instructed her solicitor to begin divorce proceedings against her absent spouse.

It wasn't unusual for Frank to pack up and head off somewhere without telling her and she had let people know that. Once he had taken off without saying a word to go to an Expo in Queensland. Heather kept intermittent contact with the police, at one stage telling them she suspected he might have been transporting drugs interstate and that might explain his disappearance. A bloke had been coming around saying Frank owed him $10,000 for drugs, she claimed.

The pretence was to go on for three-and-a-half years. 'Things had gone fairly well from the accused's point of view,' said Mr Morgan-Payler later.

But not so well for David Albion. A few months after the killing, he had confessed to his brother. They were at Paul's house in Nolan Street, Bendigo. 'We were just drinking and having a bit of a laugh and that's when he came out and said: "Paul, I've done something silly. I've helped Mum knock off me stepfather",' Paul told the court.

He blurted out the details of the pills, how they 'smashed' Frank over the skull and how they had to put a plastic bag over his head because there was so much blood. 'I cried. I got upset,' said Paul.

And he talked.

Around Christmas that year Heather called a family conference. 'Paul was accusing Mum of killing Frank and Mum wanted to get it out on the table once and for all,' remembered Sharon. 'Paul sort of spread it 'round the whole town, telling his friends and that sort of thing.' Heather said it wasn't true and Paul became angry and stormed out.

But the gossip wouldn't go away and in September 1994, the Victoria Police missing persons unit began investigating Frank's disappearance. They placed phone intercepts and later a listening device inside Heather's home. Meanwhile the police Crime Stoppers program placed a story on Frank's disappearance in the local paper, the *Bendigo Advertiser*, and detectives began searching bushland nearby.

Heather was getting spooked. Yes, she told a journalist, she was a suspect: 'Well, that's what they are making me out to be anyway.' She told a friend: 'Paul's dobbed me in to the police to say that I've murdered Frank … I'm not joking, how could Paul do this to me?'

In December, some reporters arrived at the door to say bones had been found during a search. They weren't Frank's, but as she told a friend that afternoon – with the police tapped into the phone – 'I just about fell shitless through the floor, I felt so sick.'

On 12 January, Heather was arrested. Homicide squad detective Sergeant Anthony John Thatcher drove her towards Melbourne, leaving her home about 3.40 pm. Around Harcourt, 30 kilometres down the Calder Highway, he noticed she was becoming upset. She said she wanted to tell him something.

'You want me to say I did it, don't you?' she said.

'All I want to know is the truth,' he replied.

'Well, all right, I did it. I want to tell you about it.'

'What?'

'Killed Frank.'

Thatcher turned the car around and returned to Bendigo. In a short interview Heather said: 'We – I suppose you'd call the word "murdered" – him, isn't it? I don't call it murder.'

The detective asked when she first started to contemplate killing Frank. 'Just virtually the day before. We always wished he was gone, wished someone would kill him. He was a – just a menace …'

Others would later claim it went beyond wishing. Paul, who had spent two years in a South Australian jail, told the court that she had asked if he knew anybody who could get rid of Frank, or if he could do it himself. He refused. A friend, Bob Dalziel, told police she had once offered him $5000 to have Frank 'knocked'.

None of this was news to the investigators. Just lately, they knew, thanks to their listening devices, Heather had begun contemplating a similar fate for Paul.

'There's big trouble over here, David,' Heather had told her other son on 8 December, when he phoned her from his mining job in Western Australia. The police had interviewed Paul the previous morning, then they'd hauled Sharon in for four-and-a-half hours. Paul had told them she'd murdered Frank on her bed with a crowbar, she said.

That was ludicrous, she'd told Erica the day before: 'I won't even let anyone sit on me bloody bed, how could I *murder* anyone on me bloody bed?'

Three days later she spoke to David again. They needed to straighten out what he'd told Paul: 'You have to say that he was on smack … You have to say: "Right, well fair enough, I probably bloody well did say it." He, um, was big-notin' himself. He'd been in jail with armed robbery and he's gone on about Frank. And you've said in one breath: "Yeah … er, me and Mum, we fuckin' murdered Frank."

'You know? And you can't remember saying it, but he's

remembered sayin' it and he's just built on it and built on it and built on it.'

At first Heather had kept up the pretence of Frank's disappearance, even telling a journalist that she'd changed the locks so he couldn't get back in if he returned. But the constant police pressure proved too much and in late December she confessed to Erica, saying later that she felt much better for having unloaded it on her.

Perhaps she should go to the police and admit what happened, suggested her daughter. She'd heard about another woman who did something similar and only got seven-and-a-half months jail. 'I'm not going in there, Erica,' said Heather.

'They can't frighten me, Erica. I'm not admitting to it unless they get hold of the body.'

But she was frightened. And angry. 'I could fucking kill David for telling Paul,' the planted bug recorded her saying. 'Why didn't he just go out in the bush and fuckin' cry? He knows what fuckin' Paul's like … I could knock him rotten. If I thought he was going to be such a fucking sook over it.'

The next day they talked again. She told Erica how they'd buried Frank face-down and how they'd gone back the next day and she'd gone to 'a beautiful little creek' nearby where she gathered leaves, bark and orchids to cover the grave, and how she'd told David: 'He likes being buried here.'

Digging the grave had been hard work, said Heather. After hours it only came to her waist and she told David she wasn't digging any more. They should have spent another day at it: 'We couldn't go any deeper … We spent all day. We sat and planned it for a week.'

'Did you?'

'Yep. And then he goes and tells Paul.'

'Yeah,' said Erica. 'Fuckin' stupid, isn't he?'

Erica had told her mother that Bob Dalziel had offered to kill Paul and throw him down a mine shaft. 'He goes if Paul stands up in court against you … he's gonna get knocked.'

'Paul should find out all this,' said Heather.

'… that's what I want to tell him … I'll just say to him, "Look, I've heard if you stand up in court against Mum, Paul, you're going to get knocked".'

Heather told Erica that David was also threatening to kill his brother. 'David don't have to do it. He don't have to do it at all,' said Erica. '[Another friend] has been offering for a long time, Mum. It's not what you know, it's who you know.'

'I know, Erica, and I'd be really grateful to him,' said Heather. 'As far as I'm concerned, Paul's a fuckin' arsehole. He is … I feel very sorry for him. But the thing is, he could have kept his fuckin' mouth shut. It could have been a brother-to-brother secret …'

Erica should find Paul and tell him all this, and say: 'So you better retract your story,' said Heather. She should convince Paul that even if he gets four years for perjury, four years are better than none at all. She should tell him there's a lot of druggie people who respect his mum because she's not a gutter rat, she doesn't drink, doesn't root around. She knits, she crochets and 'she brought us up lovely with manners'.

And that if he stands up against his mum, he'll be dead before he even gets out of court.

'Yes, you'll have to frighten shit out of him,' said Heather.

Otherwise the police would keep searching and eventually stumble over Frank. In their whispered conversation the day before she'd predicted: 'They're going to find his whole forensic body out there, dead, the whole fucking lot.'

In the end she took them to him herself. After she was arrested on 12 January and confessed in the police car, she agreed to take detectives to the grave. At 6.43 that night Sergeant Thatcher began another tape-recorded interview on a dirt track off Durston's Road near Maiden's Gully. As they were speaking she walked them over to a spot near a tree with a forked trunk. 'It has to be here,' she said.

Frank Osland's remains were recovered the next day. His skull was grossly fractured and he had to be identified by his dental work.

Heather told the police she'd done it because of 'the violence, the mental stuff', but added: 'I'm no murderer.' It wasn't about murder, she said, 'just getting rid of all the shit out of our life … I don't call it murder'.

David Albion had been arrested by Western Australian police the night before. At their joint trial he told of the killing and what went before. He was 24 at the time and had returned to Bendigo six months earlier, after living in Western Australia with his father. In that half year he heard the shouting and arguments from the other room and, in the words of his counsel, 'lived the fear of his mother'.

He knew what Frank was capable of, claiming he had 'touched him up' as a child and raped him when he was 14. Frank belittled him for not being able to find a job and the day before the killing accused him of bludging off him. 'He wanted me out of the house before he got home tomorrow or he was going to kill me.'

When Frank came home from the quarry that last evening, David was working on his ute. He said he heard a scream and ran inside. Frank had Heather pinned against a wall. 'Get the fuck off her,' yelled David and Frank turned on him. 'That was it, he just came at me and said "I'm going to fuckin' kill you" and he hit me right in the side of the head.'

Heather had mentioned none of this. She'd told the court Frank had abused her for having her hair cut – 'he raved for an hour-and-a-half' – so she decided to put the tablets in his food to calm him down. But then she grew fearful of what he would do when he woke.

'I was just paralysed in fear … I couldn't live like this any more. There was just eye contact between David and I and we just knew … there was just no way out,' she said.

The problem for both Heather and David was that they had already prepared Frank's grave. Worse for Heather were some of her intercepted conversations.

In December she'd been caught telling a friend that she was a suspect because of Frank's violence 'you know, going back earlier'. But she added: 'If I was going to do anything I would've done it years ago when the kids were little, not now that, you know, I was living me own life with me dogs …'

She told another friend: 'You know 10, 15 years ago, yeah, I could've throttled the shit out of him. But not the last couple of years, we just didn't talk. You know there was just – there was just nothing. Well, ah, there was the pleasantries: "You want a cup of coffee?" Yes – no. You know, that was it.'

And later still: 'If I wanted to kill him, I would have killed him fuckin' years ago. We had no gripes these last couple of years.'

Heather Osland was found guilty. Justice Hedigan told her that there was little doubt Frank's continued physical violence and psychological terrorism had a potent and devastating effect on her sense of security. But he said the jury had rejected her defences of provocation and self-defence and that she believed it was necessary to kill him because she feared for her life.

'Whilst Frank Osland was a cruel and violent man, his life nevertheless had value and the taking of it was a fully premeditated act done by you to turn your life around and preserve your situation.' He sentenced her to more than 14 years jail, with a minimum of nine-and-a-half years.

The jury could not reach a verdict on David and he was sent to retrial. In December 1996, despite having admitted to striking the fatal blow, he was acquitted.

Heather appealed both the verdict and sentencing, contending Justice Hedigan should have informed the jury differently about the definition of provocation and self-defence. In August 1997 the appeal was lost, the judgment stating that as far as self-defence was concerned, the digging of the grave was an 'insuperable hurdle'.

Meanwhile Heather Osland was turning – or being turned – into what one commentator would later call 'the *cause celebre* of battered women'. Two campaigns – Release Heather and Women Who Kill In Self-Defence – had sprung up in support of Heather and other women in her situation.

A spokeswoman for both groups, Chris Momot, first met Heather when she was in Fairlea Women's Prison. Momot had worked with victims of domestic violence for 13 years but later said Heather's story had affected her profoundly.

While on bail, Heather had volunteered at the Brimbank Community Centre and took a 16-week course on family violence. Only at its end did she reveal she had been charged with murdering her husband.

'The class was shocked,' Momot said later. 'Heather didn't look like a murderer. She is a gentle soul and the other students had grown to love her.'

The justice system persisted in viewing both provocation and self-defence only as reactions to immediate threat – the bar-room brawl scenario, said Momot. But battered women can suffer and live in constant fear of being killed, 'simmering' for years but unable to escape the relationship. They might kill their abuser in response to apparently minor acts, but that did not mean they did not believe they were under immediate threat.

'Heather believed Frank was invincible, I don't think there's any doubt she killed in self-defence,' she said. 'She was under immediate threat. She was under real and immediate threat of being killed by him almost every day of their life together.'

But others had misgivings. One commentator claimed Heather had been 'embraced by the feminist legal sorority' to pave the way for more lenient treatment of domestic violence victims – 'hijacked by her feminist supporters' eager to test the legitimacy of battered women's syndrome or self-defence. Less inflammatory observers, including feminist lawyers, simply noted that given the intercepts and the grave suggested premeditation, there might have been better vehicles for such campaigns.

In February 1998, as her growing band of supporters cheered, Heather Osland won special leave to appeal to the

High Court. But in granting leave, presiding judge Justice Mary Gaudron pointed out a fact that had barely been alluded to in the 16 months since the original verdict. It seemed a glaring contradiction: what was Heather's crime if David, who wielded the fatal iron bar, had been acquitted?

In the constant focus on battered women's syndrome, said Justice Gaudron, fundamental legal issues had 'gone out the window'. Fellow Justice Bill Gummow described the disparity between the verdicts as a potential 'knockout point'.

The day before the High Court appeal began, on 23 April, an optimistic band of supporters – 30 or so community workers, housewives and students – rolled out of Melbourne for Canberra on what they had dubbed the 'Free Heather' bus. They detoured to the women's jail in Deer Park, where Heather was now locked up, to tie balloons to the fence to show their support.

Outside the court the next morning they displayed life-size cut-out figures made by women who had survived family violence. In one, a woman displayed the battered women's symptom of 'learnt hopefulness', hunching over a set of rosary beads with the mantra: 'I kept praying he would change, I kept praying he would change, I kept praying he would change …'

But inside, opening the hearing, feminist barrister and author Dr Jocelyn Scutt had taken Justice Gaudron's advice, telling the five judges: 'We say that the inconsistent verdicts are wrong and that they are illogical and it's on that basis that Heather Osland's conviction should be set aside and an acquittal entered.'

Justice Michael Kirby considered the point the following day, conceding the community might well be 'affronted' that Heather was in jail while David walked free. In convoluted legalese he noted: 'You have standing before the public the person who strikes the blow acquitted and the person who does not strike the blow convicted.'

But Mr Mark Weinberg, QC, for the Crown, said there was no inconsistency and that different evidence was given in each trial. In Osland's case, that included telephone intercepts about 'knocking' Paul and admitting she had not been abused for three years. It was possible for mother and son to have planned the killing together, but it was also possible for David Albion to have snapped at the last minute and acted in self-defence.

The High Court delivered its judgment in December. As expected, Justices Gaudron and Gummow ruled Heather deserved a new trial because of the inconsistent verdicts. 'The jury's failure to convict David Albion reveals a flaw in reasoning which requires that Mrs Osland's conviction be set aside,' they wrote.

Their fellows disagreed. As Justice Kirby put it, the evidence in the first trial left it open for the jury to conclude Osland was the leading participant. 'There are many explanations for the jury's verdict in her case and their failure to agree on the verdict in the case of Mr Albion.'

None of the five agreed the trial judge had failed to properly direct the jury on the significance of expert evidence that she suffered battered women's syndrome. Justices Gaudron and Gummow said: 'Given that the ordinary person is likely to approach the evidence of a battered woman without knowledge of her heightened perception of danger, the impact of fear on her thinking, her fear of telling others of her predicament and her belief that she can't escape from the relationship, it must now be accepted that the battered wife syndrome is a proper matter for expert evidence.'

But they said that in Heather's case, the expert evidence of the syndrome had been given in too general terms and was not sufficiently linked with the circumstances of the case. Justice Ian Callinan wrote: 'That this court should adopt a new and separate defence of battered woman syndrome goes too far for the laws of this country.'

Justice Kirby warned of the need for caution in accepting evidence of battered wife syndrome, saying: 'It is not a universally accepted and empirically established scientific phenomenon.' Nor, he said, did the mere raising of it in evidence or argument 'cast a protective cloak over an accused ...'

He had earlier noted that evidence of a long-term abusive relationship still didn't give Heather, or any other battered woman, a blank cheque or legal carte blanche to 'engage in premeditated homicide ... No civilised society removes its protection to human life simply because of the existence of a history of long-term physical and psychological abuse'.

After the judgment David told a reporter his mother had not been given justice but the injustice of a sort of double sentence: 'To live 13 years with a bloke that beat her up ... and now to spend the next seven years reminded of it ...'

A couple of weeks later Heather sat in her cell at Deer Park and penned an article for Melbourne's *The Age* newspaper: 'I've gone from one type of prison to another,' she wrote.

Her dauntless supporters refused to give up hope. They canvassed taking the case to the United Nations under the

International Covenant on Civil and Political Rights and organised a petition of mercy to the Victorian Government. But Heather Osland's luck must have deserted her completely that day she bumped into Frank in Karratha. In September 2001, Victoria's Attorney-General Rob Hulls ruled against her petition, saying she would stay in prison until at least 2005. And there she remained, until 22 August that year.

In her newspaper article Heather had written: 'I ask, in my wisdom now: should my original counsel have persuaded me to plead manslaughter? Should I have had a strong, aggressive, male barrister to fight my defence in the Bendigo Supreme Court? Would my life be different now? I might be lucky and home free. But I never felt I was guilty of murder. Frank was the guilty one – he "murdered" us every day we were with him. Frank raped my mind and my body and now he is raping my soul.'

CRIME IS HIS MISTRESS

This is The Fear. It's the thing you feel as you rise, step between that one in the dock and the 12 of the jury, and begin to talk. It is the churning in your stomach and the turmoil in your mind. Most of all, worst of all, it's the weight on your shoulders.

The Fear drives John Smallwood. It's what motivates and debilitates him. It makes him dry retch in the shower on the mornings of a trial, kills his appetite and destroys sleep. It's the always whispering reminder of why he does what he does.

Other criminal barristers might know it by another name but they all have it, or at least all the good ones. In the end, he says, it's like your robes stink. With him, it's nerves, nicotine and spilt beers after a loss: the smell of The Fear.

It's what fires you and what wears you down, both your enemy and your friend. It's the adrenalin and it's got to do with terror and with excitement. It's about the enormity of what you're doing.

But most of all, it's about the consequences.

He remembers great Australian judge Cairns Villeneuve-Smith telling him this: 'Those who criticise our justice system have never put on the robes and stood between an accused man and his ruin.'

Wednesday, 31 January 2001: The pre-trial conference
There is no argument that Gabriel Chang killed Dianne Psaila. He did and he admits it. But did he murder her? There's a difference and it hangs on intent. Under the strict definition of The Law, the question is this:

Did he mean to kill her or cause her really serious injury?

No, he tells John Smallwood, the same as he told the police over and over. He never meant to hurt her at all.

They are in the QC's small chambers, sitting opposite each other on a pair of green couches, surrounded by the photos of 14 Collingwood premiership teams; seven cover-driving cricketers; a thespian grandfather doing Shylock; a plaster saint and the old crim Archie Butterly's first mug shot. Smallwood, in shirtsleeves and bushranger beard, takes notes on one of four spiral binders. Both burn cigarettes in endless rotation.

Chang is dark, his Chilean ancestry in his aquiline, Incan features. Less than 48 hours from trial, he is nervous, almost defeated. Once more though, he says this is what happened:

Dianne was a friend with a heroin habit. He'd been lending her money, but this time he told her no more. She lost her temper and lit into him, slapping with both hands. He fended her off, throwing out an open right hand he thinks might have hit her under the chin. He remembers her falling back, spinning and hitting the left side of her forehead on the wooden arm of a sofa.

When she hit the floor she just lay there. At first he

thought she was joking, but she wasn't breathing and he couldn't find a pulse. She was dead.

And then? 'I was panicking,' he says. 'Shittin' meself, to be honest. I didn't know how I'd got myself into this. It was like, this can't be real, it just can't be.'

And that's when he did all the dumb things. Not just hiding the body in her car boot or burgling her father's place, probably for running money, or even trying to bury her four days later on the south coast of Victoria, near Lorne and assaulting the copper who discovered him there. But the thing with the meat tenderiser. He doesn't understand quite why, but to see if she was really dead, he hit her with a small aluminium meat tenderiser. Not hard. Just taps, he says, demonstrating with little forward prods.

'I don't think a jury's gunna wear that,' says Smallwood. 'I think they'll find it very hard to accept the contact with the meat tenderiser was as gentle as you say. I find it difficult to accept myself.'

Yet while it was a very, very odd thing to do, it didn't kill her. If Chang believed she was already dead, and it did happen by accident, no matter how bizarre the actions that followed, they don't make it murder. He doesn't even think it's manslaughter.

But Chang is staring at 13 or 15 years jail, and wavering. Maybe they ought to offer to plead to the lesser charge and cop three or four. 'The truth of the matter is I'd rather do a bit of time than take the risk and do a lot of time. I don't mind doing a bit, but I want to have it where I can come home and be there for me kids before they're married.'

'I understand that, Gabe,' says Smallwood, 'and this is where we part company. As a lawyer I can't advise you to plead guilty on this scenario. But it's not me that's going to be doing the time.'

Chang says he'll think about it. 'But, you know, the way I feel inside,' he says softly, 'I do feel guilty for what I've done. I feel in myself that I need to do some time for what I've done.'

Smallwood watches him go. 'It's funny, first impressions aren't good, but you talk to this bloke for a couple of hours and it makes a sort of sense. There's an irrational explanation for all this.'

But he'll offer the plea. He's almost convinced he can win this one, but he won't even try to persuade Gabe. 'I've got to live with it,' he says. 'If I said "No, I can win this, mate", and talked him into it, and then didn't, I'd spend the last 10 years of his sentence thinking this bloke is in jail because of my ego. But he didn't do it. You can smell it. After a while it gets so you can smell death on their hands, and I can't smell it on him.'

There's something sepia-toned about Smallwood. Imagine a faded tintype print cured by roll-your-own tobacco and gumleaf smoke, redolent of a simpler, straighter Australia. He is narrow as a split rail, with greyish eyes, long, curving nose on a face gullied in comfortable creases, and earth under his nails.

But it's the beard you notice first and remember most. A wiry briar patch of greys and browns, a foot-long scrub (that ought only ever be mapped in imperial measure) tumbling down to hide his crinkled jabot and usually punctuated by the ember of a smouldering Winfield. A growth that always evokes the same descriptors: it's a Ned Kelly/swagman/maybe Henry Parkes beard.

His wife, Liz Gaynor, also a criminal barrister, puts it best, laughing: 'He's such an Aussie. If you look at John, he's a bit like you'd expect a tramp to be in the 1890s. He'd be the sort you'd sit down with, he'd boil a billy and tell you a few yarns. He's like something out of the old *Bulletin*. He's the greatest yarner of all time.'

Watch him in court some time, standing, his right foot on his chair, his elbow on his knee, leaning into the jury, just talking it through. 'Um, Mr Tipstaff,' he says in one case, 'can you get us 13 beers please. It's time we sat down at the bar and had a bit of a yarn about all this.'

'Oh, sorry,' he adds, 'and a shandy for the prosecutor.' The blokes love that one.

Yarning's what got him into the game. Back at St Patrick's College in Sale in the 1960s, the boarders would be expected to stand up and give a short speech every Sunday. He got to love it. 'I like arguing,' he says. 'I like the logic of it, or lack of it, and I like the feeling. So I just said, yeah I'll do law. All I knew was that it involved arguing, talking.'

Ask if there's law in his background and watch it happen as he spins a long, entertaining genealogy. Yeah, there was his maternal great-grandfather, a police magistrate in Hobart, but he was the only one. His grandfather on that side had been a touring actor with JC Williamsons since he was 16, played League footy and was an accomplished painter. 'But he became a chemist when he was about 40 and I'm told eventually his attraction to the white powder got a bit the better of him.'

On the other side, his grandfather was the bandleader in an outback circus. Smallwood's dad was a radio announcer and met his mother when they were both radar operators in

Queensland during the war. They married and moved back to her hometown, Foster, in South Gippsland, and he became a pharmacist.

Smallwood initially attended Melbourne's Xavier College as a boarder. He hated it, but it provided one formative influence: he was briefly suspended after being wrongly accused of pinching a watch. 'Ever since I was tiny, I've had this absolute hatred of being falsely accused. Mum reckons that when I was little, two or three or so, if she accused me of something I hadn't done, I'd just become stricken.' It's an emotion, honed by the experience at Xavier, that he now taps into when defending someone. That feeling of unfairness and helpless desperation. It's why he despises 'give-ups' – prison informants.

It was only a matter of time until he and the school 'parted company' and he moved to St Patrick's – 'a footy team with a couple of classrooms attached'. The team slept in the one dormitory, with the coach in charge and the beds virtually arranged by jumper number. They trained every day and played on Sundays. Smallwood revelled in it: 'The team concept, the loyalty … it was just absolutely my element, mate.'

After school he did four years of articles, took a year off hitch-hiking in the United States with his first wife, then in the mid-70s, started working as a part-time solicitor in the Melbourne bayside suburb of Beaumaris, doing corporate and workers' comp cases with a mate, Adrian McKay, who was chalk to his cheese: McKay smooth, Smallwood already with the beard and hair down to his waist. They took to running conferences out the back of the local bakery, with a flagon of red and steaks grilled by Ferdie, the baker. The clients loved it, but it couldn't last.

About 1980 they both gave it away. Smallwood and his wife started a second-hand shop, Zucchini Sisters, in Richmond. 'I did that for a few years but started to feel I was wasting my time,' he says. 'I was doing something I enjoyed, but the adrenalin wasn't running. I thought I'd go to the bar and see what happened. But I decided I'd only do crime, because I'd never touched it before, never even cross-examined a witness. In my first 47 days at the bar I got one brief, and that was for my sister: a smash-and-bash, a bloke running a red light out in Broady [Broadmeadows]. And I won it and the feeling was sensational.'

But it helped put an end to his marriage. His wife was from the country too, and wanted to go back. He didn't. 'But I agreed when I shouldn't have, bought a place down Bairnsdale, and eventually it fell apart.

'I just couldn't leave this. I'd found something that satisfied a whole lot of stuff in me.'

Wednesday 7 February: The final address
'I'm scared,' says Smallwood, pacing and burning a chain of smokes. 'Not as scared as Gabe, but bloody scared.'

In the end it comes to this. The DPP has refused their offer to plead to manslaughter and a stink of circumstance has hung in the hot, closed courtroom all week. Now he is forced to confront the seven men and five women with it head on.

Remember a night in the middle of November 1999, he tells them. The evening news shows dramatic footage from a helicopter of a man being arrested in the bush near Lorne. There's a half-dug grave, a body in a car boot. 'Undoubtedly some of you saw that, sitting at home having your tea and a beer, and when you saw it what were your thoughts?'

He answers for them. 'This bloke's been caught red-handed.'

This is The Fear. That the jury will work backwards, rewinding from the prime time visuals of the capture through the bizarre behaviour of the previous days, with its burglary and meat tenderiser; until it comes to that moment of the killing with its mind made up: if he did all the dumb things, he did the murder.

That's been the premise of the prosecution, he says, indicating his opposite number Ray Elston. But that's not evidence, it's just creating a feeling, and you cannot conduct a trial as a sneering match. 'You can't convict somebody of a crime because he *feels* guilty. You just can't do it. It's wrong.'

This is the first time he's been on his feet for any length of time in the three days of the trial.

Ninety-five per cent of the facts aren't in dispute, so there's no point doing hard cross-examinations.

A murder trial is like a bushfire, he says later. The central allegation is the great wall of flame coming at you. Fight that and don't start little spotfires over inconsequential matters. But it's meant he hasn't been able to build a relationship with the jury.

All that's left are admissions and an admonishment. Gabriel Chang has behaved abominably; the grief he has caused is reprehensible; he has stolen and lied; he has done stupid, inexplicable things; and yes, on his own admission he is guilty of killing his friend.

But not of murder.

'You are not appointed as avenging angels, you are not appointed to get revenge,' he reminds them. They may not like it, it may stick in their craw, but 'despite the horrible, nasty, bizarre surroundings to this, if you are not satisfied *beyond reasonable doubt* ... you have got to acquit him'.

And, he might add, me too.

Talk to Smallwood about his cases and it's 'we' this or 'my boy' that: he doesn't just defend clients, he adopts them. Makes it personal. 'People such as myself do it so personally we put ourselves on trial and say to a jury, "Hey, convict me. Not him, because he couldn't string three words together. C'mon, convict me".'

A judge, who admires Smallwood's approach, says all counsel 'constitute a bridge between the dock and the jury and engage in a psychological linking process'. But turning that link into a relationship extracts a cost. 'Whether you are successful or not, in an emotional sense you receive a belting.'

Smallwood knows that too well. 'That's the way I run them, but the danger is when you get convicted, it's you too, not just the client. They reject you personally – or it feels like it.'

You win a couple and you fancy yourself sensational. Lose one and it's like it's never happened before. It comes as a massive shock. What he does then is sit outside the court, under its brooding, ancient sandstone walls, and imagine a hundred years of broken prisoners being led past, so he doesn't feel one out. It rarely works.

'Every trial John's ever done, he's done hard,' says Liz Gaynor. 'I guess most barristers do, but John seems to put the whole load on his shoulders and trudge along with it.'

Gaynor and Smallwood met in 1985 when she started a reader's course after a few years in journalism. She jokes about how she walked in with a friend, surveyed the room and said,

'Well, Jools, no talent here.' But she liked the bloke with the beard's energy and supportiveness. They became friends and married in 1989. A person of large enthusiasm herself, she loved his kindness and humour and passion for his work.

Increasingly, she worries about that passion's toll, though, typically, she hides her concern behind a gentle dig: 'John's the sort of person you feel sorry for because he didn't get to be an old digger at Gallipoli and then live sadly through the Depression. It's almost like sometimes he welcomes adversity.'

But since taking silk in late 1999, he's had what she calls 'the really heavy, hopeless brutal cases', and they're starting to drain him. Smallwood says half a dozen of his murder trials last year were 'doomed' from the start. 'But once the ball's bounced and he says "Not guilty", as The Villain says, the only thing between that man and ruin is you. And the consequences are extraordinary. And you've got to do it.'

Not that he's any romantic about his clients. 'I'm extremely cynical. To protect myself as much as anything, I assume they're guilty. What that does is make me very careful and very objective.

'I don't believe my client until 30 seconds before I give my final address. But by the time I've stood up, pushed that chair in and faced the jury, I believe everything. Because I can't convey it otherwise. Doesn't matter what side of the fence you're on, if you haven't got that personal conviction the jury knows straight away. And it's not method acting, that person is totally dependent on you.

'You might fail and you're bitterly hurt when you do, but you personally can do something very effective in a situation you very strongly believe in. And that is this:

everyone has the right to be represented and you cannot have an innocent person in jail.'

Thursday, 8 February: The verdict
'Guilty.' The jury foreman's single word is a clear, crisply enunciated blow. Smallwood, sitting at the bar table, looking straight ahead, takes it like a jolt to the head, his jaw dropping, flinching despite himself.

As someone among Dianne Psaila's relatives hisses 'Yesss!' and Chang's wife Veronica blanches and begins to cry, he sucks in air and his eyes slowly slide shut. He shakes his head almost imperceptibly, mutters something to himself.

The jury went out at 11.30. Barely past 4, the word comes back that they are returning with a verdict. Smallwood, waiting in the courtyard, doesn't know what to make of it. 'It's hard to believe they can pot him for murder that quickly,' he says.

But they do. 'Indecent haste, Shakespeare called it,' he will growl later, 'indecent haste.'

But now he cannot even watch as Gabriel is hustled out, looking suddenly anaesthetised.

He sits with his head in his hands, the balls of his thumbs kneading circles into his temples.

A long time later, well after the court has emptied, he is still there, bent forward in his seat, lost deep inside himself. Then something very unusual and very decent happens.

Justice Frank Vincent returns to his court and pulls up a chair beside him. 'How're you going?' he says softly.

The doors close and they talk for 20 minutes or more. About what, Smallwood won't tell. 'Just a bit of parental care,' he says.

* * *

Murder can kill you. It obsesses you, starts to own you. It gets so you talk it and dream it and neglect your children for it. Do murder, and you'll be lucky if you've got a 10-year lifespan.

We've all got a homicide in us, he argues. Very few murders, but a hell of a lot of manslaughters. It's why he specialises in it. It's his gift to be able to explain to a jury those infantile acts, those moments of rage and passion and their unforeseen consequences.

'But I think I've just about had enough,' he says now, sipping Melbourne Bitter under a pear tree in his Thornbury backyard. About two years ago he found he was starting to hit the wall and said he'd put a limit on it. He's never really added them up, probably scare him to do it, but he'd average between eight and 15 a year.

'And every one of them takes something out of you,' he says. 'You leave some part of yourself behind, because of the stakes you're playing for, the intensity of it. Win, lose or draw, eventually you are weakened by leaving those pieces behind.'

Liz has watched it starting to wear him out. He sleeps badly, doesn't eat much until he comes out of the end of a trial looking like a skull. 'He's getting tired and, I think, it's becoming almost joyless for him. It's like dragging great sacks of stones uphill at the moment.

'It's not just us, most of the barristers I know treat their work that way. It's huge and it does take years off their life, particularly the good ones. My experience of criminal barristers is so un-stereotypical. They're very angst-ridden, anxious people whose guts are hanging out on the table all the time and who care enormously about what they do.'

The history of murder barristers is 'a pretty chequered one', says Smallwood, reeling off examples of upper-level mortality rates, alcoholism, cancer, 'the early-death rate, the burn-out rate'. He talks about old hand Bill Lennon doing 25 murder trials in a row, with the death penalty hanging over every one. 'He went about it the same way I do – put your heart and soul on the line – and it broke Bill.'

This is The Fear. You do crime and it will do you. He remembers criminal barrister Freddy James worn out and dying and telling a friend: 'Crime's been my mistress and she's murdered me.'

LOST IN THE FACE OF EVIL

T wice in the winter of 1969, a little boy looked deep into the eyes of a young man called Derek Percy and got lost there forever.

The first time, that crisp Sunday in July, Shane Spiller was 11 and strolling down a dirt track at Warneet, a coastal village on Westernport Bay, south-east of Melbourne, with his friend Yvonne Tuohy. When they got to the beach at the end of the trail they were going to make a little fire of driftwood and have a picnic lunch.

But Percy got there first. He grabbed 12-year-old Yvonne and pressed a red dagger to her neck. He told Shane to come too, but the boy knew better than that. In his belt he had a small hatchet that he'd brought to chop firewood and now he waved it at the man and began backing away.

'Come back or he'll cut my throat,' begged Yvonne. Instead, Shane sprinted 200 metres through the tea tree scrub yelling for help. As he got to the road he saw Percy driving away. He had Yvonne wrapped in a blanket.

The second time was at Russell Street police headquarters. Shane had been able to describe the car, an orange station wagon, and gave detectives a drawing of a sticker he'd seen on its rear window. It was a Royal Australian Navy insignia and pointed the police to the nearby base at HMAS Cerberus. They found Percy in the laundry, trying to wash Yvonne's blood from his clothes.

He took them to Fisheries Road, Devon Meadows, where he'd left her under some bushes. He had tied her wrists behind her, stuffed a balled cloth in her mouth, strangled her and mutilated her body and throat with long, deep cuts.

But now the detectives needed Shane to look into those killer's eyes again. They put him in a room where the 21-year-old naval rating with the long, narrow face had been placed in a line-up. 'I had to pick him,' Shane recalled later. 'I had to walk up and point right at his nose.'

After 30 years he still shuddered: 'The look he gave me ...'

The police were very pleased with their young witness. They had a sketch artist do his portrait and gave him a show bag of gifts. The newspaper photographers were happy too: they'd captured a terrific image of the boy in his army-style jacket, epaulettes and turtle-neck jumper, holding his steel tomahawk in both hands, his wide hazel eyes staring straight down the lens.

'And for all the world,' remembers former police victim liaison officer Robert Read, 'that was the end of Shane Spiller.'

The world had a lot to distract it that day. On the moon, Neil Armstrong had taken a small step onto the Sea of Tranquility. But as Read now points out, that was a word that would never again apply to Shane Spiller: 'That little boy was traumatised for life by Derek Percy and by what he'd seen.'

At his trial a year later, Percy was found not guilty on the grounds of insanity and sent to prison for an indefinite term. He is still there. Shane went home to Armadale and tried to resume his life. 'He went back to school after the holiday and seemed to be doing all right,' says lawyer Michael Clark. 'The effects didn't really catch up to him until he was about 14 or 15.'

From the beginning he had trouble sleeping and grew afraid of the dark. His parents had been advised that he'd get over it and not to mollycoddle him. These were the days before trauma counselling, says Clark. 'Back then, if you saw something you didn't like you bit your tongue and took it like a man. He wasn't able to do that.'

He got lost in guilt, loneliness and fear and began drinking at 14. 'He'd been a pretty good student but very quickly his results went from good to pathetic, he fell out with his parents, left school and basically went walkabout. From that time on, he was a wandering, lost soul.'

One day, years later, and by then a heavy drinker and drug user, Shane Spiller washed up in the little New South Wales village of Wyndham, in the hills and bush 30 kilometres west of Merimbula. It must have seemed the perfect place to escape to. The trouble was, he took Derek Percy with him.

Wyndham is a pub, a general store and a couple of dozen modest houses tucked into the dips and folds of the Mount Darragh ridgeline, between Whipstick and Rocky Hall. In the 1860s it was gold country but now yields mainly cattle and timber, with some sidelining in small-plot cannabis plantations hidden in the surrounding national park.

The Robbie Burns Hotel is the district's social centre. A twin-gabled weatherboard built in 1891, it is decorated with traps, maps, a long leather bullwhip, old logging photos and Scottish-themed bric-a-brac. Its public bar is homely and welcoming with a log fire and a couple of fat lounge chairs, its only concessions to modernity a plasma flat screen and a clutch of pokies.

This drizzly Thursday, the back dining room hosts the weekly Stitch 'n' Bitch, where the local womenfolk bring their crafts and gossip to lunch. The men start drifting in to the bar about 3.30. They're taciturn but not unfriendly and when a stranger raises the puzzle of 'Stick' Spiller, the theories, stories and suspicions spill out.

Ever since he suddenly disappeared that Monday, 9 September 2002, what might have happened to skinny Shane Spiller has exercised the minds – and imaginations – of Wyndham. 'It's a real mystery. Everyone still talks about it,' says general store owner Bryan Hunter, the last person to see him alive.

That morning, Spiller had walked to the store from his two-bedroom shack around the corner to pick up his mail. A few days later, when worried neighbours broke into his house they found his boots in the middle of the living room, dinner set for two on the table, his wallet, and his medications untouched. His motorcycle was locked in his shed. They called the police and joined in the search for him, on motorbikes and horses, checking old mine shafts and lookouts.

Every so often they still go out looking, but have never found him.

The police have settled on two probabilities: in one, Spiller suffered an accidental morphine overdose and someone panicked and got rid of his body. In the other, more likely scenario, after years of post-traumatic stress, substance abuse and paranoia, he went into the bush and committed suicide.

The blokes in the pub won't have that. 'Not a hope in hell,' says David Thoroughgood. 'He could have done it a hundred times before and he didn't want to.'

What got him in the end, they reckon, was bad company. He'd become involved with 'a bullshit scene' of morphine abusers, junkies and thieves. One in particular, who'd arrived not long out of prison, scared people. 'A bad egg,' says one. 'Black, empty eyes,' says another. When he first came to the pub, looking for Stick, the barmaid told her boss: 'If ever I've seen evil, it's just walked into the bar.'

For the second time in his life, Shane Spiller had come too close to a killer. 'We've bandied this about for years,' says Tony Boller. 'Somebody disappeared him, that's for sure.'

But however it ended, they insist, Derek Percy had already stolen Shane Spiller's life all those years ago.

In 20 years Robert Read looked into the eyes of thousands of victims of violence. As head of the Victoria Police victim advisory unit, he counselled survivors of rape, assault and armed robbery and families who had lost loved ones to murder and road toll. He dealt with the community fear instilled by serial killer Paul Denyer, who murdered three women in outer-suburban Frankston in 1993, and, last year, the emotional aftermath of the Mildura crash that killed six teenagers.

But in his scrapbook of hard memories, Shane Spiller has a special place.

They first met in 1998, when he began helping Spiller seek criminal injuries compensation. Read liked the 'loveable sort of bloke' from the start. 'He was a knockabout sort of fella, a wild and woolly little character, very thin, with this big Ned Kelly beard. There wasn't much of him, probably more beard than anything.

'He was quintessentially a little Aussie bloke from the bush. But that was the façade. Underneath that he was a shattered individual and Derek Percy still controlled him. He was vulnerable and he was extremely fearful. Beneath the face of Shane Spiller lived a deep and dark cesspool of emotions.'

And they were the baggage he carried when he drifted into Wyndham in the late '80s. Next-door neighbour Andy Morris believes that from the time of his fatal beach holiday, Spiller had never felt safe again. Friends were asked to note the number plates of cars parked outside his home; he cut a trapdoor into his living-room floor; and slept with a baseball bat by his bed.

He had become convinced that Percy would come after him or had put out a contract on his life.

'He was the most paranoid person I've ever met,' says Morris. 'Shane suffered all his life with post-traumatic stress disorder. There was this overwhelming dark cloud over his life and he was basically self-medicating with drugs and alcohol.'

In mid-1998, Percy began moves to have his case reviewed by the Supreme Court of Victoria, seeking to be freed under recent laws relating to people serving indefinite 'governor's pleasure' sentences. Of 46 people under such rulings, he was the only one held in prison and had become the longest-serving prisoner in Victoria.

Police had long been totally opposed to Percy's release, suspecting him of involvement in the notorious murders of eight other children: Christine Sharrock and Marianne Schmidt on Sydney's Wanda Beach in 1965; the disappearance of Jane, Arna and Grant Beaumont in 1966;

Alan Redston in Canberra later that year; Simon Brook in Sydney; and Linda Stilwell in St Kilda, both in 1968.

They began seeking statements from people who had been involved with Percy and Bega police were asked to contact Spiller. 'It brought back all the memories and he went into stupefaction again,' says his Melbourne lawyer Michael Clark.

The police were so concerned they put him in contact with Robert Read, who found him in utter distress: 'In fact, he was almost out of control. He was utterly petrified of Percy. He'd had a wretched life.'

Read would telephone him at the Robbie Burns, where he had a regular seat at the end of the bar. In long night-time conversations, he says, Spiller poured out his heart. 'Derek Percy had absolutely ruined his life. He took a young innocent and turned him into a runaway – and it was Percy that he was running from.'

Wyndham, with a floating population of less than 100 people, seemed a good place to run to. It was a mix of long-termers, logging workers and alternative lifestylers – or as one local puts it, tree-cutters, tree-changers, drop-outs and dole-bludgers. 'It's a different sort of place,' advises a policeman a few jurisdictions away. 'Real Deliverance country. It's out in the scrub and the banjos are playing.'

That's unfair, says barman Peter Cox. 'This is a place where you can be who you like. People mind their own business but look out for each other. Stick was a nice bloke – he fitted in and everyone accepted him.'

They laughed at his hoarding and his constant tinkering in his yard full of car parts, old washing machines, bike and boat hulls and his never-fulfilled plan to open a laundromat. And celebrated his skill and – perhaps uncharacteristic – fearlessness on his GSX1000 Suzuki.

'He was a manic rider,' recalls Bryan Hunter. 'He'd scream past here standing on the seat, arms spread wide. He came off a few times, scraped off a bit of bark, but never really hurt himself.

'It's hard to say exactly what twisted Stick's whistle. He was a normal bloke in many ways, just a larrikin motorcycle rider who liked a beer and smoked a few cones too many.'

In 2000, Read helped Spiller apply for compensation for his decades of emotional trauma. He was awarded $5000, but appealed to the Victorian Civil and Administrative Tribunal and received the maximum $50,000. It was more money than he'd ever had, but it couldn't buy him peace of mind.

'People liked Stick, but there were times his melodramas and paranoia could give you the shits,' remembers a local woman. Shane was having a whinge in the store one day when she called him a drama queen. He turned and quietly walked out.

'He came back a little while later and plonked a file down in front of me and said, "This might explain why I'm like I am,"' she recalls. 'It was full of cuttings about this bloke Percy and what he did. I sat down that night and read it all. After that I was a lot more sympathetic.'

Detective Sergeant Mark Winterflood from Bega police had helped track Spiller down for his 1998 statement. Every so often after that Stick would ring to talk about Percy. Winterflood knew he was an alcoholic and that he grew and smoked a lot of dope. (In 2006, after the bank sold Spiller's house, the new owners pulled out the ceiling and a bunch of rat nests fell out. They were all made of marijuana.)

But Winterflood had a strange fondness for him. Shane was harmless, considerate and for the most part honest, he says. 'He was an unusual sort of bloke. But he lived on the fringe – and he didn't pick his friends very well.'

Which turned into a problem when he became addicted to morphine. 'He mixed with this circle of substance-abusing people. Anywhere he could get morphine, through shonky scrips or other friends who could scam it, he'd grab it. People took advantage of him.'

Locals took to calling a section of town past Stick's, where the junkies, bludgers and thieves lived, the Bronx. 'It was a bullshit scene,' says David Thoroughgood.

'There was a lot of people around here then that … well, they aren't here any more,' adds Tony Boller.

One of those was Andrew Paul Kraaymaat, a 38-year-old who'd spent most of his adult life in and out of jail for a string of violent offences. He wasn't long out of prison when he came to Wyndham in 2000. He scared a lot of people, but was soon spending a lot of time at Spiller's.

In August 2000, after a night of drinking, Kraaymaat and a mate, Brian Peebles, 'borrowed' Stick's Nissan Patrol, purchased with his compensation payout, and rolled and wrecked it. Two nights later the pair went on another drinking binge at Candelo, about 25 kilometres north, with another mate, Lee 'Mick' Petrie. When it was over, Petrie was dead with a filleting knife sticking out of his chest.

'The murder was three drunks in a room,' says Winterflood. 'Their alcohol readings were all around the 2.5 level – Kraaymaat described himself as virtually paralytic.

One of them winds up dead and the other two can't really remember what happened. But they're able to shove a plastic bag over his head, drive him to a lookout on Myrtle Mountain, pull him out of the back of a car and dump him there.'

They were arrested after Kraaymaat had a rare attack of conscience. He phoned his mother and said he'd committed 'a cardinal sin … I've killed a bloke'. Reverting to type, he added: 'he was a mongrel bastard and he deserved to die.'

Kraaymaat was sentenced to a minimum of 15 years for murder. Peebles, who turned Crown witness, was convicted of being a witness after the fact. But while he was locked up awaiting bail, some of his friends from the Bronx broke into his house.

'They've stolen his tools, his washing machine, anything of value,' says Winterflood. 'And one of the people he blames is poor old Spiller.'

Spiller began getting threats. A man rang and said he'd shoot him in the knee if he didn't name the thieves. Stick immediately phoned the police. 'The uniformed cop races around and while he's there, this bloke rings again and says, "Me and my pistol are 15 kilometres away." It wasn't real bright, but it caused Shane a lot more stress.

'No-one was really out to kill him. But the fear played on his mind constantly.'

There is an out-of-focus photo of Stick from just before he vanished. He is standing at the bar of the Robbie Burns in a torn and dirty blue windcheater, looking away from the camera. His long beard is gone, replaced by a five-day growth. He is skinny and haggard, looking much older than his 44 years. He seems distracted and unhappy.

In the four-and-a-half years since he disappeared, Mark Winterflood has arranged searches, pumped out a flooded mineshaft at Devil's Hole, scouted the lookouts where he had his cannabis crops, conducted all the relevant death checks and checked immigration. This year he sent a brief to the New South Wales Coroner.

'There's nothing. He's never accessed any funds. The bank chipped away at his savings and when that ran out they foreclosed and took the house.'

Winterflood suspects there are two possibilities. One is that he suffered an overdose at someone's home and they panicked and hid the body. 'What doesn't fit with that scenario is that Wyndham is such a small place where everyone knows everything and sooner or later the word would have got out.

'The other theory is that he's gone to a place of his choosing, a nice lookout or whatever, and done it there. Suicide.'

Spiller had already made two unsuccessful attempts to kill himself. In the last he had pulled a plastic bag over his head and injected an overdose. His psychologist booked him into Bega Hospital but after a few days he walked out. Not long after, he was gone.

But Robert Read, who knows too well the lasting damage done by trauma, says the suicide scenario doesn't sit right. 'This was a bloke who talked night after night of killing himself, but it never happened. If I was honest with my emotions and my intuition, I'd have to say I don't believe he killed himself. Something else happened to him. Because, deep down, I thought there was a resilience in Shane.'

And despite his fears, there was a bravery about Spiller, says Peter Cox. 'He was a very clever boy. Look what he did way back then,' he says. 'If it wasn't for Stick, that bloke could still be killing people.'

Adds Andy Morris: 'In a sense Shane was a Derek Percy murder victim as well. To me he was a very brave man. I like to picture him lying in a hammock with a banana daquiri, that'd be heaven to Stick.

'But wherever he is, I just hope he's happy at last.'

THE POLICE KILLERS

I n the kitchen, a tap can be heard running hard into an empty sink. There is the clatter of dinner dishes gathered up, the brittle chatter of television voices, later the hum of what might be a dishwasher, and there is conversation, much of it whispered, yet all of it clearly audible.

In the courtroom, 15 jurors follow this on their headphones and on transcript, turning pages in unison as the recording advances.

Amid the mundane, household routines of cooking, eating and cleaning, extraordinary things are said. A father is calmly discussing with his daughter the prospect of killing two policemen.

Not all the recordings are as clear as this one. Those from the garage at the front of the house compete with passing traffic as cars labour through their gears rounding the corner of Springfield Avenue, and those from one of the bugged cars are punctuated with the metronome-like ticking of what may be a dashboard clock.

At other times the incessant yapping of a little dog called Pebbles threatens to obliterate conversations from the house.

During the four-month trial of the two men accused of killing police officers Sergeant Gary Silk and Senior Constable Rod Miller during a robbery stake-out at Moorabbin, south of Melbourne's CBD, on 16 August 1998, the jury hears from 161 witnesses. But the prosecution has no smoking gun and no confessions – the case is built around the secretly recorded words of the suspects.

In the courtroom, the red-cloaked Justice Philip Cummins leans towards the jury and stresses that the transcripts are not evidence. It is the recordings that count as evidence; the transcripts are merely an aid to understanding them.

In the kitchen, it is shortly before midnight on 11 February 2000. The Narre Warren home of one of the two accused men, Bandali (Ben) Debs, has been bugged for nearly three months, but police investigating the killings have recently begun a strategy of encouraging conversation among their suspects – the middle-aged Debs and Jason Joseph Roberts, the 18-year-old boyfriend of his daughter, Nicole. Since the case is 18 months old, police believe the two men may need some prompting.

So earlier on that day, detectives visited the New South Wales home of Debs' brother, Robert Rutherford. Rutherford then rang Debs from a public phone to alert him of the police visit.

The eavesdroppers heard that conversation, picked up by a telephone intercept, and they have heard Debs and his family attempting to discern its meaning, since Rutherford spoke guardedly.

Debs reckons it must be about the matter where 'two CPs' – police – have gone down. Rutherford would not ring otherwise. Debs adds, however, that the 'things' that were used have gone – one was destroyed, the other was thrown into a lake. After the water gets at it, it will give a different reading if it's ever fired again.

Now Debs and his eldest daughter, Joanne, hold a hushed conversation in the kitchen, but their words are so clear they could be whispering into a microphone.

'I don't want you to worry or anything, but I'm telling you straight. Within the next six months we're going to have to get rid of another two CPs, listen,' Debs tells her.

It will confuse the investigation, he says, but Joanne seems to suggest that he is already in the clear.

'Yeah, but what for?' she says. 'They've already been here … They've questioned, taken the car. If they found anything on that car don't you think that they would have been fuckin' pullin' youse both into the police station by now?'

At the time, her logic may have seemed impeccable. In December 1998, police scientists cleared sister Nicole Debs' Hyundai Excel – an 18th birthday present from her father – of involvement in the police shootings. But events had moved on.

Everything had begun to change the previous winter, when police had no breakthroughs, no clear leads, and the first anniversary of the killings was approaching.

At the time of the shootings the lack of evidence and clear suspects suggested police faced a protracted investigation. The then head of the homicide squad, Rod Collins, told relatives of Gary Silk that if there was not a breakthrough in the first two weeks it could take two years.

Paul Sheridan was heading the murder investigation. Sheridan, then a detective inspector in the homicide squad and a graduate of the prestigious FBI National Academy, agreed the case would be a marathon.

When senior police want results they usually turn to their most experienced detectives. Sheridan defied convention when he created the investigating taskforce called Lorimer. He turned away from the comfort of veterans and drafted young detectives, reasoning that energy and stamina would be more valuable than experience.

By mid-1999, almost a year after the shootings, they had gathered enough intelligence against five suspects to persuade courts to allow them to bug telephones and plant listening devices. But each lead ended in disappointment.

They were running out of time. There had been too many false leads, too many dead ends. Some senior police were losing confidence and patience. There was talk of scaling down the taskforce or changing tack to introduce a 'harder edge' – a tougher, kick-down-doors approach.

Instead, Sheridan ordered a review of all material held by the taskforce. He was prepared to start over.

Among the thousands of tips, interviews and false starts, they found a glimmer.

It was not a eureka moment. Just one small thing that reignited interest in Bandali Michael Debs, hard-working tiler and middle-aged family man.

Debs had been under notice within days of the shootings. Shattered automotive glass at the scene had told police the killers fled in a small Hyundai with a broken rear window.

Police asked parts suppliers to alert them to anyone seeking a Hyundai rear window. Which is why, when a young couple arrived in a Mazda mid-morning on 26 August 1998 – 10 days after the shootings – to pick up a

Hyundai Excel replacement rear window, the sales assistant at Grant Walker Parts in the Melbourne suburb of Bayswater noted the registration number of the car.

The Mazda was registered to Joanne Debs. Questioned, Bandali Debs said he had broken the Hyundai's window, claiming he closed it on metal strips used for tiling.

He said the accident happened at a work site on 19 August – three days after the shootings. Police took his mobile phone records to check his movements over the time of the shootings, but when glass from Nicole Debs' Hyundai was tested in December 1999, and failed to match crime scene samples, he was not pursued further.

A police surveillance crew was set on Debs and trailed him when he left for work and when he returned home. Nothing untoward showed up. Debs appeared to be an early riser and hard worker at his tiling trade. Nothing in his background or his behaviour suggested a double life. If anything he was too busy on work sites to have the energy for armed robbery.

On the night of the shootings, Silk and Miller had been taking part in Operation Hamada, an investigation into a series of 'soft target' robberies – raids on isolated restaurants, take-away stores and shops.

It was not the first such operation. During the review, an officer noticed from phone records that in the days after the shootings, Debs had made a series of calls to a man suspected of involvement in a series of armed robberies strikingly similar to the Hamada raids.

This earlier sequence of robberies, investigated by police under Operation Pig-Out, hit 28 targets between 1991 and 1994. There were two bandits, a heavy-set man with a younger assistant, and the robberies occurred in Melbourne's outer east. In most cases the victims were tied up. But on their last job, on 9 October 1994, at the Palm Beach Restaurant at Patterson Lakes, they had too many victims – 17 diners and three staff – to bind them all.

As usual, both bandits were dressed in dark pants and jumpers and balaclavas, and were carrying handguns. The robbery went badly when one of the patrons started abusing the robbers and would not shut up. Panicked, they bailed out of there.

But one of the diners trailed their getaway car, a white Ford Meteor, closing in sufficiently to take down the registration number, although he lost interest when one of the robbers pointed a gun at him.

About three-and-a-half hours later, the owner of the Ford Meteor walked into Dandenong Police Station. It was 4.05 am, 9 October 1994, and 18-year-old Jason Manuel Ghiller had come in to report his car stolen.

He had been at a local nightclub earlier, he said, while his car was nicked. In fact Ghiller had spent the previous two hours running through the Nu Hotel in Scott Street bailing up his mates to tell them he had been there all night and where the fuck had they been? He was almost certain someone at the Palm Beach holdup had sighted his car's registration so he was building an alibi.

Ghiller's Ford was later found burnt out in nearby Lysterfield and he lodged an insurance claim. The Pig-Out robberies stopped after that and Ghiller sweated through hours of interviews with Pig-Out investigators.

There had been an earlier close call, although it was not then seen as a Pig-Out incident. Two cops on uniform patrol pulled over a Nissan Bluebird at Hallam, in Melbourne's south-east on 19 September 1994. But when one of them started to approach the Nissan he saw a man pointing a gun at him.

Three shots were fired at the police car before the Nissan sped off as the cops fired back. They lost the Nissan which later was found burnt out behind the Fountain Gate Shopping Centre. It proved to have been stolen from a car yard three months earlier. Its number plates were stolen too. Since it was untraceable, the robbers felt confident enough to go out again the next month.

They ended up with their bungled job at the Palm Beach. This time their getaway car was traceable and Jason Ghiller was scared out of the business.

It would be four years before the Pig-Out-style robbers struck again.

When, in 1998, two bandits launched a similar series of raids there was a difference. While the older gunman seemed the same, his partner was colder and more aggressive.

They thought, rightly, that the original, younger robber had been scared off by the near-capture after the Palm Beach Restaurant raid, and the older man had recruited a new apprentice.

Hamada was launched, and police identified 60 possible targets for the pair, with 10 restaurants highlighted as the most likely. The Silky Emperor, a licensed Chinese restaurant on Warrigal Road, Moorabbin, was in the top 10.

Now, during the review of information by the Lorimer Taskforce, police found that Debs had been in phone contact with the young suspect from Pig-Out. Jason Manuel Ghiller was Debs' nephew.

The link was strong enough to demand another look at the hard-working tiler.

Further phone record checks showed that Debs had, on 16 August 1998, rung a man near Bendigo who advertised Hyundai parts for sale in *The Age* and *The Trading Post*. This was just hours after the murders, and three days before he claimed to have broken the window.

Olivia Coffman almost had to laugh. A sales assistant at Sportsmart in Noble Park, she had left the store to move her car, only to walk blithely into an armed robbery when she returned. She came through the front door, and was met by the barrel of a revolver.

Herded with the other staff and customers into an upstairs storeroom, she was, like the others, bound with her hands behind her back and her ankles together.

It was terrifying, and gut-wrenching. A female customer who was there with her little girl was told they wouldn't be hurt if they didn't do anything stupid.

But the bigger robber, the one whose revolver greeted Coffman when she returned to the store, whose gaze she avoided because he was clearly more dangerous, had also warned the store manager: 'I'll kill you if I have to.'

Lying there on the concrete storeroom floor, Coffman – an attractive, elfin, 20-something – could still see the joke: she knew the second younger robber. He had been walking into the store undisguised as she went out to her car.

Maybe he had been a customer before, because she had recognised the long face and the dark, heavy eyebrows. As for that stocking he had since pulled over his face, it was a pathetic attempt at disguise. Amateur hour. Almost comical.

'I very clearly remember almost having not to laugh at the fact that I could still see and recognise the face through the stocking,' Coffman said.

The next day she went to police headquarters and worked with an artist on a face likeness of the smaller robber who she reckoned was aged about 19.

Coffman was not happy with the likeness, but insisted she would always recognise him if she saw him again. In the flesh or a photograph.

The Noble Park robbery, in March 1998, was the second of 10 committed in a spree over five months at small businesses in Melbourne's eastern and south-eastern suburbs.

The crimes occurred at 'sitting duck' targets with poor security, which were cashed-up at the end of a week's trading and were robbed late at night or on weekend afternoons when other nearby outlets were closed.

Two robbers carried out the offences. Almost always, both carried handguns. They herded their victims together and taped their hands and feet.

One offender, taller – about 182 centimetres (six feet) – heavier, seemingly older, was in control, making demands and taking money, while the other, the short, lightly framed one, used the tape.

Two weeks before Coffman had a clear look at the smaller offender, Tracey Chadwick was able to observe his older, heavier accomplice at close quarters.

Chadwick was working at a car parts suppliers at Carrum Downs and found herself staring down the barrel of a gun. A big one. A .44 Smith & Wesson. A hand-held cannon.

For a time it was held to her head, but despite his black

cap and sunglasses and her terror, she formed a view of a sculptured face, drawn and angular.

Just as the Pig-Out robberies had ended suddenly in 1994, after the robbers were pursued by a victim, so too did the Hamada robberies, in August 1998, after Silk and Miller were shot.

The way they died has tied Gary Silk and Rodney Miller together inextricably. Yet their pairing on the night, and even their appearance at The Silky Emperor, was almost accidental.

Silk was based at St Kilda and Miller at Prahran. Both had been seconded to the Elwood Regional Support Group, which was seen as a bridge for young police to gain investigative experience before becoming detectives.

Silk, 34, was picked for the job as a supervisor because he was a trained detective, Miller because he had shown a flair for investigation. Silk was the senior man, with 13 years' experience. Miller, who was a year older, had joined later after serving in the army.

They were assigned to watch over a Korean restaurant, but after it closed they were reassigned to The Silky Emperor.

It was a routine job. So routine that both men kept their bulky bullet-proof vests in the boot of their unmarked car.

Two other police, senior constables Frank Bendeich and Darren Sherrin, were already there, but unable to watch the rear car park, which was located down a narrow access way. Silk and Miller took up a surveillance position in the car park.

About 12.15 am on 16 August 1998, a small Asian-built coupe drove into the car park, and drove out again almost immediately, followed by Silk and Miller in their unmarked police vehicle. The two vehicles turned out of Warrigal Road into Cochranes Road, an industrial estate that shuts down at night.

Bendeich and Sherrin followed, and drove past Silk and Miller, who had pulled up about 90 metres along Cochranes Road. As they rode by they could see that Silk was out of the car speaking to a male driver in front of the Asian-made car.

It did not look suspicious and Bendeich and Sherrin continued along Cochranes Road until they could turn right in the median strip into Capella Court. From there, they were about 200 metres from the scene. Their car's headlights were switched off, so neither Silk and Miller, nor their killers, knew of their presence.

Bendeich and Sherrin heard the volley of gunfire. They saw the muzzle flashes. They saw a Hyundai drive off slowly along Cochranes Road and they went to the aid of their colleagues.

They found Silk, clearly dead, on the roadside's grassy verge. Miller was missing, but finally he was found in front of The Silky Emperor, having struggled back to the main road, fatally wounded.

'Silky's dead. Silky's dead,' Miller told Senior Constable Glenn Pullin who found him. He was in pain and afraid. 'Help me, help me. Don't let me die.'

Asked how many offenders there were, he said, 'Two. One on foot … dark Hyundai … I'm fucked, I'm fucked … I'm having trouble breathing.'

Three hours later, he died.

Once Debs' telephone records linked him with one of the suspected Pig-Out robbers, police scientists re-checked the glass from Nicole Debs' Hyundai.

There was a complication. The windscreen bought at

Grant Walker Parts had not lasted long. Debs fitted it himself to save money, but it blew out when the car was being driven and a second replacement was professionally fitted about a month after the first.

Investigators queried the original glass examination by scientist Edward Kennedy-Ripon. He had taken two pieces of glass from the car and one from Cochranes Road. When he examined them in December 1998, he found small differences in the way they refracted, or bent, light.

He took the variation to be significant, and concluded that the vehicle was unlikely to be the source of the Cochranes Road glass. Was it possible he inadvertently tested glass from the first replacement window installed by Debs?

In September 1999, overseen by Peter Ross – a team leader at the Victoria Forensic Science Centre – Kennedy-Ripon conducted another analysis, this time using a much larger sample of glass fragments: 46 fragments from the car were tested. This time, a significant match between the Cochranes Road and Debs' Hyundai fragments was found. The Debs car was back in the frame.

Almost by chance, Jason Roberts, the boyfriend of Nicole Debs, entered the picture.

Mark Butterworth fixed on the young man's face. The picture jumped at him. An armed robbery squad detective sergeant seconded to the taskforce, Butterworth had seen Olivia Coffman's impression of the younger Hamada robber, and this man looked right for it.

Once Debs was elevated from a person of interest to a suspect, a police analyst compiled a profile of him and his associates.

Among pictures of Debs and his family was a photograph of Roberts, who qualified for inclusion by way of his relationship with Nicole Debs.

As it happened, he had been with her to pick up the rear window from Grant Walker Parts. While Debs claimed to have broken the window at work, Roberts told the salesman a thief had smashed it 'and stole the sub-woofer' from the car's sound system.

The day after his discovery, Butterworth went to see Coffman with a photo board of 12 faces. Coffman identified Roberts from his driver's licence as the younger robber with the heavy-set eyebrows.

Miller's dying declaration was that there were two offenders. That was confirmed in police thinking by Miller's shooting pattern as he returned fire in the brief gunfight: two of his bullets, fired presumably in the direction of Silk's killer, hit the roller door of a nearby panel shop, while another, which hit the rear of the Hyundai, was fired towards the killer with the Magnum.

Two weapons, two targets for returned fire, and the fact that the Hamada robberies were committed by two offenders, led to the conclusion that both had been present and both were involved in the gunfight.

Now, with Coffman's identification of Roberts, there were two clear suspects.

Bandali Michael Debs had an unconventional upbringing. He was born Edmund Plancis on 18 July 1953, the son of Helga Anna Frank and Silvester Weipnikowski.

Helga Frank had married Olgerts Plancis in Germany and the couple migrated to Australia in the late 1940s. They had one son, whom Olgerts took with him to Adelaide after the marriage broke up.

Helga Frank then had a series of partners – Silvester Weipnikowski, Dennis Reynolds and Albert Rutherford, whom she married in 1977. She had two further children by Weipnikowski – Robert Rutherford, who adopted his surname as a young adult, and Christine Weipnikowski.

Edmund Plancis proved to be a difficult adolescent. Unable to get along at home, he befriended a father figure in a man who ran a nearby boarding house, Bandali Michael 'Malik' Debs. When he was aged 17, the older man formally adopted Plancis, who in turn took Debs' name and shrugged off his family name.

Debs met his wife, Dorothy, in Melbourne. They married when he was about 26 and had five children – Joanne, Nicole, Kylie, Michael and Joseph.

Jason Joseph Roberts met Nicole Debs in a karate class. A couple of years later, when he was 17 and she 18, they met again at a party and soon after began dating.

Roberts lived at home in Cranbourne in south-east Melbourne with his mother. His father had died of a heart attack when he was 10. By the time he began dating Nicole Debs, he had left school and drifted into the building industry as an apprentice glazier and builder.

When Lorimer investigators looked closely, they were surprised at Debs' close relationship with his daughter's boyfriend. Just as Debs in his youth had gravitated towards an older man, he now became a father figure to Roberts.

In the space of a few months, the investigation had gone from a series of dead ends to one promising lead: the re-examination of Debs' phone records linked him to an armed robber; the review of the glass placed one of the Debs family's cars at the scene, and a witness had placed Roberts in the Hamada robberies.

In most of the Hamada robberies the victims were tied up with a type of tape commonly used in the glazing industry, with which Roberts was familiar.

It was promising, but it wasn't a case. For example, placing Nicole Debs' Hyundai at the scene was one thing, proving who was in it was something else. Police remained cautious.

'We weren't too excited,' Sheridan said. 'We had seen strong leads before that had gone nowhere.'

During October 1999, police began to monitor their suspects' bugged telephones – including Nicole and Joanne Debs' mobile phones; a public phone box in New South Wales used by Robert Rutherford; Rutherford's home telephone; and his partner's mobile phone.

In November, two bugs were placed inside the Debs' house. Bandali Debs' Commodore station wagon was bugged on 9 December, and Nicole Debs' Hyundai sedan was wired up on 13 December.

A further listening device was installed at the Cranbourne house under construction for Jason Roberts and Nicole Debs, as well as another at Roberts' mother's house.

Almost from the beginning, the police monitoring the listening devices – a crew headed by Detective Sergeant Dean Thomas – knew they were on to something. Criminality was evident in a conversation picked up in December 1999 between Bandali Debs and his young son Joseph, then 15, who was working at a local Hungry Jack's store.

It began with Debs asking if any money was counted that

day. The teenager told him: 'I swear that joint is so easy to fucking rob ... All you got to do is fucking knock out their guard ... fucking walk in ... they leave the safe open when they count the money.'

Debs responded: 'Is there only one guard now, or two?'

Moments later, Joseph suggested his father rob the joint when 'the black cunt's working. Beat the fuck out of him.'

Debs asked: 'Would it be all right if I, um, cut his fingers off?'

Joseph replied: 'Fuckin' oath. I hate the cunt.'

Weeks later the pair returned to the subject, with Jose – as his father called him – asking how long the raid would take. Told it would be 40 minutes, he told Debs: 'I want an apprenticeship off you.'

Debs answered: 'Well, I can tell you, after the first 12 months you'll be making big money.'

It was this series of conversations that convinced police Debs was the older gunman. They had connected him with younger suspects for the Pig-Out and Hamada robberies. Now they knew he was planning jobs.

Throughout the investigation, Sheridan briefed the Silk and Miller families every two weeks, even when there was no news. Now he could tell them there had been a breakthrough.

Gary Silk's father, Morrie, was dying of cancer. Sheridan knelt beside Morrie Silk's bed to comfort him with the news they had identified his son's killers. Within two weeks, Morrie Silk was dead.

Over time, the investigators would become familiar with the group's vernacular: police were 'CPs', detectives were 'Ds', firearms were 'articles', the Silk–Miller shootings were 'that other matter' and their victims were 'our friends'.

The surveillance revealed crimes being planned, and carried out, such as when Debs and Roberts carried out late-night burglaries, unaware that Debs' station wagon was bugged.

Other conversations, unheard by the jury for legal reasons, were boastful recountings of past glories: of Roberts using his car to run a motorcyclist off the road; of terrifying victims during robberies; of people soiling themselves in fear; of a man threatened with emasculation and something about smashing a woman's face; and how when Debs screamed at them 'people just dropped like fucking spaghetti'.

Some of the stories clearly came from the Pig-Out series of robberies. Their ruthlessness and appetite for criminality seemed insatiable. According to another tape played to the court, while riding in Debs' Commodore in June 2000, Roberts tells Debs that someone called Rodney 'wants to know how far we go'.

They are discussing becoming hitmen, of killing Rodney's estranged wife, a mother of three. They agree it will have to be an overdose: 'Take it out of the packet, wipe up all the gear, double check, take the syringe out, have it already filled. Boom, boom, boom,' says Roberts.

Debs confirms it – one good hit. 'Remember, that particular person's been taking a lot of drugs and they need a massive hit … The person's out of it, and just make sure they're holding it in their hand and that's it. When CP comes they say, ah, had too much.'

Roberts says their client 'will pay good'. Debs replies: 'Oh yeah, I reckon five big ones.'

And it seemed any reference to police shootings sparked conversation. Sheridan decided to exploit this, using press statements as a prompt as well as specific police action, which in one case included having two officers pull over the suspect Hyundai, with Roberts and Nicole Debs aboard, for a roadside check.

In February 2000, three months after the electronic surveillance began, and after police nudged him with their visit to Robert Rutherford in Sydney, Debs had his incriminating conversation with daughter Joanne in which he talked about another two police having to be shot, and in which she talked about it being done out of their area.

Getting to and from the shooting would mean taking back roads to avoid City Link's e-tags, he said, but Joanne urged him to wait to see what Rutherford knew. For at least a moment Bandali Debs also considered killing Miller's widow, Carmel, and her son, then almost 20 months.

'Seriously. Do you think I should get rid of the kid and the mother? ... So they try and get the investigation to think that it's drug-related or anything like that?' This was also a comment the Supreme Court jury did not hear. Justice Cummins ruled it inadmissible on the grounds that it could be prejudicial to a fair trial.

From all of this it emerged that Debs made confidants of his young daughters, but mostly not his wife, Dorothy. After discussing killing police with Joanne, for example, he cautions her not to talk to her mother, who he said was 'fuckin' very nosey'.

Talk of shooting police and Carmel Miller had immediate repercussions. Sheridan knew he did not have enough evidence to make an arrest, but would be forced to move if Debs went ahead with his threats.

A unit of the Special Operations Group was moved to the Police Academy in Glen Waverley. Debs and Roberts were under constant surveillance and would not be allowed to leave the region to conduct an ambush.

More difficult listening than the conversation with Joanne, but still audible when it was played in court, was Debs' conversation with his adoptive father, 'Malik', a few days later at home on 15 February. While his lawyer, Chris Dane, QC, argued that many of the details of the shooting had featured in media reports and knowledge of them did not imply he was present, Debs appeared to describe the shooting in detail. His was an account that the prosecutor Jeremy Rapke, QC, described as 'unnervingly accurate'.

According to the prosecution, Silk, who approached the gunmen's car, was shot first – in the chest by Roberts – with a .38 calibre revolver. And from less than two metres, he was shot in the hip and head, effectively executed, with a .357 Magnum, while lying helpless. Silk's pistol remained in its holster.

Miller was shot once in the chest with the Magnum fired by Debs from within the car, but he fired several shots from his police revolver before crawling several hundred metres to Warrigal Road where he was found.

'He was on the ground – laying on the ground, firing in the air … he just shot up in the air and things went everywhere … and you know where they found the other one, a long way away,' Debs told Malik.

'They don't know. But the other one never got to pull his, it was still in the pouch.'

Debs also appeared to describe what went before, the police staking out The Silky Emperor restaurant and the robbers' car trailed out of the car park.

In words clearer than those that preceded them, Debs was recorded as saying: 'No, no those were the ones that were sittin' there, when we drove in just to quick look, they seen us so they drove behind us, and drove down the street to stop us. They stopped us. Then it's not good.'

This was followed by an account of the immediate aftermath of the shooting, including a reference to police messages picked up on a scanner: 'A few shots, it's no worries, a little thing … as soon as that happened we went. But then they came, after everything happened they come in one minute … oh yeah, we heard it on this … they said, "Oh one is gone, we can't find the other one".'

'After we left, they come in 30 or 40 seconds they were there, that means they had a few cars in the area.'

Justice Cummins told the jury this account could be used only against Debs, but not Roberts, since he was absent when Debs used the words 'we' and 'us'.

'Roberts wasn't there for this conversation between Mr Debs and his father, so Roberts can't put his hand up and say "That's wrong. I don't know what you're talking about" … you can't use it against Mr Roberts,' Justice Cummins said.

Roberts, however, provided his own moments of self-incrimination, among them the expression 'I kill Ds' in a conversation taped at his Cranbourne house on 19 February 2000.

And after reading from a newspaper article, which quoted Sheridan as saying the younger of the two suspects may be in danger, Roberts remarked: 'I didn't know that. I had so much fun. Fuckin' hell.'

Seeing police attending a road accident on the Eastern Freeway, Roberts also seemed to offer an insight into an intense hatred of police. As he passed the scene, Roberts yelled 'Bang! Bang! Suck on that cunts,' before breaking into a laugh, his taunt clearly caught on the Commodore's bugging device. But to some investigators this shout was more than a statement of hatred – some reckoned it was a re-enactment of what had gone before.

That Debs and Roberts were insular – in effect, an independent crime cell – made the investigation difficult. They did not talk to outsiders and had no contacts among wider criminal networks.

But once identified, their clannish culture helped police. While they trusted no-one outside their group, privately, at home and in their cars, they spoke with a brutal honesty. Even the youngest daughter, Kylie, was able to speculate about where this was heading. Shortly after he told her that another two police would have to be shot to distract the investigation she asked him: 'What about when they shoot you – do you have a plan?'

The tapes revealed Debs rehearsing what he would say to police if they tried to re-interview him – he had made a formal statement to police to explain the broken rear window in his daughter's Hyundai.

He would also be heard talking about stuff hidden under the stumps of his mother's house – where a gun and stolen jewellery from one of the Hamada robberies would later be found, and another eight guns besides – and he would be heard paying an inordinate amount of attention to police shootings anywhere in the country. When a gunman shot three police in Queensland, Debs hoped that he might be blamed for the Silk–Miller shootings.

On 29 May 2000, six months after the electronic surveillance began, Sheridan announced a breakthrough in the investigation, claiming that an anonymous caller had declared they may be able to help identify the killers, especially the younger and smaller one.

On 31 May, at Roberts' house, Debs was overheard saying: 'I don't reckon they were talkin' to somebody … no-one was there but us.'

The conversation continued for minutes, with Nicole and Joanne Debs joining in. Joanne said: 'The police have an idea, they think they know how it happened of course.'

Jason: 'Yeah and I've seen two of their ways that they think it happened and it's fuckin' backwards.'

Nicole Debs tried to calm herself. 'It's someone fuckin' shittin'. Why would they … ?'

Police prepared a face image of the younger suspect – suggesting they wanted to know the person's identity. The image was taken from Roberts' driver's licence. Sheridan released the image on 16 July – a quiet Sunday. He wanted headlines and had cancelled two news conferences because of competing news stories, including a coup in Fiji and the introduction of the GST.

He was looking for maximum coverage to unsettle his targets.

Sheridan said: 'Somebody must know this person … this man is not a recluse. He cannot hide forever. This is the best lead we have received. I feel fairly confident that this will lead to the solution of this case.'

It prompted extensive conversations over several days among Debs, his daughters, Roberts and other associates. Nicole said repeatedly that she felt sick.

Debs said, accurately, that the police were trying to build up the pressure. 'They're trying to make something out of nothing … If people show 'em they're scared they get caught.'

Within days Roberts had contacted the taskforce. 'That's my picture, mate … ' he told Detective Sergeant Andrew Burgess. 'It looks exactly like me.'

During the trial, Ian Hill, QC, representing Roberts, called an expert witness who challenged Sergeant Thomas' interpretation of the expression 'I kill Ds'.

Speech pathology expert Professor Andrew Butcher said he heard the words 'I'll' and 'kill', but could not make out 'Ds'.

In cross-examining, Rapke produced compact disc recordings of the phrase. One was enhanced to remove background noise, the other left unenhanced.

Rapke was able to emphasise the expression, playing it 20 times to the jury, and he had Butcher agree that familiarity with a voice made it easier to accurately interpret sounds on a tape.

And the person most familiar with the voices on the tapes was the police witness, Sergeant Dean Thomas, who had spent thousands of hours listening.

In terms of voice recognition, Thomas had the advantage of having met Debs in person. The first time was when the Hyundai was examined in 1998. Then, they met by chance in an outer-eastern suburbs supermarket.

Thomas was there to buy milk. Debs was shoplifting that night's dinner, and had secreted a $15 tray of chicken in his jumper at the time.

He later bragged to his wife that he walked up to Thomas and said: 'How ya goin', mate? … Have you caught those pricks who … um … killed those cops?'

Debs was annoyed that he could not continue shoplifting and speculated that Thomas lived nearby: 'I'll have to get rid of him … find out where he lives and kill him.'

Roberts, meanwhile, had done his predecessor as Debs' sidekick a big favour. When he was first linked to Debs by telephone records, Ghiller had been a suspect for the police shootings, but Roberts had clearly taken over Ghiller's subordinate role.

It would emerge much later that this was not because Ghiller was scared out of the business, but that Debs knew the kid's cover was blown by the car registration link to the Palm Beach restaurant. It was Debs who had decided not to go out any more with Ghiller.

While Sheridan was making statements to the media, and using police operations to spark conversation between Debs and Roberts, an entirely different operation was aimed at Ghiller in the first half of 2000.

After keeping his secret for almost six years, Ghiller found himself with a new mate with whom he felt he could share everything. He would not realise, until far too late, that his mate was an undercover cop and that their conversations were recorded.

On 30 April, he related the story of that bungled last robbery fouled by an angry customer. 'But he came up to attack us … we were just rounding all the people up to move them aside … and he's goin', oh he's fuckin' he's going shit and I looked at me partner … and he sort of lunged for us and he just, he just knocked him out and then we fucked off.

'And all of a sudden there was a car behind us with its high beam on, and that's it, got away and that's it … I ended up going to a nightclub … I had a good alibi. Like I said, I went and got clothes, went to a club and all me mates were pissed.'

He showed the same lack of compassion for his victims as Debs and Roberts. One of the jobs he did with his 'Uncle Ben' was an early-morning raid on a newsagency in Clayton, near Moorabbin, on 29 November 1992.

A middle-aged couple, Shawki Yacoub and his wife, were opening up for the newsagent.

About 4.20 am, Mrs Yacoub saw two men wearing balaclavas and armed with handguns in the rear work area. Aiming the guns at her, they told her they wanted money. Mr Yacoub walked back into the work area, and, seeing his wife threatened, pushed her to the ground as he called to the robbers not to hurt her.

As he lay on top of his wife to shield her, Debs took aim and shot him in the back, severing his spine and crippling him. Years later, when the undercover cop asked Ghiller if he lost any sleep over that episode, Ghiller answered: 'Nah. Are you talking about the wheelchair cunt?'

Springfield Drive in Narre Warren marks out the furthermost boundary of a metropolitan fringe housing estate south of the Princes Highway. It mixes established homes with well-tended gardens with a few vacant lots.

From the Debs' house the view is of suburban rooftops and open paddocks to the Pakenham rail line a few hundred metres away.

Residents must have wondered what was happening to their quiet little neighbourhood in July 2000, when, within two weeks, a Springfield Drive man was shot while walking to his car early one morning, followed by a bomb scare in the street a fortnight later.

At least one family, however, knew the bomb scare was 'sus', as one of them put it.

'Anne' was stopped by police in Springfield Drive and held up for more than an hour on 11 July as a police robot examined a suspicious package. At least, that is what people were told since the roadblock prevented the dozen or so locals stranded by the operation from seeing much.

The plainclothes detective who stopped 'Anne' wore a name tag distinctive enough to stay in her mind: Sol Solomon. When she related the story to a family friend who is in the force, he remarked that it was odd that a senior, St Kilda Road-based detective like Sol Solomon – a member of the Lorimer Taskforce – would be on an operation so far out of town.

Her family decided the whole thing was suspicious. They felt vindicated in their judgement when Debs was arrested. They did not know him personally, but he was known to them as 'Fucking Michael', since those two words, a reference to one of his sons, often emanated in an exasperated shout from the Debs backyard.

The bomb scare was a cover to enable police to replace a failing battery in one of the listening devices inside the Debs home. By the time of the bomb scare, the devices had done their work in terms of gathering evidence, but police still needed to know what their suspects were thinking.

The shooting was unrelated to the Lorimer investigation, but it offered plausible cover for the bomb scare. Two weeks later, on 25 July 2000, Debs and Roberts were arrested by the Special Operations Group in co-ordinated raids. Debs stuck to his original story and was vague on any other questions.

Jason Ghiller was arrested six days later. He was planning a visit to the Lonely Planet brothel in Elsternwick when his mate, the undercover cop, and another bloke made a surprise diversion and delivered him up to the St Kilda Road police complex.

'I've got some bad news for you, buddy,' his mate said. 'It's a set-up, and we're from the government.

'Co-operate with these blokes. They are from the Lorimer Taskforce. It's your last hope. We're just doing our job, and that's it, all right? If you give them what [they] want, everything will be fine.'

Faced with armed robbery rather than murder charges, Ghiller would plead guilty.

Roberts was released and then finally charged on 15 August. Sheridan had considered delaying the final act for a day, to coincide with the second anniversary of the shootings, but felt that would be too contrived.

In the courtroom, the families of the victims and the accused sit a few metres from each other.

Opposite the nine women and six men of the jury, Gary Silk's mother and brothers, and Rod Miller's widow sit along one wall. The Lorimer investigators occupy the row in front of them.

At a right angle to this, a single form has been placed in front of the dock for the families of the two accused. Nicole and Joanne Debs, often joined by Kylie, sit here in conservative dark suits.

Once, they were rebuked by the judge for rolling their eyes and exchanging glances during Olivia Coffman's testimony, which placed Roberts as one of the Hamada robbers. But apart from that indiscretion, the Debs daughters remain impassive.

Meanwhile, Debs is placed at the scene of one of the robberies by Tracey Chadwick, who identified him from a videotape line-up after observing the older robber at gunpoint during the first of the Hamada raids.

Chadwick said that she looked three times at a police videotape recording of 12 men in September 2000, to see if she could identify either robber.

Number eight on the video flipped her stomach. 'When I saw [the video] a second time, I said: "Number eight gave me that hair-on-the-back-of-the-head, stomach-doing-somersaults kind of feeling",' she said. 'After seeing it a third time, I said it was definitely number eight.'

Number eight in the video parade was Debs, recorded during an interview after his arrest for the Silk–Miller murders.

Debs' sons join the daughters – a family united – when Chris Dane makes his closing argument to the jury. Behind them, Debs cuts a studious figure, taking notes throughout. Debs and Roberts show no emotion as the tapes of their conversations are played to the court, but by now there are no surprises. Just as there were none for the police who interviewed Debs.

They had, after all, listened to him outline his interview strategy with his father, Malik.

'They don't like it when you talk tough to them,' a laughing Debs had told Malik on 23 July 2000, two days before his arrest.

'And when you say I dunno, I dunno – that one, they hate it. You know that one? I dunno. I'm not sure … Happened so long ago. I didn't take much notice.'

Debs and Roberts do not testify in the trial. They stand by their right to remain silent, but have, in a sense, already testified.

Less than a week before his arrest, Debs had asked his family: 'Listen, do you think our phone's tapped?'

On 24 February 2003, Bandali Debs was sentenced to two terms of life imprisonment for the murders of Gary Silk and Rod Miller. He was refused a minimum term. This one-man crime wave, who with his youthful apprentices raged through Melbourne's south-east in two rampages, killing two police and shooting at two more, is never to be released.

Jason Roberts was also sentenced to life, but was given a 35-year minimum term which will see him released a few years before he could claim an old age pension.

Nine months after his mentor in crime, his Uncle Ben, was jailed, Jason Ghiller arrived at Melbourne's Supreme Court carrying an overnight bag. He was packed and ready for prison. Ghiller pleaded guilty to 22 offences including 13 counts of armed robbery, one of intentionally causing serious injury and two of reckless conduct endangering life. He was jailed for 10 years, with a six-year minimum term.

Joseph Debs never did win that apprenticeship, as an armed robber with his father, or in any other trade. In December 2003, not quite 12 months after Debs and Roberts were convicted of the police killings, the body of a young man was found in a house in Greensborough, north-east of Melbourne. It was Joseph Debs, dead of a drug overdose.

Nor was the justice system finished with Bandali Debs. In April 2007 he was back in court charged with the murder of troubled 18-year-old and occasional prostitute Kristy Harty.

Harty was shot once in the back of the head overnight on 18 June 1997 near a bush track in outer-suburban Upper Beaconsfield. An unused condom was found near her body. She was known to offer sex to motorists in the area and she was desperate for $90 in the hours before her killing.

The guns found under Debs' mother's home in Sydney included a .357 Magnum, the type of weapon used to kill Harty, although damage to the lethal bullet prevented conclusive identification of his gun as the murder weapon. While digging in the backyard the new owner of the house had uncovered two glass containers containing ammunition. Included among the bullets were 69 Winchester .357 Magnum cartridges of the type used to murder Harty. Semen at the scene further linked Debs to the killing. Forensic scientists found there was only a one in 370 billion chance the semen came from anyone other than Debs. The police case was that Debs killed her before, during or immediately after having sex with her.

On 11 May 2007 a Supreme Court jury convicted Debs of Harty's murder. Despite speculation that Debs' daughters could be legally viewed as accomplices in his second crime spree, they were not charged. The Debs family, however, was forced to surrender the Hyundai Excel used the night of the police killings.

Finally, in April 2005, the Court of Appeal refused Debs and Roberts objections to their convictions, and confirmed their sentences.

With John Silvester and Peter Gregory

CHASIN' — STORIES FROM THE HEROIN PLAGUE

1: WORKING THE GOLDEN ELBOW

I f this is the Golden Elbow, we must be a little way down the inside of the forearm, about where you need to start slipping in the needle when the veins up higher have scarred over. In other words, that scabby section of Russell Street, Melbourne, maybe 50 metres from the corner of Bourke.

It's quiet, no-one much around, and the girl with the dirty blonde hair is dozing. She lies on her back, her knees up, right arm over her eyes to keep out the insipid morning sun. No need to get moving just yet, the business around here starts sluggishly, too.

But it's beginning.

9.50 am, Russell Street
It could be one of those kiss-and-ride zones at a suburban railway station. A little silver–grey sedan pulls in to a no-standing spot, the guy in the passenger side leans over, gives his partner a peck and gets out. She buckles up, drives away and he goes off to work.

It is a short, nervy amble around the corner into Little Bourke Street. Under the Chinese gate he meets a teenager dressed all in black, they chat for less than a minute, and shake hands. Watch how it goes: the hands slip softly into each other, slide out, the fingers tucked over the palm, and head straight for a pocket. You see a lot of handshakes like that around here.

He continues his stroll. Three police are coming and he does a U-turn and disappears. A lot of U-turns here too, especially when the jacks are about.

10.10 am, Russell Street
A divvy van is nose-in to the kerb, its crew questioning a girl, making her empty her handbag on the bonnet. She's about 18, with wavy, fair hair, dressed nicely, quite pretty. They spotted her asking people for money on the corner. She's got a bagged hot dog and sausage roll and about $200 in twenties and fifties.

'She reckons she just got her dole,' says the constable. 'We told her to go home, to stay away from here, but what can you do? The place draws 'em like flies. They're all on the methadone, they say, every one of them on the program,' he laughs. 'And they're all going to get fixed – first thing tomorrow.'

Down the street the other three coppers have roused the sleepy blonde. She's sitting up, head down, elbows on her knees, rubbing the sleep from her eyes with the heels of her palms. She sees the camera. 'Aw shit, don't take me photo,' she says. 'I don't want me parents to know.'

10.30 am, Bourke Street
The green steel benches on the north side of the street, between the Nike Store and the Village Centre, are filling

with regulars. Walk this strip often enough and you get to know the faces: lazy-eyed, lank-haired girls bumming change; burly, close-cropped young men in exercise-yard huddles by the amusement parlours; hip-looking, watchful young Asians catching people's eyes. There's a sense of community.

Look at this one: stocky, a blotchy blue tattoo on his neck. He cocks his head at a long-haired fella walking past and, out of the corner of his mouth says, 'Chasin'?' The other guy pretends not to hear. He shrugs, says his giddays to the fruit-barrow man, and gets on with his rounds.

Across the road the foot patrol has pulled up two Kooris in flannelette and a tall, unshaven, white guy in paint-spattered tracksuit pants. They check IDs, write down the details, while the three men smoke, apparently unfussed. Been there, done that. The police move on.

The counter assistant at Priceline grins. Reckons he sees it every day, all day. 'You want a real scoop,' he says, 'go to KFC and ask how many deaths they've had in their toilets in the last 12 months.'

10.45 am, Bourke Street
Suddenly, the three police are back, scanning the street like meerkats, looking for the bloke in the painted tracksuit pants. A call has come back on the radio, something about an outstanding warrant.

There he is, outside the Subway store. They try to explain, but he gets a bit mouthy. Next thing his arms are up his back and he's frogmarched down Royal Lane and into a car park. Hands up, he's patted down, made to get out of his shoes and drop his trousers.

Handcuffed, he's led back into Bourke Street to wait for the police car to come and take him away.

11.10 am, corner of Bourke and Elizabeth
But for the pin-prick pupils and sagging shoulders, he could be one of those living-statue artists busking further up the mall. Five minutes and counting and he's barely moved. He's sitting at the top of the GPO steps, trying to roll a smoke and keep from nodding off at the same time. Someone wanders up to bot a smoke and ends up rolling it for him. As soon as he leaves the smoke falls from his hand and he begins the whole near-comatose process again.

Nearly 10 minutes now. In the end we go and do it for him. 'Ta, mate,' he slurs. 'For some reason I can't get me fingers to work.'

11.20 am, Elizabeth Street
There's mumbling from the middle cubicle of the underground toilets next to the GPO. Two teenagers, boys really, one on the floor, the other on the seat, sharing a stall and a hit.

Joe Buttigieg, the toilet attendant, works around them. He's been here for eight years and he's not stupid enough to interfere. 'I mind my own business, what else can I do?' he says. 'I'm scared if I say something, they might whip the needle out and jab me.'

Besides, he's used to it now. Sometimes they're in and out every five or 10 minutes. He cleans up their puke, asks them to take their fits away and when they don't he picks up the used syringes with a set of barbecue tongs. Sometimes four or five times a week, he calls the ambulance when they overdose.

The kids come out, none the worse for wear, and hare off down Elizabeth Street, yelling at each other. Two minutes later their spot's taken by another user, and soon another pair. 'It's a procession,' shrugs Joe.

12.15 pm, corner of Bourke and Russell
Talk about presence, this is a police overdose: two uniforms on the Darrell Lea corner, three others outside Hungry Jack's, two bicycle patrolmen quizzing a man at the end of Bullens Lane.

A woman and her little boy make a late crossing against the lights and a policewoman pounces, drawing her aside and taking her details. When she lets her go the woman still looks confused. This is Operation Pedestrian, targeting jaywalkers.

Maybe 50 metres back down Bourke Street, two of the users from the GPO toilets are squatting sleepily in a doorway. The guy arrested earlier is back, already bailed on his outstanding traffic matter. He sees the coppers and does one of those U-turns.

12.45 pm, corner of Bourke and Swanston
The sleepy blonde from this morning and a dark-haired friend are working the crowd at the tram stop, asking for change. A young woman shakes her head and edges away. Surly, they move on to the next mark.

'At least they didn't try and spin a story,' she says. 'Just asked if I had any change. It must be me because every day I have them coming up and asking. Either here or down the other end near Spencer Street Station. It drives you crazy.'

1.30 pm, off Russell Street

Call them John and Chloe. He's 23, wiry and blond; she's 19, also blonde, almost skeletally thin, with an 18-month-old baby back home with her mother. Nice, friendly kids down in Melbourne from the country for a few days on a sort of junkies' holiday.

They're squatting in an alley doorway of the Greater Union cinema. A little stream of urine runs from the alley. They've just gone halves in $50 worth of gear they scored over on the corner. Couldn't wait to get into it, says John, but it did nothing. Have to get some more later.

Chloe dumps the used fits in a wheelie bin. They've got standards, she says, they never shoot up alone, always use clean needles, and carefully dispose of their syringes.

John has been using for about three years. 'I discovered this shit and it was downhill all the way,' he says. 'I was drunk and a bloke said, "Try this," and I said, "Sweet." Next morning, when I sobered up, I thought I'd like to try it while I was straight and I thought, "Shit, that's nice." So then you have that third one. And it's got you …'

They finish each other's sentences: 'See the problem is, it's too nice,' says Chloe. 'It takes away all your problems and that makes it so easy to go back to, 'cos it's so nice.'

John says he's got a job, 12-hour shifts in a factory back home, but it's never enough. 'You've got to do a few rorts here and there to get enough … just shoplifting and stuff like that. I've never been gutsy enough to go out and do holdups, but I've thought about it. I've thought about selling myself too. I never have, but I've thought about it and that's bad enough.

'They need to find some legal way to control it. There's no control, that's what causes all the problems.'

2.45 pm, off Little Bourke

Croft Alley is about as seedy and scary as it gets. It runs off Little Bourke, dog-legging a couple of times past the back doors and stinking rubbish skips of some very good restaurants until it ends at the back door of a cinema. The alley is piled high with the detritus of deals and hits: syringes, swabs, capsules of distilled water, plastic spoons and human filth.

Part-way down there's a little graffiti: 'I'm going to bom Swanson police station son and you will all die, coper scum.' The misspelling has been corrected in white chalk. You get a hint at why such sentiments come about when the three plainclothes officers surprise you there.

City Patrol Constables Mike Maybury, Simon Bourke and Kasia Bartnicki are working a shift, patrolling byways like Croft, Payne's Place and Celestial Avenue, the makeshift shooting galleries of the CBD. The expandable batons are out because an hour ago someone threatened them with a syringe.

Suddenly a girl with deep-set, shadowed eyes bumbles around the corner. 'Oh, this doesn't go through to the shops,' she tries, as if lost, and spins on her heel. No such luck.

Gently, politely, she's made to empty her handbag and out tips the usual kit: syringes, swabs, toilet paper and spoons. She slings the bag over her shoulder, but Maybury asks for another look. And extracts two tightly packed foils of heroin. Out come the cuffs.

While they wait for the van, Bartnicki says she's only been in the job since February: 'I had no idea, but my eyes have been opened, it's everywhere.'

'It's a classic example of what's going on around us, of how these alleys and lanes are being used,' says Maybury.

'You might look at people like this as the poor victims, and that might be true, but obviously someone's getting rich off them. And they're just over on the next corner.'

5 pm, corner of Bourke and Russell
Right on the Golden Elbow, a trio of undercover police have pulled up three young blokes after watching a transaction go down. They find a cigarette filter soaked in smack. 'It's like trying to plug the dyke,' says one, 'when there's [sic] leaks popping out all around you.'

A regular, Sam, wanders up to chat. Says he's been away, meaning in the nick, for three months. Now he's trying to stay clean. 'Thirty years old and look at the torment it's done to my body,' he tells one of the coppers.

'But I did use today. Got offered a $50 rock for 20 bucks,' he says, giving a sheepish never-look-a gift-horse smile.

'See you around,' he says. And, of course, they know they will.

THE HOUSE OF HORRORS

You need a reason to go to Reservoir's Summerhill estate, a sad, lost pocket of once-public housing deposited among the unfashionable sweep of Melbourne's northern suburbs. Newly arrived migrants have it. So does anyone on social services or in need of cheap housing. People with choices do not.

Joel Russell thought he had it. But it cost him his life.

Like nearby West Heidelberg, Summerhill has a rep, a 'name', but during the late spring twilight it settles into a benign quiet. Daylight saving is kind to this place. Residents tend neat little gardens or sit out on the front steps with VB longnecks. It's a reflective time. The sounds of kids playing hang in the still, evening air. Families of the newest arrivals, East African refugees, play soccer on their front lawns.

Down by what passes for the local shopping centre, the quiet creates a different mood, of loss and resignation. Most of the businesses have fled, hiding their failure behind heavy metal shutters now scarred with under-done graffiti. The car park is deserted.

Up the hill and along Nisbett Street it used to be different.

Business boomed there. Lance Franklin's business: dealing 'smoke'. Thirty, 40 cars a day, maybe 50 on pension day.

Joel Russell was 14 and a regular client of Lance Edward Franklin's drug business – mainly marijuana but occasionally speed.

Lance is a little man, sharp featured, with a body as hard and lean as a wild hare and a record of burglary, theft, drug and firearms offences. Franklin dealt dope, the currency of the Age of Aquarius, but he was no blissed-out flower child. Cross him, and you're a dog, a fucking lying dog.

What was the Franklin house is pre-fabricated concrete, 1950s Housing Commission stock, part of an estate that is being progressively privatised. It is on the low side of the street, so the property falls away to the south creating a kind of enclosed basement under floor level. It was down here that Lance Franklin and five other men took Joel Russell and beat him to death.

Who said so? Well mostly Joel's 17-year-old brother, Wade Russell. Wade was down there too, having been forced to crawl through the house on his knees and led down into the sub-floor area where he was flogged with a baseball bat and made to eat dog shit by Lance's son, Alan. Lance in miniature, Alan has the same high cheekbones, hollow sculpted cheeks and tight frame as his dad, and he is working on his mean streak.

Joel and Wade knew the house well. They had lived there before the Franklins and had taken to making regular visits to buy marijuana. Their mum, Lorraine, knew Lance Franklin, and was able to put names to the descriptions of his associates that Wade would offer up but could not himself identify.

Joel and Wade began their ordeal about 2 pm on Tuesday, 14 January 1997, but Joel set out on that path about 14 hours earlier when, with a friend, Chris Hexter, he paid a late-night visit to Nisbett Street to buy a small quantity of marijuana for $25.

Alan Franklin was supposed to be relaxing with friends, all grouped around the glass tank in the lounge room that served as a coffee table, but which also housed Lance's pet snake. Trouble was, someone had brought along a mouse in a box. It had eaten its way to freedom so they were running around looking for it.

Lance was in and out during the evening, and was visiting his girlfriend when Joel arrived, so Alan sold him the dope. Within minutes of Joel leaving there was a knock on the door answered by Alan's mate, Luke Bird.

'We're running through,' he was told when he opened the door to two men, one wearing a balaclava.

'No you're fucking not,' he shouted back, slamming the door.

Seconds later the raiders broke through the back door. There were four of them. Four men. Two whites and two Aboriginals.

Alan, his girlfriend Kristy Edwards and Luke fled. Their mate Robert Carpenter was unable to get away, and was held by the burglars until they left. They made off with an impressive haul: gold jewellery, 14 pairs of runners, $250 cash, 135 grams of marijuana, most of Lance Franklin's clothes and a video player. They left behind three of Lance's T-shirts.

When Lance got home and the others had returned to the house, Robert Carpenter's brother brought over some dope. They had a smoke and started canvassing who might have done the run-through.

Suspicion soon fell on Joel Russell because he had left just minutes before it happened, Luke Bird told police. 'They didn't go on about Joel, it was more that his name was mentioned, along with a lot of others,' Luke said. One other thing he could say: the white guys he saw during the run-through did not include Joel Russell.

At about 10 am, Lance went to Neville Honeysett's house in Preston. Shane Kelly and his girlfriend Dallas Sweetman were also there. Lance was badly shaken, Sweetman recalled later.

Later, after she had obtained her methadone dosage and Shane had reported to police as he was required, the couple went to Lance's home. By now, the conversation had turned to 'how they thought that it was Joel and Wade'.

Joel and Wade were in the frame, but they didn't see it coming.

About 2 pm on 14 January, Lance Franklin drove up to the Russells' house down near the Yarra flood plain in Alphington. The first Wade saw of him, he was pulling up in Alan's two-tone green Holden Calais. Through the driver's window Lance asked if Wade had seen a bloke, Andrew Werner, who was supposed to owe Lance $2500.

Wade agreed to help Lance look for him, but Lance insisted Joel come too.

'I said that I would know all the places Andrew might be. Lance said just to get him to come anyway in case we forget a place,' Wade said later.

They drove to a series of addresses without finding the man, and then, Wade made it easy for Lance. He asked to buy a couple of grams of dope. Lance said: 'Yeah sweet, it's at home, you'll just have to come home with us.' It all seemed so ordinary.

At Nisbett Street Wade and Joel and Lance went straight into Lance's bedroom because that is where he always stored the smoke.

As he led the way into the bedroom, Wade noticed Alan and a cluster of others in the lounge room but he ignored them. Alan's girlfriend Kristy was lying on Lance's bed, but she left immediately: 'Sorry. I'll leave,' was all she said. Lance headed to the right side of the bed, Wade figuring he was going to get the smoke.

Time moved too slowly once Wade saw Lance pick up a silver baseball bat, walk behind Wade and up to Joel, carrying the bat alongside his right leg.

Dallas Maree Sweetman had known Lance most of her life, from when she was 11 or 12 living in the high-rise public housing flats in Collingwood and when her older sister Kylie was dating him. Dallas was an aunt to Lance's youngest kids Trent and Samantha, born during the 10 years Kylie shared with him.

Although the relationship with Kylie had hit the rocks five years earlier, Dallas still saw Lance, practically every day, to buy smack. This day she was visiting with her boyfriend Shane Kelly who was just out of jail.

In the lounge room, Dallas heard a sudden, distinctive sound from the direction of the bedroom. Like a bat hitting a baseball, she said later.

Alan Franklin was facing the bedroom, watching through the open door like he knew something was coming: 'Fucking beautiful,' Dallas heard him say. 'Straight across the head.'

The bedroom door closed. Then she heard shouting. Lance mostly.

In the bedroom, Lance backed up with a verbal barrage: 'Where's me gold chains? The clothes, the shoes? I want the smoking dope as well … you little cunt, you set it up last night … two minutes after you walked out four guys ran through the place with knives.'

Wade later told police: 'When we said we didn't know, that's when the second blow to Joel's head came.'

Lance turned on Wade next. 'And you little cunt, I'm gunna shiv you four or five times for knowing about it and not trying to stop him.'

Shortly after, the three of them emerged from the bedroom, Wade and Joel crawling on their knees, and Franklin announced, 'I've got me culprit.'

Franklin ordered the boys down into the sub-floor area. 'Get the fuck in there, you little cunts.'

Alan Franklin, Shane Kelly, Robert Carpenter and Paul Cassar – the boyfriend of Alan's sister Tracey 'Sissa' Franklin – followed like very interested spectators. Carpenter had lost some gold chains when he was held captive during the run-through and Sissa had lost all her runners and gold as well.

It was too low under there for an adult to stand upright, but Lance lifted the bat as high as possible to hit Joel several times to the legs and body. The low roof cramped his style but Lance did the best he could. Then he ordered Alan to take hold of Joel's arm and hold it to the ground.

'Right, I am gunna ask you one more time and then I am gunna break your wrist,' Lance told Joel who screamed that the gold was in the roof, and that Chris Hexter, his friend who was with him when he bought the dope at Nisbett Street, had everything else and was going to sell it. Lance brought the bat down anyway, just like he said, on Joel's wrist.

'I could hear the sound that an aluminium bat makes,' Wade recalled. 'It is very hard to describe the sound.'

Alan Franklin laid into Joel next, kicking him in the ribs as he writhed in pain from the blow to his wrist. Lance told him not to dirty himself by getting in too close: 'Use the bat.' Alan told Joel to lift his arms above his head so he could take a clear swing at his ribs. 'Shut the fuck up, you little dog. My girlfriend was shittin' herself pretty bad. Shut the fuck up and cop it sweet.'

There was more of this. Paul Cassar rushed under the house and punched Joel. Kelly kicked him as well. Alan laid into Wade with the metal poles of a dismantled trampoline, and when he went down, Cassar kicked him in the head, maybe three times. Wade covered up so Cassar shifted target, kicking him in the chest, and stomping on his groin.

'These cunts aren't talking. Go up and get me a couple of shivs. I'm gunna shiv these bastards until they start talking.'

Cassar disappeared, returning soon with a couple of Staysharp knives. Lance Franklin stabbed Wade in the buttock and sliced Joel across his collarbone.

This time Joel said the gold jewellery was in the roof of his home, but the bashing did not stop immediately.

Alan joined Lance in bashing Joel while Shane Kelly straddled Wade, forcing a curved section of trampoline framing into his neck. Shane was working hard, his sweat dripping onto Wade. A few metres away Alan was holding Joel's arms and Lance was flailing at him with the bat.

Lance finally ordered that Joel be tied up, and Neville Honeysett, who had just arrived, helped out by showing

Alan how to hogtie the teenager, leaving him suspended from one of the floor bearers, slung sway-backed with his stomach touching the ground.

Before he left, Lance belted Wade with the baseball bat half a dozen times. Joel was frantic. If the gold jewellery was not in the roof, then Wade must have moved it, Joel told Lance. If the stolen goods were in the roof, Lance said he would let them go: if not, 'I will fuckin' kick the living fuck out of you.'

Carpenter re-appeared suddenly, demanding Joel return his mobile phone that was pinched in the run-through. He kicked Joel and stomped on his head.

There was a surprise waiting for Lorraine Russell when she returned home from shopping. Lance Franklin was in her roof.

'He came out with a telephone in his hand,' the boys' mother said. 'He said he was looking for gold.' The boys were in Broadmeadows, he claimed, 'with some nasty men'. Then he was gone.

He had already made his phone call. Alan took it back at Nisbett Street. 'Hang on, Dad. I'm having trouble hearing what he is saying,' Alan told the others under the house. He picked up the bat and twice swung it into Joel's shoulder blades. Joel said to tell him to look near the veranda at the front door.

Alan put the phone away and nothing much happened for half an hour. Upstairs they were blowing a few bongs, and Alan kept the business going as Lance's regular customers turned up to buy dope. There was a steady flow of visitors to the house and Alan took many of them into the backyard to have a look. Twenty-eight deals were done that afternoon. In total, about 50 people were said to have come and gone during the day.

In this lull, Wade could see some of them standing around the backyard.

Alan Franklin's sister, 'Sissa', came home during the afternoon and was told to turn up her music. Loud. The television was tuned to cartoons on pay TV to amuse Lance Franklin's five-year-old niece, Karen. The cartoons didn't hold her though, or maybe those under-floor noises caught her curiosity, and she ran out to the driveway and over to the side of the house. Her dad, Lance's brother Shane, called her back in each time.

Returning from the futile search, Lance took up the bat. 'I could see the expression on Lance's face. He was pretty much trying to give it everything he had,' Wade said.

Lance was furious. 'I hate climbing up into roofs because of spiders and shit like that,' he said.

Alan had Sissa bring down a sock and a shoelace to tie a gag into Joel's mouth. Joel's T-shirt was stripped off him to mop up the blood streaming down his face. His shoulders and legs were marked red and purple.

The thumps could be heard from inside the house, coming it seemed from directly below the lounge room. Six or seven at a time, then a pause of maybe 20 or 30 minutes, Dallas Sweetman said.

Lance was gone again when Alan ordered Wade to eat a piece of dog shit that was under the house, where Lance had tied up his pit bull. It was dry and crumbled in his mouth and Alan refused him a drink of water. Wade said he had started to choke on the dog shit when Dallas Sweetman appeared with some water.

During this time Lance was back at the Russells' home, with Robert Carpenter waiting by the door with a baseball bat for the return of Chris Hexter who was living at the Russells' unit.

Lorraine Russell asked him what he was going to do with the bat. Lance said that depended on the answers he got. But when Hexter arrived he said he did not know anything about any gold. Carpenter had a good look at him and said, 'That's not the bloke.' Lance pulled down the neck of the kid's T-shirt and then the pair took off again.

At Nisbett Street the torturers became a little more inventive. Shane Kelly hit Wade with a second baseball bat to coax him into hitting his brother.

'I then hit Joel twice around the top of his right shoulder area. I didn't do it hard and I told Shane I was sorry it wasn't hard. I had to hit with my left hand because I couldn't move the right one that well. The next thing I recall was feeling a kick to my right side around my ribs. Alan said something like "don't say sorry to your brother" so I thought that it was him who kicked me.'

Lance returned home, still convinced Joel knew more than he should about the run-through, but this time when Joel offered up Chris Hexter's name Lance said he ripped down Hexter's T-shirt and 'he had no gold at all'.

But it was slowly dawning on Lance that Wade had no part in it. He decided to take the older Russell home.

When Wade was led away, Joel's shoulders were black – 'not purple, literally black' – his legs dark purple, his body suspended and motionless, his breathing a rattle and he had blood streaming from his nose and mouth and the back of his head.

Wade's return was Lorraine Russell's worst fears realised. She burst into tears at the sight Lance Franklin and Robert Carpenter brought with them.

To Lorraine, it seemed her son's head was swollen like a discoloured pumpkin. His face was misshapen. Unrecognisable. He could not walk unaided. He was dirty and bloodstained. Lance Franklin told Lorraine Russell: 'This is nothing, the other one is worse.'

He said he should take the family's TV, fridge and freezer as compensation for what the boys had organised. The boys' little sister, Leah, 11, called Lance an 'arsehole' for what he had done to her brother. 'Get upstairs, you little slut,' he told her.

He left, but came back yet again, with Wade's wallet. He said that he had dropped Joel off with a bottle of coke and $10 for a taxi. An ambulance was called for Wade and Lorraine went off to Faye Street, where Joel was supposed to have been dropped, but he did not turn up for three days.

Joel may still have been alive, according to medical evidence, when Wade was dropped at home. He probably died about eight hours after his ordeal began, from either asphyxiation or blood loss, or a combination of both. He had five broken ribs, a ruptured kidney, a broken collar bone, a broken vertebra, internal bleeding and massive bruising.

About the time of his dying, Wade was being picked up by an ambulance. The police were about to arrive at the Russell home.

When the police went on to Nisbett Street, a little after midnight on Wednesday 15 January, and two hours after they spoke to Lorraine Russell, Joel was gone and so was Franklin's car.

Questioned at the local police station, Alan Franklin said he had been home all day but had not been involved in any assaults on Joel or Wade.

Lance arrived home, saw the police heat and drove on to stay at his sister's. He was picked up 30 hours later, walking along High Street, Preston, early on 16 January. Interviewed at the homicide squad that day, Lance denied having anything to do with either of the Russells being bashed. 'As for getting rid of his body, or both their bodies or whatever, well, you've gone a couple of miles past me, chief,' he said.

'You know the mentality of them two kids. Are you trying to say I'm stupider than them? You're trying to get me for some bloody, double fuckin' murder or something. And I'm not gonna cop that.'

Lance did make certain admissions to an undercover cop who was in the cells with him, however, including the revelation that, 'Every time I go to jail, some cunt fuckin' dies'. This was believed to be a reference to the death years before of his father.

In court even Lance's lawyer would marvel at the obscenities that poured from his mouth: 'Some of it is not English, it's simply saying profanities,' he observed.

Justice Frank Vincent responded: 'It's certainly English. Very old English – some version of Anglo-Saxon.'

Joel's body was found floating in the Yarra River at Hawthorn, the opposite bank to Alphington, two days after he disappeared.

When they went to trial in July 1998, Alan Franklin, then 20, Shane Kelly, 40, and Robert Carpenter, 20, pleaded guilty to the manslaughter of Joel Russell, and to unlawfully imprisoning and causing serious injury to Wade Russell.

Paul Cassar, 19, pleaded guilty to causing serious injury to Wade and to Joel Russell. Neville Honeysett, 32, pleaded guilty to assisting Lance Franklin to avoid arrest.

Lance Franklin, then 40, pleaded not guilty to murder but guilty to false imprisonment and to intentionally causing serious injury.

He had been charged with murder because he was different to the manslaughter defendants, argued prosecutor Jeremy Rapke, QC. He had suffered the personal loss of the run-through; he lured the boys from their home; he struck the first blow; he directed the others; he was the only one to use a knife on either victim; and he had the obvious power to put a stop to the attacks. After all, said Rapke, 'he extricated Wade Russell and restored him to his mother'.

The jury agreed and Lance Franklin was sentenced to 22 years.

But for Lorraine Russell that could never be enough. She retreated from the inner suburbs to a small unit in country Victoria where she is unknown and might construct something of her life.

There, at the far end of the narrow lounge room, where the curtains are drawn against the spring sunshine, is a small table with a formal arrangement of photographs and candle holders. Its backdrop of rich burgundy curtains gives it the look of a shrine, and so it is. A shrine to a family history of violent loss.

There is a little girl, maybe 12 months old, with plump red cheeks, turned towards the camera as if someone just called her name. Next to this is a larger portrait, a teenage girl, bright, attractive and confident.

These are unremarkable images, typical of any family album, not intended for strangers. But the next portrait many have seen, in newspapers and on television: an adolescent boy stares evenly out of the frame. Joel Russell, tortured and bashed to death under a house in Reservoir, aged 14.

The little girl, Michelle, would have been Joel's eldest sister had she not died in a Thomastown house fire 24 years earlier, shortly after the photograph was taken. The teenage girl is Joel's twin, Ruth, who died of a deliberate drug overdose eight months after he was murdered, deeply troubled and unable to cope with her brother's death and the manner of his dying.

Sometimes Lorraine lights a candle for each of them. She is a religious woman despite the layers of horror her God seems intent on visiting upon her. But she is not forgiving. She speaks heatedly, angry and bitter. She had hoped to put some of the pain of Joel's dying behind her. Now she says she cannot, because the sentences of those who killed her lovely and loving boy, her best friend, seem to hold his life in contempt.

Two walked free from court. Lance Franklin, the ringleader, got his 22 years with a minimum of 17, and Shane Kelly received a minimum of eight years. Two others, Franklin's son, Alan, and Robert Carpenter, received seven years with four-and-a-half-year minimum sentences.

Lorraine Russell's emotion threatens to overwhelm her. Her hands tremble constantly, her voice occasionally breaks and she fights off her tears. These men did not just kill her son, she insists, they destroyed a family and mocked the boy's memory. They mocked him when they tied a blue shoelace like a bow tie around his neck before they threw his trussed body into the Yarra River. And they mocked him when they exchanged smiles and thumbs up signs with their friends at their sentencing.

'I am absolutely so angry about this,' she says. 'Fair enough for what they did to Wade, they've been sentenced for bashing Wade, but where's Joel's justice?

'I was told they were going to come out old men: the older two would die in jail; the younger ones would come out old men.

'They have tortured him with iron bars, bats ... and Paul Cassar used an iron bar and walks with a two-year suspended sentence. Honeysett walks away. Nothing whatsoever. He tied up my boy by the feet and hands upside down, and he walked free.

'There was no justice done. And the horrific way he died, tortured for five hours and dumped in the river. Even after I saw him, I still couldn't believe it because there was no resemblance.'

While Lorraine and the remnant of her family have been moved from Melbourne for their safety, there is talk of another move, interstate, with new identities. She does not want it. She wants to retain some semblance of normality for her youngest daughter, Leah.

She knows better than most that you cannot run or hide. One of her brothers, Patrick, was murdered while hitch-hiking in 1985. Another brother, just 13, was killed in a hit-and-run accident. And her first husband, the father of Michelle, was killed by Cyclone Tracey a few weeks after Michelle died.

It was while she was in a psychiatric hospital being treated for depression after Michelle's death that she discovered marijuana was more effective for her than conventional medication. It is an awful quirk that marijuana introduced her and her boys to Lance Franklin, who was running a thriving drug business out of that Housing Commission house in Reservoir.

Now Lorraine Russell is consumed with bitterness. 'You can't see the inside of me. I'm tough,' she says.

So what is the inside like?

'It's indescribable, it's agonising, it's black, bitter. It really disturbs me how I feel and think about these people that did this to my family. It's eating me away. I know when I get the strength I have to hand it over to God … he'll take my pain, but I have to feel good and ready to hand it over. At this stage I can't, because they got away with killing my son. And the way they killed him.'

While Wade Russell provided the account of what happened under the house, in sentencing the men Justice Vincent said that Wade's 'observations were made during a period when he himself was being beaten, terrified and humiliated'. This could have resulted in an 'understandable error' in his recall. The judge said he must be careful in attributing particular acts to specific people.

Court observers said this doubt about exactly who did what probably influenced the sentencing of Cassar in particular, who was regarded only as aiding and abetting the assaults and who received a suspended sentence.

Although Neville Honeysett was alleged to have advised Alan Franklin on the tying of Joel to the sub-floor of the house, he was sentenced on the grounds that he had attempted to hinder police after the event by planting false leads to protect Lance Franklin. He had, however, served a 'substantial period' on remand, Mr Vincent said.

None of this can console a mother for whom the unthinkable has become reality: 'I want to see them properly punished so I can get on with what's supposed to be a life. I could deal with my pain a bit better.'

Lance Franklin appealed against his conviction and his sentence. On 28 May 2001 the Court of Appeal unanimously rejected his appeal. It still wasn't much comfort for Lorraine.

POLICE STORY

P icture this. If you can. An eight-month-old baby girl, pretty as a pixie, is taken to hospital with a fractured femur. Her mother tells the doctors it happened when she fell out of bed, less than 30 centimetres onto a pile of towels.

But a full skeletal X-ray survey has revealed other healing fractures: one to each humerus – the bones of her little upper arms – and a couple to her tiny ribs.

What it looks like, someone observes, is that for the past five or six months – most of her life – this baby has been going through hell.

So now a pair of ugly detectives have the mother, 17 and scared but sticking to her story, in a cramped interview room at Kingsville police station in Melbourne's west, laying out her options before the official taped interview begins.

They good-cop/bad-cop her a little, one leaning in close and telling her she's a liar and how if she doesn't tell the truth she's likely to lose the kid for good, the other taking her out into the courtyard for a cup of coffee, a smoke and a chat about both their beautiful babies.

And suddenly the tears and the true story fall out.

She didn't mean it, she says, never wanted to hurt her. Just snatched her up too quick and too hard, maybe grabbed her a couple of times too roughly. Done in by the utter frustration of a baby she loves madly but who too often just won't stop crying.

The policemen read her rights and roll the tape.

But now picture this. A couple of days later and one of the detectives is in the young mum's kitchen, taking coffee and dropping off a couple of dummies and a list of places she can go for help. Saying yes, he'll go to court with her when she tries to get her baby back. Even wishing he'd brought his tool box to fix that dribbling tap over the sink.

And to think she'd always reckoned all coppers were arseholes, she says. Says she's going to get help to make sure it never happens again, that she's going to work one day at a time at becoming a good mother.

In the car on the way back to the station, one detective tells the other that he doesn't consider himself naive but he believes her. It's true, says the other: now she's got her awful secret off her chest and is getting the help she needs, she's taken a giant step towards a better life. That's one mum, they'd bet, who's not going to damage her baby again.

But, of course, it's not up to them any more. They've done their job.

When you work on Victoria's Community Policing Squad, you come in every day thinking you've already seen the worst that can happen, and every day you're wrong. There's always something worse.

There are times when you're dragged down among society's bottom-feeders, that particular breed of monster that devours its own children. Down to a world of hurt, full of broken babies.

Down here a de facto bites a little boy all over his body because he won't go to sleep, chomping down on his toes so hard they fuse together. One man rapes an eight-week-old baby and another a 97-year-old great-grandmother. Pensioners French-kiss paperboys in public bus shelters. A father and his daughter live as husband and wife and all the relatives come to the birthday party of their vegetal offspring.

Here there are pederasts and pedophiles, battering babysitters, fondling schoolteachers, and parents who chastise their naughty children with fists and boots, lit cigarettes and boiling water.

'Sometimes you just have those days,' says Sergeant Linda Bennett of the Newport Community Policing Squad. 'Those days when you get the worst that people can throw at each other, all laid on your doorstep in the course of one shift.'

Sometimes in this line of work, she adds, there are no blacks and whites. Only shades of grey.

A too-young mother with no parenting skills, alone and at her wits' end from depression, shakes her screaming baby too hard. Another, the subject of a protection order when she was a child, now lashes out at her own. A dad goes too far and takes a shoe to his boys.

Is this an abuser? Or someone crying for help?

So you care about victims before crooks, about giving people quality time and personal contact, you counsel victims and point offenders to the services that might help them break the cycle. And you ponder the awful dilemma of knowing when it's time to take away a baby or put a parent behind bars.

Says David Walsh, a soft-spoken, considered senior constable at Newport CPS: 'You have to look at the overall picture. You don't want to break up a family. You put the main caregiver, the breadwinner, in jail and the repercussions and consequences can be ongoing and just blow that family right out of the water.'

Senior Constable Sharon McKinnon, 25, says she has been awed by the extent of abuse she's seen in the six months she's been posted at Newport. The mother of a small daughter and now four months pregnant, it has made her more protective: 'But you've got to keep it in perspective. I think you're more aware and more wary but, once you start losing faith in the human race, you might as well get out of it.'

It has to be hard. Thousands of Victoria's children live in that world of hurt: abused physically, sexually, emotionally, even chemically, or neglected in all manner of ways. Since 1981, it has been the job of the 210-member Community Policing Squad to protect them and bring to book their tormentors.

And of the 27 community policing squads located across the state, Newport is the busiest. A humble, dirty-white, triple-fronted weatherboard place in North Road, just down from the overpass and the railway yards and well screened by a couple of scraggy gums and a paperbark, you'd be hard-pressed to recognise it as a police station. Its 18 members, and the two permanent CIB detectives attached through its sexual investigation unit, serve almost 400,000 people across Juliet district, stretching from the Maribyrnong through Footscray, Williamstown, Altona, Sunshine and Melton to the hinterland country communities of Little River, Bacchus Marsh and Toolern Vale.

They respond to calls of truancy, missing persons, neglect and abuse of the elderly but the staple fare is child abuse, domestic violence and – more than any other police district in Victoria – rape, incest, indecent assault and sexual penetration of minors.

Over the past three years, since the squad moved to Newport from the red brick police complex at Altona North, the number of complaints has slowly fallen. Nevertheless, in the past 12 months it has inquired into 1120 complaints, 819 of them involving children. It investigated 448 sex crimes and 319 assaults – more than 80 per cent of them involving victims under 16.

But the Community Policing Squad and the Department of Human Services, with whom the police work in partnership, may only be scratching the surface. Worldwide research suggests that only 10 per cent of sexual assault of children is reported.

In a single year the CPS will take statements from more than 1000 children regarding sexual abuse – which implies that there are actually 10,000 instances of child sexual abuse in Victoria every year. Likewise the rest of the country. In other words, 10 times as many of our children as we suspect – and few of us suspect even the extent of the official figures – might be having their innocence brutally stolen away.

The coppers at Newport know it. It's just the tip of the iceberg, says Senior Detective Gary Carson. The bulk of horrible stuff floating beneath the surface just doesn't get complained about. And it can make you jaundiced, turn you cynical. 'Yeah,' he says. 'You tend to think everybody's either A: a victim or B: a sex offender.'

'It's rife,' adds Senior Detective Paul 'Robbo' Robson, on seven weeks' secondment to Newport from Footscray CIB. 'Not just the sexual abuse but the physical stuff. The sexual, you can't say it's out of hand but the files we're getting of the historical stuff, incidents from 20 years ago, show we don't know what's going on today.

'These people come to us. We're not out there fishing for complaints, because why would you? Why would you fish for these sorts of complaints?'

Because, of course, they keep rolling in anyway.

Tuesday, 11.26 am
He's a lined and leathery Italian in his late 60s wearing a blue pullover, cheap check shirt and old grey trousers, incongruous against his nice white Nike Air runners. A little bloke and getting littler as he fidgets and looks around the interview room at the triple-deck tape recorder, the fingerprint gear and the two shirt-sleeved detectives sitting opposite.

Robbo and Terry 'Keg' Keating joke a bit and bring him coffee while they wait for an interpreter. He tries to join in but it's only the brave-face bonhomie you put on with coppers when you know you've done something wrong. And he admits it: smiles and says he's shitting himself.

Last week, after a Department of Human Services notification, the police were called to his immaculate little house in Footscray. He'd found out his 15-year-old daughter had been wagging school to see some boy, so he beat her. 'What else could I do?' he'd told them.

Later that day, in a VATE (video and audio-taped evidence required for all sex or assault witnesses or victims aged under

17) interview, the girl said she was on her bed when her father came in, started kicking at her and hitting her with the buckle end of his belt, calling her whore, slut and prostitute in Italian, 'Puttana!', hitting her on the arm, thigh, leg, everywhere. Twice, she alleged, he left the room to calm down but returned and started in on her again.

The beating went on for an hour, she said, and left her covered in welts and bruises, one on her thigh black and swollen up like half a football. A doctor who examined her at the Royal Children's Hospital's Gatehouse Centre stated it was the worst assault on a child he had seen all year. The girl had been placed in emergency accommodation and now she wanted her father punished.

Senior Detective Keating flicks on the recorder and the old man begins talking. He admits hitting the girl: 'I was unhappy; I lost control and what happened, happened.'

He was worried she would get out on the street with the boys, maybe the drugs, he says through the interpreter. He wanted her to have an education and a future. He begins to weep. 'I love my children very much and I want her back whatever the cost.'

Keating puts it to him that the beating went on for an hour. 'No, no,' he says. That he went outside to get his breath? 'No comment, I can't comment,' he repeats over and over. He lost control, he can't remember. He buries his head in his arms and weeps hard now. He's so ashamed; 'Molto pentito,' he sobs.

Robson takes over, less patient, pushing harder than Keating but getting no further. You remember all sorts of details, he tells the old man, what you were wearing, all sorts of things, but not a single thing about the beating. 'Now you say you're sorry. You're not sorry. I put it to you that you're only sorry you've been caught.'

They tell him he is to be charged with recklessly and intentionally causing serious injury and drive him home, outwardly friendly but unfooled.

'Crocodile tears,' Keating sneers later. 'Mate, I saw that poor kid's bruises.'

They call Keating 'Keg' for obvious reasons: he's barrel-chested all the way down to his hips. 'You look like a keg on legs,' yelled one of the instructors at the academy a dozen years ago and it stuck.

Likeably gruff, with an equally exuberant moustache, he's been a copper for 12 years and with the sexual investigation unit for the past 14 months. Keg came to the force as a 30-year-old after working as a rep for health insurance company HBA. Got bored doing the same thing day after day, decided it was time for a change. 'It's amazing what you can get used to,' he says. 'I try not to let it worry me any more but when I first came here I thought "Crikey". You really don't believe how much of it goes on. Certainly the general public wouldn't have a clue.

'There are cases where, yeah sure, it depresses you a bit, but your main aim is to get them down the end of the track, to get them into court and convicted.

'It's just a shame to see, especially with a lot of the baby files – they're the worst ones, babies going to hospital with broken bones and burns and bits and pieces and no-one's saying anything. If an eight-month-old baby could talk we'd be laughing in this job.'

Born and bred in Newport and a mainstay of the lawn bowls club just over the rusty railway lines, he derides the view of Melbourne's west as some sort of Appalachia – an epicentre of abuse. 'The western suburbs, it's a working man's area, some spots within the district are pretty rough and you get a lot of physical abuse but there's no set area, no set social class where these things happen.'

Tuesday, 2.30 pm
The phones have been ringing hard since 9 am, batches of notifications from the Department of Human Services rolling in. Since the implementation, in 1992, of a system designed to end confusing and risky duplication of child abuse investigations, the department has clear child protection responsibility but must involve the squad if there's any suspicion that a crime has been committed. So sometimes you get calls like this.

Sharon McKinnon smiles wryly at the apologies of the department worker on the other end of the line. Had to let you know, he says, about a woman dobbing in her neighbour for abusing her eight-year-old son. Reckons she yells and shakes him and he's so scared he hides up a tree, says she saw bruises on his face three weeks back.

'But it's the worst notification I've ever received,' he says. When he asked why she'd waited three weeks to make the report, the woman says she had an argument with her neighbour while putting out the bins that morning. 'And, besides, she owes me $200.'

Thanks but no thanks, says Sharon. The squad will sit this one out for now – like the other notifications: a school reporting a boy who claims his mother hits him with a belt, yet has never been seen with a single bruise; a nine-year-old boy touching a schoolmate intimately; two Koori sisters, 13 and 14, found sleeping rough in the city who say they've run away from home in Albury because Mum and her de facto belt them with cords and frying pans. Victorian and New South Wales missing persons are contacted, the LEAP computer scanned, but the names the girls have given can't be matched. No Community Policing Squad involvement. For now.

Meanwhile, Keg and Robbo are at Kingsville for their first interview with the 17-year-old who hurt her baby. She's tiny and pretty in a striped knit top and jeans and now, finally having rolled over and admitted hurting the child, she smiles shyly as Robbo regales her with stories of his new daughter, 11-week-old Annie Isobel.

Robson, 30, has been 11 years in the job, six as a detective at Sunshine and Footscray CIBs. A self-confessed motormouth, he reckons he was born with the gift of the gab but turned it into an art form in his previous life as a car salesman. This is his second relieving stint with the Community Policing Squad and he says he's enjoying it more than many other detectives who get roped in: 'Some coppers like doing armed robberies, others like doing arson or homicide, some coppers like booking cars. I prefer to help out the victim.

'The victims you get in this job are more victims than anybody else you deal with. These are people that, when they come to a place like this and ask for help, they *want* that help, *need* that help more than anyone else.'

And not always just the victims. That's why he's prepared to help out this kid. 'What comes first, the chicken or the egg?' he says later. 'I wasn't prepared to look at her as a crook and say "You're a rotten bitch, you've punched the shit out of your kid" – though she has, she's damaged her child, we've now got a broken baby. But she might be as much broken as the child.

'I think I've been around long enough not to be too naive but now that she's admitted it I can't see her even contemplating doing it again.'

Wednesday, 10.25 am
The kid doesn't like the jacks much, in fact she almost did a bolt over the back fence when they rang up this morning, thinking for a minute they were chasing her for something. But all they want is to take a quick witness statement.

She's a freckled redhead, 17 going on 13, nervous and distracted, not too sure how to react to having two policewomen, Sharon McKinnon and Senior Constable Kylie Towk, in her cluttered, footy-trophy-decorated living room. She covers her mouth with her hands and talks between the fingers.

On Monday, just before midnight, Kylie Towk and David Walsh, out in the van on night-shift, were called to a report of an alleged rape of the girl's mother.

The mother told them she had gone to her ex-boyfriend's house the previous Friday to borrow some cigarettes. She said he had kept her imprisoned in the house over the weekend, assaulting and raping her a number of times and cutting her clothes and shoes into strips before taking them out and dumping them. She fled when they went to a bank in West Footscray on Monday.

The woman said she remembered her daughter coming to the house on the Friday, knocking on the doors and yelling for her. She said she was not allowed to answer.

Now the girl tells Sharon she was trying to drop off some shoes for her mum. She left them at the door and they were found with the other dumped clothes. It is strong corroborating evidence, a good result in less than 30 minutes.

Back at Newport, the notifications keep piling up. A woman reports her husband for punching their 16-year-old son but neither will press charges. Counterpunching allegations from a couple in a custody battle over a three-year-old girl, a claim of physical assault trumped by a counter-claim of molestation, the child a pawn in their nasty game. Nevertheless, a joint visit is arranged.

A school reports a little girl with a cigarette burn on her hand. She says it was an accident when she reached across to get a drink from her daddy. Plausible except that Dad's known to police and the LEAP file shows he has a scar from a burn in exactly the same spot. That's too much of a coincidence for Sergeant John Flynn's liking, so he and Senior Constable Jane Walsh head out to the school. In the end the story stands up, but there's no point taking chances.

Flynn, 37, and 21 years a policeman, came to Newport from Ballarat in April 1995 and immediately felt the culture shock: 'I thought "My God",' he says. 'And the sex – at the time I started there was a hell of a lot of sex abuse and child sexual offence is arguably the worst offence you can imagine, the worst experience a child could go through. But I think just recently the physical abuse has increased – and mainly against children.'

You can see why people get stressed. 'Police, we don't deal with happy people. You go to a burglary you don't see a happy person there, you pull over a car and they're not too happy with you, you go to thefts and murders and you don't find anyone glad to see you …

'But here you go to the extreme, dealing with the tragedies really, absolute life tragedies. Kids, and adults, dealing with us are not going to forget it overnight, it's a long-term thing. We've got to help them get through it as best as possible.'

Wednesday, 1.30 pm

The two little boys are highly strung at the best of times and it was their first visit to a cemetery, so you can see why they had the night terrors. They started talking about ghosts and monsters and couldn't sleep. They kept crying and sooking and carrying on until it all got too much for their dad.

They arrived at school on Tuesday and the teachers couldn't help but notice the bruises, one all over one boy's upper arm, and a six-by-six-centimetre welt on the other's thigh. Daddy had hit them, they said. With his shoe. His very best shoe.

But the school hadn't reported the incident until today and now Kylie Towk is reading the riot act to the welfare co-ordinator. It's mandatory reporting, she reminds, *mandatory*. All it needs is a teacher to pick up a phone. Who knows what else could have happened to those boys in the intervening 24 hours?

Kylie, Dave Walsh and two Department of Human Services workers conduct separate interviews with the brothers, who repeat their story. Walsh asks one how he felt about being hit. 'Half happy, half sad,' he answers. Sad he had been hit but happy that he would learn not to be naughty.

At 3.40 the parents arrive at the school. Dave and Kylie introduce themselves and, before they can say anything else, the mother walks into the foyer and collapses, crying loudly. Curled up in a ball, she sobs that the boys are lying and their father never hits them. The father is calm and says he understands he must be investigated.

Eventually, the mother settles down and accompanies the boys to the Gatehouse Centre where they are examined and pronounced fine, except for the bruises. They are then taken to Newport for their VATEs.

One of the boys says he loves his dad and knows he loves them very much too, but sometimes he hits them, though never before with a shoe. He says he wishes his family was happy and that Daddy could get a job.

Late that night they are allowed to go home. Though a department officer says one bruise is the biggest she's ever seen, they decide not to 'apprehend'. She believes it would distress the boys too much to be taken from their parents.

'One of the common things people say is "I hit you because I love you",' says Dave the next morning. 'You can't take the hard line and say don't ever, ever hit your children, but people have to learn what's acceptable and what's not. I think, in this situation, the father's realised he's been, um, over-zealous. We can't stop what's happened but hopefully this will stop it happening again.'

'I don't know,' says John Flynn. 'You sit down and say, "What has that fella done?" It only takes one incident to be a child abuser, whether you're angry or not, and this one I think goes well beyond legal chastisement.'

Thursday, 7.30 pm
'He'd be the best teacher in the world,' says the girl, 'if he just didn't do these things.'

She's 18, tall and coltish and terribly embarrassed, just days away from the start of her VCE. She has come in to Newport with her mother to make a statement about one of her teachers who has become far too familiar with her and another girl. He has been touching her, making suggestive comments and, on her birthday, kissed her on the neck. The final straw came the other day when he bit her ear.

She reported him to her principal who, under mandatory reporting provisions, contacted the Community Policing Squad. She's nervous now, doesn't want to get him in any further trouble because he can be like her best friend at times, and makes an official request, as she is entitled, that police take no further action.

Sharon, painstakingly tapping the details into an ancient ValueMagic computer, explains there is little chance the matter will be ignored. 'This is a person in a position of authority and trust and, if this is true, he has abused that trust,' she says.

The mother is surprised the police would take their time over something 'so trivial'.

'I don't think it's trivial at all,' says Sharon. 'Frankly, I'm appalled.'

It's her second complaint involving a teacher this evening – but the first, at 5.45, was about a student. A female teacher from Sharon's old secondary college calls to report a campaign of harassment. A 14-year-old girl has been making phone calls and sending pizzas to her home. The harassment has gone on for six months and the school has failed to act and now the woman is at the end of her rope. But she is reluctant to seek an intervention order.

'Linda and I might go speak to the girl in the morning,' says Sharon later. 'Hopefully that will wake her up to what she's doing. 'Cos basically it's stalking.'

Friday, 8.30 am
'Oh, fantastic. As if I really need this,' says Gary Carson, looking into the mouthpiece of a telephone and seeing months of careful investigation disappear into the ether.

The kid was only in yesterday afternoon, reviewing his VATE tape, and travelling pretty well. They gave him a can of Coke and he thought it was Christmas. A 13-year-old, with attention deficit disorder, he had alleged that when he was about nine, his uncle had begun forcing oral sex on him.

The uncle had been charged with sexual penetration of a child under 10 and they were due in the Melbourne Magistrates Court for a contest committal hearing. But now the local divvy van boys were on the line, saying the kid had climbed onto the roof of his house and wasn't coming down. 'I'm not goin' to no court. I'm not goin' nowhere,' he'd yelled.

Carson, a copper for 15 years, 10 of those as a detective, got on the phone to the boy's home and slowly, softly cajoled him into coming down. Now he's heading out to chauffeur him, hostile and reluctant, to court, but seeing his case slip away.

Meanwhile, Terry Keating and Jane Walsh are shepherding a florid-faced old man, in his late 70s, across Sun Crescent, Sunshine, and up the stairs of the local CIB offices. He's shaking so violently that Keg fears the poor old couta's going to have a heart attack.

Earlier this year his daughter came in and alleged that, in about 1980, when they lived in New Zealand and she was eight, he began having sex with her – once a week, when her mother was at a women's committee meeting. The abuse continued until she was 14 and after they came to Australia.

The police all arrive back at Newport about the same time that afternoon and – surprisingly – everyone's grinning. 'The old fella rolled right over, made full admissions,' says Keg. And Gary's uncle, after half an hour of debates between lawyers outside the court, decided to stick up his hand and plead guilty.

And now the father of the boys hit with the shoe comes in and makes admissions as well. Unshaven and harried, he says he 'cracked the shits. To tell you the truth, I didn't realise I hit them so hard'.

'Not a bad end to the week,' says Keg, heading out to the bowling club. But it's rarely this good. Sometimes you go home wondering if it's all worth it. On those days, he sits down and talks it through with his partner. Then he goes out and plays bowls.

Carson takes the exact opposite approach: 'You start taking it home and it'll drown you,' he says. 'My family wouldn't have a clue about what I do, I don't talk about it. I don't want them to be part of this type of life, sexual abuse, physical abuse, incest.'

And anyway, there's always something worse tomorrow. 'We're never out of work,' says Linda Bennett. 'That's the sad thing here.'

PRIME SUSPECT

A fterwards, the thing she could not credit was how normal he had seemed.

Through the trivial chat with the glasses of lemonade, and the roast chicken dinner, and the pancake dessert and him showing her the snaps from a trip to Queensland to visit his mother, through all that his manner had seemed so unremarkable.

Fleetingly, it occurred to her that the scratch on his left cheek might have been left by a fingernail, but she let the thought slip by without comment. But she did ask, the way she always did, whether he had told his live-in girlfriend about his past. He told her he had a new life now and added: 'Don't ask me again, please, Sister Clare.'

What Sister Clare meant, was had he told his girlfriend his criminal history, but she did not press him because he seemed upset.

What Peter Dupas had told his girlfriend was that he had been married, which was true, and was now divorced, which was also true, and that his divorce led to a breakdown and time in hospital, which was a sort of half-truth to the extent that he was familiar with the workings of mental hospitals.

The rest of it, the rapes and knives and balaclavas and convictions for loitering and peeping and threatening to do harm to babies if their mothers did not submit to being raped, and attacks on teens and the elderly, he left out.

The failed attempts to suppress his twisted sexual urges by taking the drug Depo Provera, and the teenage engagement that lapsed when he was jailed for rape, and the refusals to admit his attacks on women while privately fantasising over them, and his resistance to psychiatric treatment, all this he left out too.

Had she asked about the scratch on his cheek, and the other one on his neck, he would have told her he scratched himself on a piece of wood in his workshop. That was the story he told his other friend, a former priest called Patrick O'Brien who had commented on it the day before, the Monday, when it was still fresh.

He complained to O'Brien that he had not had a good day. The car alarm was acting up and then he had gone and scratched himself on a piece of wood.

That was a half-truth too: the car alarm had been wailing intermittently all morning while the Toyota four-wheel drive remained undisturbed in the driveway of the rented Pascoe Vale weatherboard in Melbourne's inner north. No-one was home.

Dupas had gone out shortly after his girlfriend left for work about 8 am, buying petrol in nearby Bell Street soon after. A neighbour saw Dupas return, driving his girlfriend's other car, a brown Mitsubishi Lancer, about 11.45 am.

O'Brien arrived about an hour later and did not stay long. They had known each other more than 20 years, from the time Dupas was a prisoner at Ararat Prison, where the sex offenders were housed, and O'Brien was the local parish priest. He started to visit Dupas because Dupas' parents asked him to.

All these years later, and these two are his only real friends, Sister Clare and ex-Father Patrick, professional carers. This day, O'Brien went to Dupas' place to pick up some camping gear. They had spent the weekend together, camping at Wilsons Promontory with their partners. Dupas and the two women had explored the bush while O'Brien took it easy.

It was the first time they had done anything like it, but Dupas did not want to dwell on it.

O'Brien did not stay long because Dupas seemed keen to get back to working on the half-built bar unit in his workshop. 'He seemed quite normal,' O'Brien said later.

O'Brien left Dupas' home soon after 1 pm on 19 April 1999. Five hours later, while Dupas waited at Pascoe Vale station to escort his girlfriend safely home, a friend of Nicole Patterson arrived, as arranged, at the 28-year-old's home in Harper Street, Northcote.

Harper Street, Northcote is narrow and lined with single-fronted weatherboard homes – workers' cottages from the Victorian era when Northcote was a bustling suburb housing workers for the factories of the inner suburbs.

Harper Street lies at the foot of Northcote Hill, the highest point in Melbourne, where the period homes are bigger, grander two-storey terraces. But in Harper Street the houses follow a pattern. The front door opens onto a bowling alley hallway that runs past several rooms before opening into an old sitting room, with the kitchen tacked on at the rear.

When Nicole did not answer the knocking, her friend peered through the front window into the room Nicole used as a lounge. The horror of what she was looking at did not dawn on her at first. Nicole Patterson was lying on her back. Asleep? She was naked from the waist down and the clothing on her upper body was in disarray and looked unfamiliar and odd.

She rapped again but Nicole did not stir, and realisation overcame disbelief as the mutilation of her friend's body dawned on her.

Dupas and his girlfriend were heading home to share a tuna casserole about the time police investigators began analysing Nicole Patterson's murder.

She was killed at about nine that morning. She had known, or been expecting her killer, they reasoned, and had left the killer briefly in the front room while she brewed coffee. She returned up the hallway, carrying a coffee plunger, two cups, sugar and milk.

He attacked without warning, flailing at the defenceless Patterson with his knife. Police interviewing neighbours found one who had heard a woman cry out, in an instinctive shout of shock and fright: 'You fucking cunt.' Twice.

After the initial shock, Nicole Patterson fought for her life, but repeatedly the knife beat her defensive parries and penetrated her chest and back. Her hands suffered numerous wounds as she tried to defend herself, but 11 knife strikes struck her lungs and heart. In total, she suffered 27 stab wounds.

Things happened in the house after the murder. Nicole Patterson's clothing was cut away in line with her sternum. Her body was stripped, and her breasts were removed. There was a series of tentative punctures near where the incisions to cut off her breasts began.

Although Nicole Patterson was found lying in the front room where she was killed, her attacker strayed. He had also been in her bedroom. There were bloodstains on the door jamb, and on the pillows, and on the bottom sheet of her bed.

The place had been searched as well, but not well enough. Under some clothing on a couch in the living room was Nicole's personal diary. On the entry for 19 April was the name Malcolm, with the time 9 am circled, and then there was a mobile telephone number: 0417 037 312.

On Nicole Patterson's body were two small, yellow pieces of electrical tape.

Jeff Maher, the homicide detective in charge, ordered a check on her telephone records. Who had she been calling lately? Who had been calling her?

The next evening, the Tuesday, Sister Clare – a Franciscan nun from the Victorian Offenders Support Agency – had her dinner with Peter Dupas. On the Wednesday, he would take his car alarm to be repaired.

Some time that week his girlfriend would remark about the scratch on his cheek and he would tell her the story about an accident in the workshop.

Meanwhile, the check of the telephone records revealed 15 calls from a Pascoe Vale number to Patterson's home between 3 March and 12 April, one week before the murder. The Pascoe Vale number was tied to Peter Norris Dupas, serial rapist and predator. His record made him a suspect. He had been known to police, as they say, for 31 years.

Police prepared to arrest him, obtaining a search warrant for his home, and three days after the murder Dupas was arrested while playing the poker machines, alone, at the Excelsior Hotel in Thomastown.

Searching Dupas' property, police found several pieces of torn newspaper in the garbage bin with a note scrawled on them. They were lucky. It was bin night that night so had they come a day later the note would have been gone.

Pieced together it read 'Nicci, Northcote 9.00 morning', 'Malcolm' and the middle six digits of Patterson's phone number.

It was later found to be a page of the *Northcote Leader* newspaper in which Nicole Patterson advertised psychotherapy services for the practice she was trying to build. The handwriting was identified as that of Dupas.

The mobile phone number in her diary was found on a note on Dupas' fridge. It belonged to a university student Dupas had hired to do some labouring. In his laundry, police found a newspaper with a story of Patterson's murder. The front page photograph of her had been slashed across the face.

And then there were the knives. They found seven in an outside storeroom, two in a cabinet in the garage, nine more in a back bedroom and six in kitchen drawers.

Hours into the search, an officer working his way through the garage found some clothing stuffed into a cupboard. There was a green jacket and a black balaclava, one of those ever-present elements of Peter Dupas' rape kits. The jacket had bloodstains on the right sleeve which, when subjected to forensic testing, were showed to be 6.5 billion times more likely to be Nicole Patterson's than that of someone chosen at random.

Neither Nicole Patterson's severed breasts nor her driver's licence were recovered. Police believe they were taken as trophies.

Dupas proclaimed his innocence, said the police had set him up and he appealed against his conviction.

It was the day after his arrest when Sister Clare told police: 'That's the thing I can't get over. He just seemed so normal on the night.'

Normal is not the usual description for Peter Norris Dupas.

Back at Waverley High School in Melbourne's east in the 1960s, if there was one word for him, it was loner. Mostly, he kept to himself, recalls Stephen Howell, who was in the same fourth form class.

'He used to try to hang around with us, but because of his nature no-one wanted much to do with him,' Howell says. 'I remember one stage he was at the sick bay. He was urinating in the glasses because he knew the teachers would use them. He would piss in them, empty them and turn them back upside down so they'd appear clean.

'I really believe that he had problems years back. When I first heard many years ago he was in jail I thought he shouldn't be in there – he should be in a psychiatric place getting help. He was weird.'

There was another word for him, one borrowed from the after-school TV sitcom 'The Addams Family'. It was the name of the foolish fat kid, Pugsley, and Dupas did not take to it.

'I don't think he was teased more than anyone else, I just don't think he cottoned on to it very well. He used to really

Mick Gatto (second from left) sometimes spoke in aphorisms, such as 'You don't know what's in a man's heart' or 'Keep your friends close, and your enemies closer'. Here, he arrives for another funeral, surrounded by friends.

'I never felt I was guilty of murder. Frank was the guilty one – he "murdered" us every day we were with him.' Heather Osland, said a psychologist, fitted the profile of a battered woman 'like a glove'.

Murder barrister John Smallwood. He remembers the great judge
Cairns Villeneuve-Smith telling him this: those who criticise our
justice system have never put on the robes and stood between an
accused man and his ruin.

PICTURES BY CRAIG ABRAHAM, USED COURTESY OF *THE AGE*

The way they died has tied murdered policemen Rodney Miller (above) and Gary Silk (left) together inextricably. Yet their pairing on the fatal night, and even their appearance at the Silky Emperor restaurant in the Melbourne suburb of Moorabbin, was almost accidental.

PICTURE USED COURTESY OF *THE AGE*

PICTURE BY SIMON SCHLUTER, USED COURTESY OF *THE AGE*

Jason Roberts (above) cuts his 18th birthday cake a week after the Silk–Miller murders. Police bugs overheard Bandali Debs (left) describe the police killings: 'He was on the ground – laying on the ground, firing in the air ... he just shot up in the air and things went everywhere.'

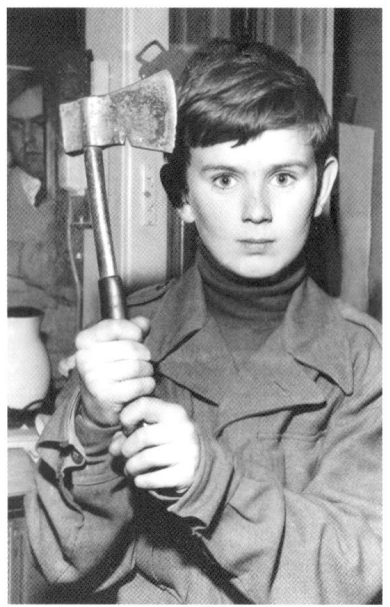

The newspaper photographers captured a terrific image of 11-year-old Shane Spiller, holding his steel tomahawk in both hands, his wide hazel eyes staring straight down the lens – the way they'd stared into the eyes of Derek Percy. Years later, Spiller (below) washed up in Wyndham, in rural New South Wales. The trouble was, he took Derek Percy with him.

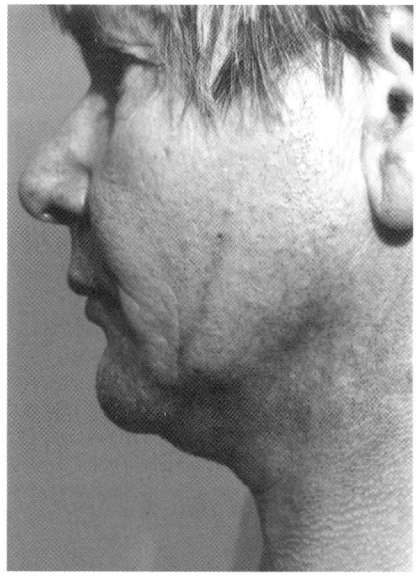

Fleetingly, it occurred to Sister Clare that the scratch on Peter Dupas' left cheek might have been left by a fingernail, but she let the thought slip by without comment.

'Look at him,' says someone as they bring Dupas by, 'he makes your skin crawl.'

Justice, goes the old legal saw, should not only be done, it should be seen to be done. Sometimes it must be seen to be believed. And preferably, seen up close. You'll find the court watchers up the back at every big trial. They are the Alternate Jury.

go off in class,' says Peter Thomas, another Waverley High contemporary student.

'He used to get razor blades out and take swipes at us – that was in form two. I'd be sitting behind him and have to put the desk lid up. [This happened] every couple of weeks. He would go red in the face. He was a pretty emotional kid. He had no set friends.'

Academically, he was mediocre. In sport, he was a non-participant. Socially, he was almost invisible. He disappeared from the school for two weeks at the end of 1968 while undergoing psychiatric assessment after attacking a female neighbour. Warren Buswell, a classmate who knew him as 'more or less a friend', says he did not even realise Dupas was out of the school.

Colin Walkerden, who lived in the next street, barely recalls him at all. 'What I can remember of him,' Walkerden says, 'he used to be a bit of a loner. Short, fat, stumpy.'

A former form teacher, Colin Mathews, remembers an isolated individual. 'I was warned by a fellow staff member that he had been interviewed by the police about indecent exposure and various sexually related offences,' Mathews, who is now retired, recalls. 'I was warned to keep him well away from the girls.'

In any case, he did not seek to sit with anyone. He was sad, lonely, almost friendless, unworthy and self-pitying.

After the attack on the neighbour, he was admitted to Larundel Psychiatric Hospital where he told Dr Julie Jones a pathetic story, about how his best friend, 'Graham' had left the neighbourhood without telling him.

Jones described him as immature, passive, dependent, fearful and anxious about his masculinity.

His story about Graham, however, is another half-truth, a sympathy ploy.

Graham, who asked that his last name not be published, says that he told all his classmates he was leaving school to find a job. In any event, he maintained contact with Dupas for a couple of years after leaving school. He might have been Dupas' choice of closest friend, but was not immune to Dupas' odd ways. He says Dupas was different.

'I was one of his better friends,' Graham says. 'He was picked on a bit at school because he was overweight. He did have some very strange tempers. I have seen him lose his temper and punch a brick wall until his knuckles would bleed. He got really wound up.

'In the classroom he would be the one trying to peep up the girls' dresses to see what colour pants they were wearing. At the time we laughed at it. We thought it was a bit of a joke.

'I can remember him grabbing one of the young teachers. You know, 500 kids crowding down the hall and he would run down and grab a handful of boob. We stood back and laughed. Well, we were 14 years old.

'I left school late in year 10. I believe it was a few months after that he attacked a neighbour. I am pretty sure I told him I would not be back to school. I started a job.'

According to Graham, a quiet kid himself, Dupas did not truly fit with anyone at school. But as a visitor to the Dupas home, it was obvious, Graham said, that his parents adored him.

Even at home, however, he was in a sense isolated. Dupas was George and Merle Dupas' third child, born in July 1953, 11 years younger than his brother and nine years junior to his sister.

A member of the extended Dupas family said the couple had separated for a period, and Peter Dupas was conceived after a reconciliation. According to accounts Peter Dupas has offered, it remained a tense relationship. George Dupas was a hard, demanding man. Self-made and proud of it. His family lived a nomadic existence with Dupas senior buying and selling a series of small businesses.

He ran a poultry farm outside Sydney but years of hand-mixing poultry feed gave him asthma, so they moved to Melbourne. He worked as a greengrocer and built a home and poultry sheds in Potts Road, Langwarrin, and enrolled his young son at Lyndhurst South Primary, a rural school with 34 students when he started.

It was remote then, and even now Potts Road is unmade, topped with loose gravel. Dupas senior was not the only self-made builder. Many families built their own homes there, although 'shacks' is a better description for what a former teacher describes as an 'unfortunate subdivision' occupied by struggling families.

Despite the low enrolment at the school Dupas left little impression. A former teacher and several fellow students could not recall him. It seems he was unattached even then.

The nomadic lifestyle resumed when the family headed to Queensland for an extended holiday in July 1964. Peter Dupas missed much of his final year of primary schooling but completed some work by correspondence.

During this trip he was an only child. His sister had left home and his elder brother, having fallen out with his father, worked his way up the east coast, occasionally linking up with the family, staying for a few weeks and then finding work elsewhere before reuniting with them farther north.

When they returned to Melbourne, Peter Dupas enrolled at Waverley High and the family moved into Bradstreet Road, Glen Waverley, an unremarkable suburban street in the ever-sprawling eastern suburbs, steadily filling with modest, brick veneer houses.

'Everybody got on well together. It was one of those nice little areas where everyone got along,' recalls a neighbour, Valda Renshaw. 'Peter had everything there was to have. I think Peter had the best of everything. He was learning the organ. He had a Gerry Gee doll and a wonderful Scalextric set of cars. All the kids used to go in to play with them.

'He used to walk awkwardly. I would not say he was handicapped. He was quite a heavy boy, but not like you see fat kids now.'

His brother urged his parents to involve the kid in football and cricket, and tried himself to develop his sporting skills but the boy known as Pugsley had neither natural talent or inclination. His brother complained to relatives that the kid seemed unwilling to give up model cars and marbles.

Mrs Renshaw remembers how Dupas appalled the amiable little community. 'We were there when he first started being peculiar. It was such a shock when he attacked "Barbara". It just happened.'

It was early October 1968. Five weeks earlier Barbara had returned from hospital after giving birth to her first child.

'What he did was totally unexpected,' Barbara recalls now. 'We were young marrieds, new to the area. We were good neighbours [with the Dupases]. We used to visit their place to play cards on Saturday nights.'

Peter knocked at the back door of the house and asked for

a knife to peel potatoes. She congratulated him on helping his mother, but he behaved oddly. When Barbara offered him a vegetable peeler, he refused to take it, yet said nothing. She then gave him a vegetable knife, and also offered to show him the baby.

Barbara left him in the nursery. Shortly after he returned to the kitchen. He announced: 'Oh well, I better go now.' He said it twice more, pausing between each sentence.

She was puzzled. Without warning, as he was about to leave, he knocked Barbara to the floor, falling on her and jabbing at her with the knife. She put her hands up to fend him off. She grabbed the blade but he kept at her. He slashed her hands and face.

When he could not get a clear lunge at her with the knife he grabbed her hair and banged her head on the floor. She screamed. He put his hand over her mouth and he told her: 'I can't stop now, they'll lock me up.'

She resisted, fighting, literally for her life. And he did stop. Suddenly it was over.

She was breathless and shocked. He was crying and docile. Harmless and pathetic.

Barbara rang Dupas' brother, who, she says, later complained about the incident being reported to police. 'I was lucky to survive,' she says now.

Mrs Renshaw recalls what happened next: '[Barbara's husband] came down and warned us what had happened. The [Dupas] family effectively did not believe it. They said there must have been some mistake. His family seemed to be such nice, normal people apart from the fact they tried to blot that out. Right from the beginning they tried to cover it up, which we thought was the wrong way.

'He seemed to have a thing about young married women with babies.'

Almost opposite the Dupas house was Amesbury Court with a handful of houses. A woman there told Mrs Renshaw he hung about, watching her. 'She was convinced he rang her a few times,' Mrs Renshaw said. No-one spoke on the phone, but she was sure the breathing she could hear was a young male.

But if he was intent on young married women with babies, he was more comfortable with maternal figures generally. In his late teens, when the Dupases had a beach house on the Mornington Peninsula, they spent time with another family.

Odd for an older teenager, but when he and his parents stayed at the holiday house in McCrae and mixed with a second family, Peter Dupas did not share their fishing expeditions. He remained behind, spending his time with the middle-aged mother of the second family. Just the two of them.

After the attack on Barbara, Dupas was admitted to Larundel where Dr Julie Jones was the first of many psychiatrists and psychologists to examine him. She observed that he 'appears to have been over protected by his mother and thus developed a rather timid approach to people. He fears sudden disturbances, car crashes and explosions.' He also had difficulty meeting his father's perfectionist standards.

So began his rush into an ever-deepening depravity. In March 1972 he was caught peeping at a woman through her bedroom window. In November 1973, feigning car trouble, he knocked on the door of a house in Mitcham and asked the woman who answered for a screwdriver.

She had her 18-month-old baby in her arms when she returned. He produced a knife, threatened to harm her baby, bound her feet and hands, slapped her, bit her breast and raped her.

Twice more he faked car trouble. Once, he stole $7 while a woman looked for a screwdriver to help him. An hour later, in another suburb he tried again but left quickly when the woman who answered said her husband had all the tools, but would be home soon.

And he was observed watching a woman with a pusher and two small children. He walked up to the driveway of the house they had just left and stood, looking after them, but returned to his car once he realised he was being observed.

While waiting to face court on the rape charge, he was caught watching women shower at the McCrae foreshore caravan park. For this, he was again admitted to Larundel for six weeks where a psychiatrist, Dr PJ Shannon, said Dupas was defensive and unable to discuss intimate aspects of his life. 'We kept Peter in hospital with a view to trying to assist him to talk about himself but really made no progress along these lines,' Shannon wrote. 'He persistently denied he had any problems.'

Just as persistently and despite being identified by his victims, he denied the rape as well as the other intrusions on women he had made under the guise of car trouble.

Underlying our penal system is the happy presumption that wrong-doers can be reformed. And from this we conclude the punishment that is meted out to prisoners should not be so onerous that it destroys all hope.

So the promise of parole, or early release, is held out, although in truth it probably is as much a prison management tool to foster a compliant prison population as it is a reward for good behaviour.

Through human error and the presumption of reform, Peter Dupas made the most of this capacity for generosity.

Following his first rape conviction, in July 1974, he was jailed for nine years, with a minimum of five years to serve before becoming eligible for parole. He was released in September 1979, just two years after finally admitting his guilt.

In July 1977, a prison officer at Ararat observed that while he no longer denied the rape, he 'still seems to have no understanding or insight into his emotions and psychological processes which precipitated the offence'.

The report went on: 'Due to his lack of insight and his belief that psychological treatment is unnecessary, it is very likely that such treatment will be ineffective.'

Yet two years later he was out. His release was a mistake, a parole officer conceded after Dupas had raped again within months of his release.

Dupas' parole officer then was Wal Soloweij, already with seven years' experience. Dupas was 26 but appeared to Soloweij as 'a scared little boy'. Usually you can look at a prisoner and see them doing the thing for which they were convicted, but not Dupas, recalls Soloweij, who has left the parole service after 27 years.

Dupas was deferential, and appeared harmless. 'At all times he was highly anxious, to the point that he shakes,' says Soloweij.

'My general approach has always been, if the situation seems to warrant it, to give the person a chance ... and of course he was, as most of them always are, insisting "I will try very hard".

'If you made it a blanket statement that they are all liars, you wouldn't give anyone a chance. It seemed he was worth taking a chance on.'

By the time of Dupas' release, his parents had moved to Frankston. They had Peter back home, but not for long. Within two months he had accosted a woman on the Nepean Highway and raped her. Armed with a knife and disguised with a balaclava he attacked three other women.

Dupas was convicted of rape again in June 1980. In a report to the County Court's Judge Lazarus, the pre-eminent forensic psychiatrist of the time Dr Allen Bartholomew said Dupas' condition would be very hard to treat even if he was co-operative. 'In this case the condition may well be highly resistant to any presently used forms of treatment,' Bartholomew wrote.

He added: 'I feel that when he realised that his hopes for parole might be jeopardised by his denials, he began to admit his guilt.' He concluded that the outlook for Dupas was poor. He was likely to remain a danger to women.

This second conviction for rape was accompanied by convictions for assault with intent to rape, malicious wounding and indecent assault. Judge Lazarus sentenced him to a maximum of six-and-a-half years, with a minimum of five years.

From Gunnamatta to Cheviot, there are kilometres of wild, occasionally treacherous, unspoiled beaches on the Mornington Peninsula's southern flank. Along here, Helen

McMahon, a 48-year-old swimming instructor, used to sunbathe in seclusion among the windswept sand dunes.

On 13 February 1985 she was found battered to death, naked but for a towel that was placed over her.

According to prison records, that was two weeks before Dupas was released from jail. With credit for time served while awaiting trial on his second rape charge, he was released on 27 February 1985 – four years and eight months after sentencing.

Five days later he was back in custody, having this time stalked and raped a young woman at knifepoint on a beach at Rye. He was caught by friends of the victim and later told police: 'I thought I was OK. Everyone was saying I am OK now.'

This attack, at Dimmicks Beach, was 4.6 kilometres from where Helen McMahon was killed. Dupas was still serving a jail sentence, which seemed to rule him out as a possible suspect.

But a closer check of prison records revealed that he was granted pre-release leave from 6 February until 14 February, the day after the murder. A police taskforce regards him as a prime suspect in Mrs McMahon's murder.

In June 1985, following Dupas' third rape conviction, Judge Leckie remarked that Judge Lazarus had previously passed an apparently light sentence having accepted psychiatric evidence from Dr Myers that suggested Dupas might be rehabilitated (despite Dr Bartholomew's opinion). Myers indicated that without treatment there was a very high chance of Dupas reoffending, and urged he be treated with the drug Depo Provera.

Judge Leckie gave Dupas a 10-year minimum term. A mental health report the next year said he was an immature

32-year-old acting out sadistic rape fantasies when he felt rejected. If he offered a bland acceptance that he had a problem, there was no evidence he wanted to do anything about it. Dupas admitted fantasising about his crimes.

He attempted suicide in May 1987 and was treated at Mont Park Hospital. He was prescribed Melleril and Depo Provera to quell his sex drive, while undergoing treatment at Mont Park. Melleril is an anti-psychotic drug used to treat abnormal thoughts and hallucinations. Depo Provera is an injectable contraceptive which, in men, lowers testosterone and sex drives. Its use is sometimes referred to as 'chemical castration'. When discharged, a hospital report noted that his dominant trait was 'an underlying anger directed towards those around him whom he sees as failing to fulfil his needs'.

He was out in March 1992, less than seven years after sentencing. At the time, prisoners were automatically granted remissions of one-third off their minimum term as an inducement to good behaviour. Yet Dupas' luck would not stop there. The system had one more indulgence for him.

From the time of his first rape conviction in 1974, until his release in March 1992 after his third rape conviction, Dupas was assessed at Larundel, Mont Park – which housed the criminally insane – and held in Pentridge Prison's G Division for mentally disturbed prisoners. He was admitted into a group for recidivist sex offenders – where he was disruptive and inattentive. Soloweij recalls that the psychotherapist, the late Margaret Hobbs, concluded Dupas did not take therapy seriously.

Dupas also had individual psychotherapy. But in 1994, after he attacked a woman at Lake Eppalock, near Bendigo, forensic psychologist Ian Joblin said Dupas was really only ever hospitalised as a suicide risk, and it was for depression rather than any disorder that he was treated. Bartholomew had observed in 1990 that: '[Dupas] really has had little or nothing to be termed treatment.'

Dupas is a timid, uncertain creature who does his prison time hard, but because he lapses into what Bartholomew called 'a reactive depression' in jail, it is for that he has been treated.

The woman who later would become Dupas' wife initiated one of his moves from G Division to hospital: 'I was very concerned about him. It was after a visit from his parents I noticed his personal hygiene had become very slack. I realised when I was talking to him he was very depressed and we had him admitted to Mont Park.'

The clinical director of the Victorian Institute of Forensic Mental Health, Professor Paul Mullen, said he doubted that Dupas was ever treated for his underlying disorder.

'Dupas in prison is self-damaging, suicidal, depressed,' Prof Mullen said. 'Any treatment he has had usually has been for depression – no-one has ever, when he has come before the courts, sent him for treatment. No-one has ever said this is the sort of man who should be treated rather than incarcerated.

'If a Mr Dupas appeared tomorrow, you can't be confident that he would be managed with any more effective intervention than the real Dupas was 20 years ago.

'Depo Provera has to be used with some therapy that changes the way they live and think about their victims.'

Joblin said in his 1994 report that Dupas attacked women to compensate for his inadequacies, to fulfil fantasies of conquest, to express mastery, strength and control. 'For Dupas the actual assault has not lived up to the fantasy which preceded the assault, and is seen at times as disappointing,' Joblin wrote. 'He does not feel reassured by either his performance or his victim's response and must find another victim, this time "the right one".

'Thus, his offences become repetitive.'

Soloweij says that prisoners with a hatred of women often had problems with their mother, but in Dupas' case the big issue was his domineering father.

'He might blame his mother for not protecting him from his father,' Soloweij speculates. 'Offenders like him, as long as they have somebody to blame, they think they don't have to change.'

Prof Mullen said that Dupas is typical of a type of sex offender who is insecure and who forms very dependent relationships. They are angry and vindictive and easily offended. They alternate between being clinging and demanding and are always likely to lose control if they feel rejected or excluded.

Seeking to understand her errant son, Dupas' mother wondered whether a childhood accident might be responsible. When he was 10 he was knocked unconscious for several hours after riding a pushbike into a tree. Tests have since shown no evidence of brain damage, but do indicate mediocre intelligence.

Yet to those who dealt with him he seemed inoffensive in the extreme. Ingratiating, excessively polite, utterly harmless, self-effacing, keen to evoke sympathy, weak, downtrodden, humble, incapable of his crimes and fantasies.

In short, he is a loathsome mixture of self-pitying and predatory instincts, aggressive and violent, cowardly and obsequious.

* * *

On the street, he was a danger to female society. In prison, he was fearful and tremulous. It was extraordinary then, that in Pentridge Prison's G Division, a psychiatric nurse 16 years older, a mother and grandmother, would decide that she loved him, and would marry him.

Sex offenders are usually condemned by their label. Dupas, however, was one of those men who brought out the mothering side of staff, male or female, a staff member recalls. So capable of manipulation is he that it almost seems a gift.

'There is something about him which is so pathetic in the way he presents ... he produced strong divisions among the staff, some finding him obnoxious and others thinking he needed care.'

The woman he married in old Castlemaine Jail thought she detected a 'beautiful nature' in him. He was co-operative, helpful, depressed and needy.

He finally moved in with his wife at Woodend, and later Kyneton, after his release in 1992. Even in hindsight, his wife struggled to explain their relationship.

'Bart [Allen Bartholomew] always said that I was his second mother,' Dupas' wife 'Mary', who has since remarried, recalls. 'I always respected everything Bart said. He was one of the best. I was a lot older than Peter, 16 years older than Peter, so what was the attraction, apart from psychiatry-wise I could relate to him? In years I was far too old to be even considering marrying him.'

While they lived at Kyneton, Dupas was reported to police for harassing a teenage horse rider. He drove alongside her and said her horse was bleeding from the leg.

After she dismounted, he got out of the car, put his arm around her and said: 'Now you're off your horse and I'm out of the car, we can have some fun.'

The girl manoeuvred the horse between them and was able to ride off.

When Mary read of the incident in the local paper she said to him: 'It's lucky they're looking for a blue sedan and not a station wagon, or they'd be looking for you.'

'He was very dependent on me. He was more or less sooky, and always around,' Mary says. Late in 1993 she resumed work, and he began to sulk. 'I was not his own personal kind of property any more,' she says. 'I had to be shared around. My work took me away, and undermined his confidence a bit, and perhaps his self-esteem.'

A visit from his parents seemed to deepen his distress. 'He had been upset,' she says. 'He had had a visit from his parents. His parents were very upright, good people. Best house. Best car. Best this. Best that. I think Peter struggled a lot to get best results from his exams right from the point where he was changing Es to As on his report card. His parents came down for Christmas 1993. He found them very hard to handle. I was not there to instigate conversation or to try to entertain them. When they left he said: "Thank goodness they've gone." They had not reached home when he had re-offended.'

In fact, they had barely left for home before he was planning his next attack. Not who it would be or where. Just that it would be.

He loaded their station wagon with knives and a balaclava. He added a plastic sheet. A shovel. In his pockets, he stuffed masking tape and handcuffs. He told Mary he was going fishing.

* * *

Ballee Bay is a generous title for the clearing on the western flank of Lake Eppalock in central Victoria. From the highway an unsealed road runs through eucalypt forest before it disappears into the hard reddish earth of the shoreline.

The bay is popular with water skiers and anglers, the packed, flinty soil offering good purchase for boat-laden trailers. The clearing is both nominally a bay and nominally a picnic area. A pair of sad, concrete tables, each with its setting of uninviting fixed stools, stands amongst the bush.

The lake seems to be on a plateau, so standing on the cleared space at its edge there is just the water, the gum trees marking the opposite shore and the big, broad blue above. More than 150 metres away, half-hidden in the native scrub, is a toilet block of dingy, grey bricks.

It was 3 January 1994. A group picnicking at Ballee Bay – two engaged couples and another young bloke, all in their 20s – ignored the middle-aged stranger who parked near the toilets and then came over and spoke to them. He said 'Gidday' and 'It's a nice day'. Nobody responded. They let the silence speak for them. They didn't acknowledge his intrusion or encourage him to stay.

He hung around briefly. He said 'See ya', as if they'd had a real conversation, returned to his car and drove away. Had he known one of the men was a Federal copper he might have stayed away. But about an hour later, on her way to the toilets, one of the women noticed the station wagon was back, parked on the dirt track.

As she was sitting on the toilet the cubicle door pushed

open. A hand and a knife appeared followed by a man, his face hidden with a balaclava.

They struggled, he waving the knife, telling her to turn around, she saying she was frightened, resisting being turned, fearing she was to be raped and feeling her hand slashed and bleeding.

Six times he told her to turn and each time she refused while fending off the knife and feeling her hand grow wet and sticky with blood.

He took her right arm and dragged her from the cubicle but finally, seeming to tire of the struggle, left the woman and returned to his car.

When they realised what had happened her friends chased Dupas 15 kilometres, catching him when he lost control turning onto a dirt track. The cop subdued him easily. Dupas was scared they might hurt him.

The year before, tougher sentencing laws had been introduced for sex crimes. Serious sexual offenders, those with more than one conviction for a sex offence resulting in a jail term, faced harsher sentencing, including: the abolition of concurrent sentences, the abolition of remissions and the possibility of indefinite sentences. Public safety was to take a higher priority than rehabilitation of serious offenders, as was the long-standing principle that penalties be proportional to crimes.

Yet despite his history, despite the handcuffs and tape in his pockets, despite the shovel in his car, the new laws were not applied to Dupas because within the Office of Public Prosecutions it was decided only the relatively minor offence of false imprisonment – not attempted rape and not kidnapping – could be sustained.

While his motive seems obvious given his history, the prosecution decided there was nothing overtly sexual in the attack and did not press sex charges. False imprisonment was a comparatively easy charge to sustain since he had clearly detained his victim in the toilet block.

Dupas pleaded guilty to false imprisonment. It was an easy out compared to the alternative of being declared a serious sex offender.

This evidently concerned Judge Hart of the County Court, who asked whether the new sentencing rules applied. He was told no, they did not, but during legal discussion Judge Hart asked: 'Is it not a proper question for a sentencing court to ask itself: clearly, why did he do this? Unless I know why it is being done, I am in a vacuum … I have got to evaluate the crime and I am looking for whatever it is that will help me do that, and one of the matters that occurred to me [which] might be of assistance … [is] to know why he did it. And if that's proper, whether it's proper to take that into account, and the discussion that we have had so far indicates that it's not.'

Despite this invitation to seek to apply the tough new rules to Dupas, the system cut him still more slack. The prosecutor, Tom Gyorffy, said that while it was possible to infer the motive behind Dupas' attack, it could not be inferred beyond reasonable doubt. This was an extraordinary break for Dupas, and it tied the judge's hands.

Judge Hart told Dupas his criminal history was 'breathtaking' and said he believed that Dupas intended to commit a sexual offence, but he was able only to sentence him for false imprisonment. Dupas received a minimum two years and nine months, of which almost a year had already been served in custody awaiting trial.

Justice failed. Here was a man irredeemably evil. He had destroyed or diminished every life he had touched by what he did or what he tried to do. He left his victims living with deep insecurity and choking fear. His brother and sister had disowned him. His parents despaired of him.

He was, in the words of a cop who knew him as a teenager, 'an unmitigated liar'. Fresh faced and fair. A bit of a Johnny Farnham look-alike, one family friend thought, but a liar all the same.

And in September 1996 Soloweij saw him again, after Dupas served the sentence Judge Hart had handed down. Soloweij was supervising his parole this time, which Dupas dutifully completed. He was a veteran of counselling courses. 'By now he would know what anybody would want to ask him. He would have the answers,' Soloweij says.

'What still puzzles me is that extreme anxiety. What is that about? You would think someone with that anxiety, that they would crack eventually.'

Middle-aged now, he remained a timid little boy. Essentially, he was unchanged.

He did not come to police attention until the check of Nicole Patterson's telephone records two-and-a-half years later. It is the longest period in which he is not known to have committed some form of sex-related offence since, as a 15-year-old schoolboy, he attacked his neighbour, Barbara.

Alone again, he lived in the northern suburbs in a flat in Brunswick. He became friendly with a South African woman who lived in the same block of flats, and together they moved into the weatherboard house in Coane Street, Pascoe Vale.

He found work, through the CES, as a general hand in a Thomastown furniture factory up the Hume Highway from home. Apart from his girlfriend, his only contacts were with Patrick O'Brien, Sister Clare and his mother.

Did he really resist his urges for two-and-a-half years? He had usually offended close to home. When his family lived in Glen Waverley his offences were in the eastern or south-eastern suburbs of Oakleigh, Mitcham, Ringwood, Endeavour Hills and Doveton.

His arrest while spying on women in the caravan park showers was over summer at McCrae, near his family's holiday house. In 1979, when his parents had moved to Frankston, he attacked women alongside the Nepean Highway. Nicole Patterson's house was a 20-minute drive along Bell Street and St Georges Road from Dupas' house in Pascoe Vale.

When released previously he attacked women within days or weeks and he was detected just as quickly. He was caught near the scene of the rape at Dimmicks Beach, Rye, as well as at Lake Eppalock. Four women identified him when he used the ruse of car trouble to approach them.

Perhaps he had decided he would not be so easily caught again.

At 4.30 on the morning of Sunday, 2 November 1997, the Greek Orthodox section of Fawkner Cemetery, on Sydney Road heading north out of Melbourne, was dark and forbidding. Thick cloud meant there were no stars or moon to provide light.

But Angelo Gorgievski took off at a run, finding his way between the graves with the faint beam of a tiny flashlight he kept in his car's cigarette lighter. It was the second time that morning that 25-year-old Gorgievski had searched the cemetery. Earlier, he and his father Nikola had climbed the fence and found, locked inside the car park, the red Ford Telstar Gorgievski had lent to his fiancée, Mersina Halvagis.

Without a torch the men had then tried to find their way to plot M33, the grave of Ms Halvagis' grandmother, calling out the young woman's name. Something had compelled Mr Gorgievski to go there, he told the Supreme Court in July 2007. 'That was a spur of the moment thing, I just wanted – something was dragging me there, something made me go there.'

But their search was in vain. They left the grounds, crossed Sydney Road to a service station and called the police. When two police cars arrived and the cemetery gates were unlocked, Mr Gorgievski led the officers to the Telstar. To the policemen's surprise, he grabbed the little flashlight and began running towards the grave. 'I … didn't even talk to anybody. I just started running through aisles,' he testified. 'It didn't look right … something looked wrong, and basically it just happened so quickly … I didn't expect to see anything, but as soon as I got there I just – from turning right to turning left it was just – she was just there. I just stumbled across her.'

Constable Andrew Garbutt, one of the officers who'd followed Gorgievski, recalled his reaction: 'It was a bone-chilling scream.'

Ms Halvagis, 25, was lying on her back, twisted slightly, at a grave site near her grandmother's. Her clothes were in disarray, Steven Reynolds, then an acting sergeant at Craigieburn, said. Her light-coloured pants were stained with blood. Her top had been pulled over her head from the back and was bunched across her chest. Sergeant Reynolds could see holes, like stab marks, in her jumper. 'Her stomach was exposed and I could see stab marks there,' he recalled. 'I shone the torch on her face and her eyes were just open and staring.'

Forensic pathologist Dr David Ranson gave evidence that Ms Halvagis suffered more than 85 separate injuries – 33 of them stab wounds and more than 20 other cutting injuries – to the chest, head and abdomen. There were a number of cuts on both breasts. Her heart and lungs had been punctured and there was a stab wound through her neck.

Sergeant Reynolds recalled Mr Gorgievski's response when he reached her body. 'He'd been nervous through the whole thing but he just became hysterical and he jumped back, he didn't touch anything. He suddenly said, "Oh my God, it's her. Who could do such a thing? Oh my God. Oh my God."'

Who? Fawkner Cemetery is within three kilometres of Dupas' house. The grave of Mersina Halvagis' grandmother was exactly 128 metres from the grave of Dupas' grandfather. And 12 kilometres south of where another woman's body, similarly mutilated, had been found a month before.

Cliffords Road, Somerton is a narrow, sealed road hardly worthy of the name. It runs by sprawling industrial sites – a steel fabricating plant and a concrete manufacturer – on one side while on the other is a desolate view of open paddocks, a railway siding and rusting rolling stock. Even during working hours there is a sense of abandonment.

The body of Margaret Maher, a drug-addicted truck-stop prostitute, was found here one Saturday afternoon in

October by scroungers looking for scrap metal. She had been dumped alongside some discarded computer parts. She was lying on her side, her black leggings rolled down over her thighs, exposing her buttocks. A piece of cardboard had been thrown over her stomach. Her purple track top and sweatshirt were bunched under her left armpit and her left breast was cut off and placed in her mouth.

Maher, 40, was well known around the truck stops and servos on the main route out of Melbourne. When she wasn't seeing men in her one-bedroom flat in Campbellfield, she would see to interstate truckies' needs in the cabs of their prime movers. She was on a methadone program supplemented with amphetamines and sedatives.

When she wasn't working to feed her habit, Maher would wander the shopping strip at Cumberland Road and Gaffney Street, Pascoe Vale. Peter Dupas used the same shops. Coane Street, where he lived, runs off Cumberland Road, five blocks away. Forensic tests found Dupas' DNA on a glove near Maher's body.

Geographic coincidences aside, police also found evidence placing Dupas in the cemetery a month later – a likeness later drawn from the recollections of another visitor to the cemetery bore a striking resemblance to Dupas.

The following month, Kathleen Downes, a 95-year-old woman who had suffered two strokes, relied on a walking frame and had difficulty speaking, was stabbed to death in the Brunswick nursing home where she had lived for eight years.

She was one of 21 residents at Brunswick Lodge, a well-run, bright and cheery place in Loyola Avenue. On 30 December

1997, she left her door open, as always. At 12.30 am, staff observed Mrs Downes asleep. But at 6.30 am, a staff member found her body on the floor beside her bed. A window had been forced, and police found signs indicating that someone had placed themselves in a position where they could watch the nursing home undetected.

Dupas knew the area, having lived nearby in Rose Street, Brunswick from late 1996 until May 1997 when he moved into Pascoe Vale. Although he was a violent sex offender he was not considered a suspect, yet police later found a direct, unexplained link between Dupas and the nursing home. A phone call, asking about placing an elderly female in the Lodge, was traced to his home.

This followed the work, three years later, of a taskforce of seven detectives which had examined Dupas in connection with 17 unsolved murders in Victoria and Adelaide. The Mikado Taskforce had been set up in February 2001. Their sparse, 10th-floor office in Melbourne's St Kilda Road police complex held more than 50 folders concerning the murders of Helen McMahon, Margaret Maher, Mersina Halvagis and Kathleen Downes. There were eye witnesses, forensic evidence and geographical links in each case.

Lobbying by George Halvagis, Mersina's father, had resulted in the law being changed to permit police to seek a court order enabling them to question a person in custody. Police delayed approaching Dupas, however. He had recently appealed against his conviction for the murder of Nicole Patterson and, based on a psychological profile of Dupas, they were advised to wait. It was thought that if his appeal failed, and he believed he would not be released, he would be at his most vulnerable.

Often when dealing with serial sex offenders police work on the principle that the offender is burdened with guilt and that if they could choose, they would be different. 'They want to confide in someone and you just have to help them find a way to confess,' an investigator said.

Dupas is different.

Senior Detective Ian Armstrong had interviewed Dupas on 30 November 1973. 'We tried everything and he would get to the point where he was about to talk. Then something would snap and he would go blank, then deny everything,' Armstrong later said.

Dr Bartholomew had warned that Dupas used denial as a coping device. 'He is to be seen as potentially dangerous. The denial technique makes for huge difficulty in treatment.'

The person who best knows Dupas, Patrick O'Brien, had thought during the period after his 1996 release that Dupas was rebuilding his life. He had formed a relationship, he had worked for a year, and was talking about starting his own furniture business from home. The 1999 killing of Nicole Patterson ended that illusion.

'I really saw him the day before, and the day of the crime, and he really did not seem any different to me, and that's the mystery,' O'Brien says.

'I just can't understand, assuming he did it, that he could be so normal. I believe that he believes himself innocent. That's how he can function the way he does, because he does not believe these things happened.'

Prof Mullen says that despite the period of unconsciousness after the childhood bike accident, there is no evidence of brain damage or mental illness, nothing at all to explain Dupas.

'His parents appear to have done their best,' Mullen says. 'They did not abuse him. They didn't throw him out. They didn't abandon him at the first sight of trouble.'

The ideal outcome, Mullen says, would be that some identifiable part of Dupas' brain could be shown to be awry, miswired in some way: 'It would be nice if it were that simple,' he says. 'It never is one thing. It is always a complex combination of genetic, social, psychiatric and most awful of all, chance.'

Soloweij says that Dupas is one of the most deceptive people he has met, comparable only to the child-killer Derek Percy who has been in jail since 1969. 'Speaking to [Percy] … is like looking into a fish's eyes: there is nothing there. Dupas is deceptively pleasant. You don't want to push him too far in case he falls apart.

'The other one is just a blank wall. Both are equally impenetrable.'

Despite the uncontrolled outbursts of rage in his school years, and the attention generated by his 1968 assault on his neighbour 'Barbara', the adult Peter Dupas had become sophisticated enough to contrive to disguise himself.

Initially he presented a front of vehemently proclaimed innocence, and later, following his arrest for rape soon after his release in 1985, a sort of bemused regret: 'Everyone was saying I was OK now.'

In the late '70s, his modest manner had lulled at least one parole officer, Soloweij, into supporting his release. Dupas had spent enough time with mental health professionals to act out a role in his telephone conversations with Nicole Patterson, telling her he needed to discuss 'family of origin issues', concerning relationships with his mother and with women.

Patterson's supervisor in psychotherapy, Andrew Cargill, said a consultation normally would be arranged with one or two telephone calls and the 15 made by Dupas would have aroused concern. Police believe Dupas made so many calls to check on her movements and the possibility of someone else being in the house when he visited.

In ordinary life, he could blend in. Among the furniture factory crew at Thomastown he was just one quiet unskilled worker. He rarely missed work, just got on with his menial chores without drawing attention to himself. In the street, he would not warrant a second glance.

His girlfriend at Pascoe Vale was utterly unprepared for the discovery of what she was living with and is understood to have left Victoria. Hers is one more life diminished by Peter Dupas.

The father of his ex-fiancée, the girl who ended their engagement after his first conviction for rape all those years ago, said his daughter had nothing to say. He remarked: 'Peter Dupas was two people. When he was here he was a fine young fellow. When he was away, he was something else.'

In August 2004, almost seven years after the killing of Margaret Maher, Dupas was convicted of her murder. The peculiar mutilation of her body, in similar fashion to that inflicted on Patterson, along with a similar cutting pattern seen in both the victims' upper clothing, were central to the case against him.

The jury needed only five hours' deliberation to reach its decision. Dupas was given another life sentence, on top of the one he was already serving for murder. Before he was led away he complained from the dock that it had been a 'kangaroo court'.

In November 2005, eight years after her death, the Victorian Coroner held an inquest into the murder of Mersina Halvagis. With circumstantial evidence, and numerous witnesses who were at the cemetery the day of Mersina Halvagis' slaying having identified Dupas, there was strong speculation he would also be charged over that crime. But the Director of Public Prosecutions, Paul Coghlan, told the coroner's inquiry into the killing that there was not enough evidence to mount a sufficiently strong case to justify a trial.

Dupas did not testify at either the Margaret Maher trial, or the Mersina Halvagis inquest. He never has liked to talk about his crimes. He has always liked to keep things close.

But then he spoke to a lawyer. The wrong lawyer.

Solicitor Andrew Fraser was a pugnacious courtroom operator known for his fierce, police-unfriendly cross-examinations. His clients included Alan Bond and fallen AFL star Jimmy Krakouer, as well as a number of permanently fallen participants in Melbourne's gangland wars. He has been variously described as compassionate and an 'arrogant ratbag' – the latter as a piece of character evidence, but only after he had fallen foul of a $1000-a-day cocaine habit.

Fraser has said he was introduced to cocaine at a party in the early-1990s. At first his use was recreational, just another trapping of success. But by the end of that decade, according to the *Australian Financial Review* in 2004, Fraser was a member of the so-called 'Negroni Commission' (named after the cocktail), a fast-moving social group of about 20 people, mostly lawyers, who allegedly had Friday lunches involving cocaine and call-girls.

In 1999, police recorded Fraser giving advice to his then drug dealer, Werner Paul Roberts, 54, over a scheme to smuggle 5.5 kilograms of cocaine from Benin, Africa inside eight wooden wall plaques. In December 2001, he was sentenced to a minimum of five years for cocaine importation and trafficking and possession of ecstasy. Allegedly in need of protection, he was taken to Sirius East, the maximum security protection unit of Port Phillip Prison.

There he met Peter Dupas and the pair became the division's gardeners and unlikely 'friends'. They took horticultural classes and watched gardening shows on TV together. Perhaps six months after Fraser arrived in the unit, he and Dupas were in the fenced-off exercise yard known as the Chook Pen. A young prisoner, possibly of Greek extraction, came up to the other side of the wire and asked Dupas, 'Are you Peter Dupas?' Dupas answered 'Yes'.

'And with that, the young bloke began to really serve it up to him verbally,' Fraser recalled six years later. He told Dupas he was a cousin of Mersina Halvagis and that he knew Dupas had killed her.

'Abuse like that isn't all that unusual in jail but Dupas was really rocked by this, you could tell just from his body language. He almost stopped as if someone had hit him, you know, and sort of was stuck for words.'

The prisoner told Dupas that if he ever got a chance, he would knock him – meaning kill him – then walked away. Fraser was struck by Dupas' response. He said, 'How does that cunt know I did it?'

'And just the whole body language, the way he uttered that word, I took that as an admission,' said the former lawyer. 'He didn't say it as a question, he said it as a statement.'

A week later Dupas told Fraser he had learnt which cell the cousin lived in. He said he had learnt the prisoner had a doctor's appointment and he would use the opportunity to kill him. He secreted a garden fork behind some bushes to do the job. Fraser quietly alerted authorities and the medical appointment was cancelled.

But in September 2002, police interviewed Dupas in relation to the Margaret Maher murder and told him they had DNA evidence – from the glove found at the scene – that linked him to the killing. Dupas was 'rattled', said Fraser, and began breaking the closed-mouth habits of a lifetime. He told the lawyer he had left no forensic evidence at Fawkner, nor 'with the old sheila down the road' – Kathleen Downes.

After Dupas was charged with Margaret Maher's murder, he showed Fraser the police brief of evidence. The lawyer had already noticed similarities with the 'fact evidence' between the crimes. As he later told police, they involved 'a frenzied knife attack and subsequent mutilation, the same modus operandi applied to Halvagis'.

Then he said: 'Dupas repeated he left no forensics at the scene and no-one, not even the deceased, would have seen him as he attacked her from behind as she was either kneeling at or bending over her grandmother's grave.' This was a dangerous admission. Police had never released the detail that Mersina Halvagis was attacked as she knelt at the grave. Only her killer could have known.

And then Dupas did something that appalled and scared Fraser. He performed 'a little pantomime' of how he'd killed her. 'I was just stunned,' Fraser later told police. 'I just put it to the back of my mind. I just wanted to survive.'

But when the homicide squad called three years later, Andrew Fraser said, 'What took you so long?'

Detectives who'd been reinvestigating the Halvagis case had uncovered several witnesses who could place a man closely fitting Dupas' description inside Fawkner Cemetery on 1 November 1997, the day Mersina Halvagis was murdered.

One was a volunteer who was approached by a man seeking details on what he said was his adoptive mother's grave. In 1998 the woman helped police produce a photofit image that bore a striking resemblance to Dupas. In 2000, while on holidays at Kyabram, the woman saw a newspaper photograph of Dupas and recognised him as the man she had seen at the cemetery. Two others had contacted police after similar experiences.

In 2003 Fraser had been transferred to Fulham Prison near Sale, in East Gippsland. Senior Detective Paul Scarlett had learnt Fraser had spent more than a year with Dupas, during which time he had acted as his jailhouse lawyer. He rang Fraser who surprised him by suggesting that he should visit and agreed to be interviewed.

When Dupas went on trial for Mersina Halvagis' murder in July 2007, Fraser was the star witness. At the opening, prosecutor Colin Hillman, SC, told the jury that Dupas' conversations with Fraser 'amount to a clear, unequivocal confession to the murder of Mersina Halvagis and provide compelling evidence that Peter Dupas was the person who murdered [her]'.

Nonsense, asserted defence barrister David Drake. He told the jury that it was not until a $1 million reward was offered that Fraser, 'a disgraced, imprisoned, bankrupt and struck-off solicitor, stepped forward'. Later, he put it to Fraser that he had invented the admissions in an effort to 'go for the gold'.

But even after six years' absence, Andrew Fraser knew how to sway a jury. Earlier that day he had re-enacted Dupas' 'little pantomime' of how he murdered Halvagis. He stepped out of the witness box and described Dupas' prison cell, where they had been sitting on the bed. He could tell Dupas was anxious, he said, because he started to fidget, clamping his hands between his legs and rocking backwards and forwards.

Dupas pointed at the intercom button on the cell wall where he believed police had planted a listening device, and put his finger to his lips. Suddenly, Fraser said, Dupas jumped up and dropped into a kneeling position, like a victim. 'Now he didn't go right down on his knees, but indicated that somebody was kneeling or bent over. And then he went …'

Fraser, facing the jury from the bar table, dropped to a crouch and lifted his arm. He plunged it down suddenly, raised it and struck again. And again.

Mersina Halvagis' family, sitting behind him, all dressed in black, bore this latest horror in stony silence.

'And then he just sat down on the bed as if nothing had happened.'

On Thursday, 11 August 2007, a third jury found Peter Dupas guilty of murder. Again he was sentenced to life with no minimum.

Many have tried to unravel the twisted mystery that is Peter Norris Dupas. That Thursday, Justice Philip Cummins stared hard at the murderer from the bench and chose to do it with crystal economy. Just two short sentences to sum him up: 'You do not suffer from any mental illness. Rather, you are a psychopath driven by a hatred of women.

'I refuse to set any minimum term,' he added. 'Life means life.'

With John Silvester

ORDINARY MONSTER

'Look at him,' someone says as they bring the murderer by, 'he makes your skin crawl.'

And it's true. There is a definite physical reaction to the sight of him: a small appalled shiver, an urge to draw away, a quick, cold welling up of strangely personalised anger. A little hate.

On first appearances it shouldn't be so. He is small, shambling and unprepossessing, with innocuous features other than that goofy Beatle mop and those over-large spectacles. Pick one word to describe him: it might easily be inoffensive.

But it's not the seeing, it's the knowing. Of the evil things he has done and the evil within.

There are monsters out there. You just don't know it to look at them.

If anyone could tell, it ought to be Justice Frank Vincent. In 40 years of this, he has seen the worst things. But now he leans forward and addresses the mystery of Peter Norris Dupas.

'At a fundamental level, as human beings,' he tells the manacled little man in the dock, 'you present for us the awful, threatening and unanswerable question: how did you come to be as you are?'

It is not a question Dupas is likely to answer. For 25 minutes he stands silent as he is sentenced for slaying Nicole Patterson in Northcote on 19 April 1999. His vacuous, ordinary face betrays nothing.

Flanked by two custodial officers, Dupas wears a blue suit, striped tie and a light blue business shirt, a size or two too large, so that its collar pokes out from his neck. His hands are clasped in front of him, his head slightly downcast, his lips a little pursed – like a barely abashed schoolboy receiving a dressing-down. He suffers from a constant, tiny trembling.

But otherwise, as Justice Vincent summarises his horrid history of sexual violence, details the savagery of his attack on Ms Patterson, even probes his peculiar inhumanity, he is motionless and emotionless.

He is, says the judge at the beginning, and with no small measure of understatement, a secretive individual with very disturbed sexuality. But there is a sort of ordinariness, too; in a life of sexual offences stretching back to his teenage years, he has possessed an ability 'to present yourself as quite inoffensive to … your targets so your unsuspecting victims are caught unawares when you strike'.

He had selected Ms Patterson as one of those victims some time before her death. 'The terror experienced by her at that moment, which you had contemplated in your perverted imagination and for which you had carefully planned, now became a terrible reality.'

There is much that is unknown about Dupas, Justice Vincent notes. But one thing is beyond reasonable doubt. 'In my opinion you regarded Nicole Patterson as nothing more than prey to be entrapped and killed. Her life, youth and personal qualities assumed importance in your mind only by reason of the sense of satisfaction and power which you experienced in taking them from her.'

Nor, he adds, is there any indication of remorse, if in fact Dupas is capable of any such human response.

And now the judge is reaching the moment for which the packed courtroom has been waiting. He leans forward and looks directly into the emptiness of the man before him. Only one course can sensibly remain, and that is that Dupas be removed permanently from the society on whose female members he has preyed.

There is a sudden smattering of applause. Even Detective Sergeant Jeff Maher, the policeman who led the homicide investigation, has turned and is now looking over his right shoulder for something in Dupas' blank face. But for a slight increase in his trembling, there is nothing.

'The sentence of the court is that you be imprisoned for the rest of your natural life and without the opportunity for release on parole,' says the judge.

The public gallery applauds, Nicole Patterson's family and friends crumple into each other's arms and begin to weep, and Peter Dupas is suddenly grabbed by the two custodial officers and roughly bundled out of the dock and from the court.

Nicole's sister, Kylie, has time to shout only one thing after him: 'You shit!'

'I AM A SERIAL KILLER.
I HAVE GOT A PROBLEM'

Another court. Another victim. During September 2004 Peter Dupas was again on trial, still his nondescript self, short and bespectacled, and with his chestnut-brown hair swept schoolboy-like across his forehead. To those who know him well, he is anxious and fearful, a frightened boy in a 52-year-old body in prison.

And, as he appeared in court charged with the 1997 murder of street prostitute Margaret Maher, there was nothing to hint of the community of grief gathered in the public gallery behind him.

Three families, three murder victims, were represented there: Pamela O'Donnell, the mother of Nicole Patterson, murdered by Dupas in her Northcote home in April 1999; George Halvagis, whose daughter Mersina, 25, was killed at Fawkner Cemetery in November 1997, and briefly, Maher's brother, Ingo, who decided to stay away to avoid disrupting the trial.

Dupas, convicted murderer and rapist and suspected serial killer, was then the prime suspect for the stabbing of Mersina Halvagis, who was killed one month after Margaret

Maher. When those suspicions were proved Dupas was to be confirmed as only the second identified serial killer in Victoria, after Paul Charles Denyer, who killed three young women at Frankston in June and July 1993.

O'Donnell was there because the Maher trial relied on what is called 'similar fact evidence'. It meant the jury heard the account of her daughter's murder. When Maher, a street prostitute and drug addict, was found at Somerton, her left breast had been severed and placed in her mouth.

Patterson – O'Donnell's 28-year-old daughter – was also mutilated after her murder. Both her breasts were cut off. They have not been recovered.

The excision of the breasts of Maher and Patterson, considering also the similar ragged, sawing action used to remove them in both cases, could be viewed as a signature of Dupas, the Maher jury was told.

And there was the similar way their clothing was cut away, down the front.

As with many acts attributed to serial killers, Dupas' treatment of his victims is shocking in its depravity, indeed almost unimaginable. It is, however, too simplistic to regard such perpetrators as simply crazed. Forensic psychiatrist Dr Lester Walton says mental illness is rare among serial killers.

Indeed, the sequence of events that led to Dupas being alone with Patterson in her house shows a level of planning not normally associated with the insane. Dupas made an appointment with Patterson, who was working from home as a psychotherapist.

He made the appointment a week ahead and he left as his contact number someone else's mobile phone, presumably so he could not be traced if he abandoned his plan.

'If you exclude people who are frankly crazy, and my instinct is there have been relatively few of those, when they are examined there's not a lot wrong with them,' Walton says. 'Clearly, they are weird people. But there's an absence of overt mental illness.'

This, perhaps, helps explain one of the characteristics of serial killers: a reliance on mentally rehearsing their crimes before committing them.

For Walton, it's a bit like incest. 'There are strong social taboos against those acts, therefore these people have to prepare themselves and get rid of a quite normal abhorrence – it seems to happen through this process of rehearsal, gradually working their way around to it.'

Another characteristic of serial offenders is they do not stop until they are caught or killed. According to FBI criminal profiler John Douglas, serial killers also tend to learn by experience and come to refine what they do, 'perfecting' each scenario from one crime to the next.

Denyer, for example, may have been disturbed preparing for a fourth murder. He had parked, in an almost deserted shopping centre car park, next to another car in which a woman was asleep on the back seat.

Denyer had his car bonnet up, and had previously pretended to have car trouble when he was stalking his victims. He was recognised when the second car's owner returned to the car park. He was arrested hours later.

Douglas, who interviewed numerous serial killers in research for the FBI serial crime unit, said in his book *Mindhunter* that 'probably the most crucial single factor in the development of a serial rapist or killer is the role of fantasy'.

And in a 1994 report, Melbourne forensic psychologist Ian Joblin said that Dupas attacked women to fulfil fantasies of conquest and control. 'For Dupas the actual assault has not lived up to the fantasy which preceded the assault, and is seen at times as disappointing,' Joblin wrote.

'He does not feel reassured by either his performance or his victim's response and must find another victim, this time "the right one". Thus, his offences become repetitive.'

Douglas also found that serial killers are usually young, white and, almost invariably, male. Typically, there will be evidence in their past of harming animals, bed-wetting and starting fires. This, Douglas called the 'homicidal triad'.

As offenders, they may try to intrude on an investigation, and since their motivation is often domination, manipulation and control, they are attracted to policing.

Denyer was a failed applicant for the Victoria Police and had been rehearsing for years by mutilating his sister's toys and torturing the family cat. He was 21 when he embarked on his murderous spree.

One of Australia's most experienced criminal profilers, Sydney forensic psychiatrist Dr Rod Milton, says: 'If we had a system of picking up these behaviours earlier in life, which people would see as going against civil liberties, we would probably identify them earlier. I think a lot of them show what they are like as quite young children, and certainly as teenagers.'

Joblin says that there are a great many more people with the psychological make-up, the sense of inadequacy and powerlessness that serial killers share, but who do not progress to serial killing.

He suggests that those who have been raised in an anti-social environment may model their behaviour on that environment. 'They have been belted by Dad. They see themselves as totally powerless, but they can kill a goat or a cat, and that gives them a sense of power. They learn from that, that they can get gratification from violence.'

Joblin says serial offenders 'mature' into becoming killers when they discover in their 20s that there is no end to their sense of inadequacy, even in the wider world.

But the generalisations about serial killers do not hold in every instance. Sydney's so-called Granny Killer, John Wayne Glover, was 58 when he launched his lethal attacks on six elderly women in 1989–90.

Ivan Milat was in his mid-40s when he murdered the first of seven backpackers whose bodies were found in the Belanglo State Forest in New South Wales. He was acquitted of a double rape when he was 26, and since being convicted of the backpacker killings has been investigated in relation to earlier murders.

Dupas, who stalked, assaulted and raped women in his teens and 20s, apparently did not progress to killing until he was at least into early middle-age. But that progression may have been delayed by the time he spent locked away – he was rarely out of jail between 1974 and 1994 as he served three sentences for rape.

Walton, like Joblin, says that the backgrounds of serial offenders are often horrific, but then many people emerge from equally difficult backgrounds without becoming serial killers.

'An inherent difficulty in looking at these types of crimes is that they are comparatively rare and have a small data base,' Walton says. 'There's nothing I am aware of that enables you to predict whether someone will become a serial killer. If it were a product of psychiatric illness, which is as rare as, that's probably treatable. But as a general rule these people are very damaged and disorganised, and there's not much you can do with them.

'They tend to be thoroughly dysfunctional in terms of family life and intimate relationships.'

An extension of the FBI's study of serial killers was the development of offender profiling – trying to read the offender's personality and characteristics from a crime scene.

Milton 'profiled' the New South Wales Backpacker Killer when the first two bodies were found, and he was able to draw a series of conclusions that were mostly proved accurate when Milat was convicted.

But, Milton says, profiling is 'more media creation than something in reality'. After attending the first backpacker crime scene he concluded two killers had been at work: one victim had been shot repeatedly in the head by a cold and methodical killer who may have been conducting target practice. The second victim had been repeatedly stabbed. The clothing of both victims was arranged differently.

'The second one was done in a much more openly aggressive way, whereas Ivan, I think, was just cold and enjoyed himself.'

As Milton describes it, profiling is often a matter of applying acquired knowledge of other murderers to the scene. Some guesses stand up, others fall down. There has been no official finding of a second killer, for instance, and his guess that Milat lived on a farm was not proved correct.

But of Milat's crime scene he correctly said the killer would drive a fast car, enjoy hunting and present as normal.

Why fast cars? 'That's the sort of person who does these things. I have seen hundreds of murderers. A lot of your knowledge is unconscious, you dredge it out of your past,' Milton said.

Why hunting? 'If you like killing people, then most likely you started with killing animals.'

And that he would present as normal? 'That's typical. They don't present as insane.

'It's possible to get things reasonably accurate, but you can have older people act in juvenile ways. That was the case with the Granny Killer. They seemed to be the crimes of a younger man because there was so much energy.'

There is a randomness about victim selection. Glover, who is suspected of having had an incestuous relationship with his mother, did not stalk his victims, but selected elderly women to kill. Milat targeted hitch-hikers, male and female. Denyer killed when he had what he described as 'that "go" feeling'.

Acting Commander Rod Wilson, the officer who led the Frankston murder investigation, says the nature of Denyer's first killing raised particular alarm. 'I am always concerned about victims grabbed opportunistically,' he says. 'There was nothing in Elizabeth Stevens' life that suggested that anybody had a personal motive for wanting her dead.'

The investigators were under immense pressure as the investigation continued. 'I remember [then Chief Commissioner] Neil Comrie telling the media we will catch this man. And we were thinking, "Gee, we hope we do."'

So great was the public scrutiny that within hours of the arrest the then-Premier, Jeff Kennett, rang the investigators to congratulate them. Kennett incidentally went public too, and the then Director of Public Prosecutions considered charging the state's Premier with contempt of court.

Denyer seemed to enjoy his status, sharing with police the fact he killed when it was raining, hoping to leave fewer clues, and telling his girlfriend after his arrest: 'I am a serial killer, I have got a problem.'

While his history of cruelty to animals fits a typical pattern, the trigger for any individual progressing to serial killing remains unknown.

'The whole thing is pretty frustrating,' Walton says. 'There's no easy answer. I think psychiatry is quite limited in being able to provide some insight into this.

'You tend to fall back into concepts like good and evil.'

The jury in the Margaret Maher murder trial needed just five hours to convict Dupas, who complained of being in a kangaroo court as he was led away.

Meanwhile, Ms Patterson's mother, Pam O'Donnell, and Mersina Halvagis' father, George, hugged each other with relief.

Nicole Patterson's sister, Kylie Nicholas, described Dupas as an evil predator. She said it was important that he be made accountable. Ms Maher's brother, Ingo, said the family was pleased with the outcome.

'Our Margaret lived her life the way she chose and no-one had the right to take that life away from her,' he said.

THE USUAL SUSPECTS

T he killer wore white. She sat in the looming dock of the fourth court with her hands pressed between her knees and her head bowed. She had lost a lot of weight and her face was pale and somehow slack. Her hair was pale too, and rambling; a couple of strands snaked down either side of her face to hide it further. Sometimes she would softly whisper, talking to herself.

Maree could see none of this from where she sat directly behind the girl and four rows back. Just a little of the back of her head, bobbing very slightly but rhythmically back and forth. And beyond that the judge, in crimson, passing sentence.

The girl was a work of self-loathing. She saw herself as the fat kid and the bad kid. The trouble-maker. The one who failed everyone's expectations. Others seemed to have good lives – Caroline had shit. Once, when she was 14, she had painted and hung a portrait of herself. It was completely black.

Maree watched the judge as he read those words. He was finding it hard. He paused, took his glasses from his nose and for long, uncomfortable seconds, seemed stuck. She thought he might be fighting back tears.

The murderer used to babysit her victim. She became obsessed with her and dreamed her as everything she was not. Rachel was gifted, intelligent, popular, perfect. Strikingly attractive with pale, clear skin and hypnotic eyes. A ballet dancer let run barefoot in the country. She wanted to be her and hated her for it.

Maree sat quietly in the courtroom, intent on the judge as he talked, for close to an hour. The girl had pleaded guilty and he needed to outline the details and complexities, forensics, the knowns and unknowns. It was sad and ugly and fascinating.

The killer had carefully planned. She had made notes in premeditation. She would lure Rachel as part of some bogus psychology project and meet her somewhere anonymous. She would get her home, drug her and when she was dead she would disfigure and dump her. Then she would take on a new identity, with a little of Rachel and nothing of Caroline in it. In effect, she would disappear them both.

In the end she strangled her with a black electrical cord, hid her body for two days in her wardrobe, and then buried it in a shallow grave on her father's farm.

Maree watched as the judge sentenced her to 20 years with a minimum of 14. She watched as the murderer was rushed angry-eyed from the dock, past the weeping relatives and out of the court. And she said, 'You know, I feel so terribly sorry for that poor girl.'

You never forget your first murderer. Theirs was Eddie. Slippery, smooth-talking Eddie Lewis, who in 1995 stabbed his girlfriend's father and mother and buried them in their own backyard so he could steal their Porsche. Eddie got 26 years for that. But it took three trials to get Eddie. And they saw nearly every day of every one.

It turned them into something like addicts. Now they habituate the public galleries of the Supreme Court, compulsive court watchers drawn to the rituals and characters they find there. Even the murderers.

After Lewis there were Camilleri and Beckett, the skin-crawling sociopaths who kidnapped and killed two Bega schoolgirls in 1997; the serial predator Peter Dupas who butchered Nicole Patterson in 1999; more recently Mark John Smith, the innocuous RAAF technician who set his wife and baby on fire in 1994; and this one, sad and sorry Caroline Reed Robertson who killed Rachel Barber.

And more than murderers: Brian Quinn, the Coles Myer chief executive who stole $4.6 million to turn his home into something approaching the Palace of Versailles. Greg Domaszewicz, acquitted of the 1997 murderer of Jaidyn Leskie. They sat through the whole Appalachian circus that surrounded that one.

But it's Eddie they remember best. You might even say fondly. After all, it was Eddie who brought them together.

Different motives took them to him. For Maree and Laurie Gleeson it was a return to old habits. For Norm Shaw it was a woman, a dangerous and notorious one. And Keith Evans? Well, Keith was just looking for a place to pee.

This was October 1996. Maree, a soft-hearted former hotel cook and grandmother of five from Melton, west of Melbourne, and her husband, Laurie, were in town to see his doctor. Laurie, an accountant, had been forced to give up work because of ill-health but for 17 years had worked in the city in Queen Street, just around the corner from the

Supreme Court. Since about 1988 and the Russell Street bombers' trial, he had been in the habit of dropping in to the courts to sit in on trials during his lunch hour.

This day, when they were done with the doctor, he said, 'Let's just nip up the court and see what's going on.' Which was Eddie.

The way Norm Shaw remembers, it was a screaming tabloid headline that got him in. Eddie had denied killing Paul and Carmel Higgins, instead pointing the finger at their daughter Amanda – the 'Drug-Crazed Daughter From Hell'. The former scoutmaster had to get a look at this woman painted so scarlet.

Keith Evans was only passing by. Not long before, the retired plumber and tyre-dealer had a couple of stents put in his heart and the doctors had told him to get a little exercise. He took to strolling a few blocks of the city. One day he wandered in to the Supreme Court to use the toilet and thought, why not duck in to a trial for a stickybeak. And there was Eddie.

Like the others, Keith was snared. And in it for the long run.

'One screaming headline started me off,' recalls Norm Shaw. 'Little did I realise that after three trials and two-and-a-half years the case would finally finish. But it became addictive. The drama, the characters, the way the prosecution and defence barristers questioned the witnesses, seeing how the judge had his say, the manoeuvring, the repartee, the to-ing and fro-ing. I was fascinated. And hooked.'

Maree found something that spoke to her sympathetic nature. 'Amanda was on the stand that first day and she came out and was crying and I felt so sorry for her. I just patted her on the arm and said, "It will all be over soon." Far from it, as it turned out, but we kept coming back.'

In the early days of that first trial they trod carefully, sitting upstairs in the gallery until they realised they were allowed down in the main body of the court where you could see and hear better. During the breaks they'd wait at the long table between Courts Two and Three, keeping quiet, observing the protocols.

Slowly they began noticing each other. When they saw Norm, with that shock of white hair and old-world decorum, the others speculated that he might be a retired judge. Gingerly, they struck up conversations and discovered they were like-minded souls.

Through that trial, the two that followed, and many since, they too were being noticed. To some of the tipstaffs, associates, lawyers and media who inhabit the Supreme Court, these four and a handful of other public gallery regulars have become almost part of the furniture. You'll find them up the back at every big trial. They are the Usual Suspects. And sometimes, less kindly, the Groupies.

But it was the barristers and solicitors from the Office of Public Prosecutions, with whom they became friendly during the Lewis trials, who named them best. The Alternate Jury.

Justice, goes the old legal saw, should not only be done, it should be seen to be done. Sometimes it must be seen to be believed. And preferably, seen up close.

Don Foster and Graeme Todd came to the 1998 trial of Greg Domaszewicz, for the murder of Jaidyn Leskie, by accident. About three months before, they had begun following cases in the Melbourne Magistrates Court, until they were on chatting terms with the deputy chief magistrate, Brian Barrow. In October they decided to look in on a trial at the Supreme Court, diagonally across the road. 'It was really only a fluke that we wandered in,' says Graeme. 'But one thing led to another and we ended up spending nearly every day.'

For eight weeks, until Domaszewicz's acquittal, they sat through the whole three-ringer. Incredible witnesses, bizarre evidence of a pig's head and puerile feuds, low-rent love triangles. Masterly performances at the bar from prosecutor Bill Morgan-Payler and Colin 'The Embarrister' Lovitt, QC, and allegations 'tossed like confetti at a wedding' of cover-up, kidnap and conspiracy.

'It was a soap opera,' says Don, a former catering supervisor and security worker, with a US marine's flat-topped brush cut. 'That was brought about I think mainly because of Colin Lovitt's happy knack of trying to bamboozle everybody, including – especially – the jury. I think they were taken in awe of his cross-examination and address. And I still say it today, my opinion differs from theirs.'

'When you first look at it, and as you learn something, well as they say the law's an arse,' adds Graeme, perhaps – perhaps not – mixing up his pronunciations. 'A lot of bull goes through it, doesn't it?'

But compelling bull. Early the next year they were back for the Bega murder trial and others. And hard to miss in their Hawaiian-style shirts. 'Well it was summer, and it gets hot in that joint in summer,' says Graeme. 'And it's a dreary old place at times so we were brightening it up a bit, I suppose.'

The pair, mates since their Essendon school days, moved to the Bellarine Peninsula last year. That and the various 'bits and pieces' of jobs they do, makes it harder to get to the court as regularly. But if there's a choice case they find the time.

It started out of a sort of half-baked interest in the law, says Don. 'Just to see, basically, how barristers operated, the defence and prosecution, all that sort of thing. I was intrigued by the mock-up court cases I'd seen on TV and such, and I wanted to see the real thing.

'I'd been on several juries through my life, I'd been foreman twice, and I'd enjoyed my experience there, but I just wanted to sit at trials and work out just how clever these beaks were.'

Nor, he admits, should you deny the entertainment factor. 'Well yeah, you do get a certain amount of pleasure, you couldn't call it therapy, but it's something you don't have to pay for, it has its heavier side and its lighter side. It's expanding. I think it broadens your outlook on life to a certain extent.

'I mean what do people do? They watch the major news stories on TV or read about them in the paper and to some extent they're interested in them, but they don't go any further. Well, we went one beyond that to actually be there and see it live.'

Justice sits somewhat sad-faced over the main William Street entrance to the Victorian Supreme Court. The blindfold is off; her right hand rests on the handle of a long sword, its point grounded in the sandstone, and her scales drape, used, across her left knee. Her head is bent forward. She looks very tired.

Justice has been done to Caroline Reed Robertson and the Alternate Jury has retired to its usual meeting place, the long table between Courts Two and Three, to discuss the verdict and the thing that keeps bringing them here.

The word pops up unbidden. 'I often wonder to myself,' muses Keith Evans, in his low, soft rumble like very distant thunder, 'am I just a stickybeak? But I don't think I am really.'

Nobody wants to look like vultures, says Norm Shaw. 'These are real people in court. Real mothers and fathers, brothers and sisters, and we feel real sympathy for them. We're not there to see them suffer. It's like a traffic accident and you see people gathered around. OK, for some it's morbid curiosity, but some people are genuinely interested in what's happening and they wish they could help, I guess.'

'Even that girl today,' adds Maree, 'I felt so sorry for her. But then I always do. That's just me, I think I'm the sympathetic type. I saw the victim's sisters crying and felt terribly sad for them, but still I couldn't help feeling something for her. The background she's had, there's something not right for her to do those sorts of things. That needs a little understanding.'

'I think some of the court officials,' puts in Norm, 'to them it's case number 145-stroke-thirty-four, the 15th or 20th murder case of the year, and they get immunised against expressing any emotion, but we can, because we're not in the court system as such, express a fellow-feeling point of view. It's life in the raw and there but for the grace of God go I.'

And there's a sense of wonder, says Laurie. 'The people on trial, they're from every walk of life … well-known people, top citizens to the down-and-outers, and you're wondering how and why they got involved in murder and manslaughter.'

But it is theatre too. The battle of the lawyers, the cut and thrust of examination and cross-examination, the strange alchemy of forensics, the stern directions, compassion and sometimes surprising humour of the judges. Other people flock to see a movie star or footballer, they'd rather see criminals and barristers.

And like most fans, they all have their favourites. The judges: Justice Frank Vincent, for his common touch, compassion, unflappability and the look he gives over the top of his glasses; Justice 'Fabulous' Philip Cummins, for his courtesy and ability to give cheeky lawyers as good as he gets. The QCs: John Smallwood, with his bushranger beard and down-to-earth nature; Bill Morgan-Payler, who always takes the time to chat; and, grudgingly, Colin Lovitt for his performance art.

'And it is a nice old building,' says Keith. 'It's just like a magnet to me for some reason. I have no intention of coming in, then I get up in the morning and, "Ah, might as well go in and see what's going on." It's better than being at the tote all day, and a lot cheaper.'

'It is the Supreme Court, of course,' points out Norm, 'and it's where the major trials are. OK, people might say you're a bit ghoulish going to the major murder trials, but look at all the people who read murder books, watch murder on TV shows, "Murder Most Foul". It's simply fascinating, it's addictive. They are big stories. They are tragic. And they're for real.'

Years back, Frank Vincent was one of them. This was the mid-1950s, before television took hold, and when the courts were the venue in which crowds of people would catch their daily dramas. The legendary defence barrister Frank Galbally was at his peak and the young law student would sit among the throng in some awe at this great performer in command of his setting.

Now a judge in the same place, he has sympathy, even admiration for the few remaining regulars taking their places among the fidgeting school groups. They are acutely conscious of the protocols, never intrusive, and know the way the courts operate. They are certainly not ghouls.

'It's said that judges and courts are remote places,' he says. 'But through the doorway of the fourth court passes almost every conceivable kind of human being, with all sorts of different personalities, with all sorts of different problems, and there is, effectively, a drama being played out there almost every day.'

Moreover, he points out, it is a fundamental tenet of our system that our courts are kept open so they can be seen by any member of the community, and what happens there is clearly a public activity.

Of course, he adds, in certain trials there are special circumstances, unusual personalities or scenarios. He smiles. 'It's hardly surprising that people may have wanted to watch the Domaszewicz trial with its parade of sometimes, ahem, different people.'

What it is, says John Smallwood, smoking another cigarette in the courtyard as he waits for a jury to come back, is better than telly. They pick and choose, watching the papers for a good case. 'It fascinates me. I've got a nasty cross-examination to do and the whole lot are there. As if some telepathy exists between them.'

At least one judge calls them Mr Smallwood's Fan Club.

And the feeling is mutual. Smallwood always feels confident when they're around. He'll be addressing a jury or doing a tricky cross and there'll be no-one there. 'It's just me against the world. And I'll look around and there's [sic] three or four of them, nodding and smiling at me. "Right, here we go, put on a show for the boys."

'Their real caper is the cut and thrust. They love final addresses and they love a decent, vicious cross-examination. I think they treat it as a whodunnit. I think they just find the mechanics fascinating. And, usually, when you talk to them, their perception of the forensic tactics and why you're doing things is pretty good.'

Sometimes they'll ask him what his defence is going to be and he'll tell them 'because there's no way known they'll dog me'. Often he'll let them know when interesting things are about to happen and will explain some of the legal technicalities, so they can follow it better.

'I think it's just a straight fascination with the process, with the whodunnit aspect of it and just with the human condition.'

Bill Morgan-Payler, who dubbed them the Alternate Jury, also enjoys having them in court. It's nice to have a couple of friendly faces around, he says, and they've become casual friends over the years.

'They're nice people, they're fascinating, and I reckon they're not bad judges of the horseflesh. They like all the big ones, they've got all the counsel worked out now, who they reckon's good and who's not, and what their good and bad points are. They're very good at picking up the atmosphere. Invariably, they have a fair idea of how you're going. It's almost as if they're writing a form book.'

And to the cynics, who see a vicarious, ghoulish, almost Madame Defarge-ish side, he insists it's the opposite. 'They are the informed members of the public that judgments keep talking about. You know, when they say, "An informed citizen would not be outraged by this sentence if one knew all the facts." That's them.'

TROUBLE IN PARADISE

You could easily miss the police station at The Rocks. It stood on a corner in rendered brick, four storeys tall but curiously narrow. It was an old pub once and, to most of the tourists, it still looked like one.

But Ronnie Thomas knew it. A lifetime of bad experience meant he probably knew every police station in Sydney. But mainly he chose to give himself up there, that Sunday, 19 January 1992, because it was closest to where his Kombi had broken down on the way into the city from Bondi Junction.

So one of Australia's most wanted men phoned his mum from Circular Quay, told her to send his lawyer down, and then walked around to The Rocks.

At 1.45 pm, Thomas strolled up to Constable Glenn Burling, standing at the counter, and said: 'My name is Ronald Thomas. I think you blokes are looking for me.'

Constable Burling said, 'What for?' and Thomas said: 'For that double murder up at Surfers Paradise. I had nothing to do with it and I want to clear my name.'

The computers were down so it took a while before Constable Burling could link his visitor to the executions on 23 December 1991 of Gold Coast SP bookie Peter Wade and his girlfriend Maureen Ambrose. But the police wanted to check one more thing.

A sergeant walked past and said – sort of smart-alecky, Thomas recalled – something like, 'Smile, will you? Show us your teeth.'

Thomas opened wide. Most of his teeth were gone and there was a chunk missing from his tongue.

'I got shot as well,' he said. He pointed to his top lip. 'The bullet went in here. Broke my dentures. I was spitting teeth everywhere.'

Now the police were convinced they had their man. Or one of them.

Peter Wade, his many acquaintances agreed, was a knockabout sort of bloke. But that was about the best they could say about him. Otherwise he was a shocking drunk with a tendency to bad-mouth people, and every so often it earned him a belting.

Wade, 50, started SP bookmaking in Sydney at 17. At the height of his 30-year career he worked up to four hotels, with up to three employees at each pub taking phone bets, and boasted of holding between 60,000 and 70,000 pounds an afternoon – something equivalent to about a million dollars in today's money. In 1989, he packed it in and moved to the Gold Coast.

On Sunday 22 December, Wade and his girlfriend, barmaid Maureen Ambrose, 53, spent most of the evening drinking at the Chevron Hotel, Surfers Paradise. About 9.15 they went home to Wade's second-floor unit at the Del Ray Apartments in Whelan Street.

Whelan Street is a tough street, known for 'fights and

blues and drunks and hoodlums', according to a local, but the Del Ray units were attractive and apparently secure.

New Zealanders Karen Renton and her husband were honeymooning in unit 22, directly below Wade's unit. At 12.15 am on 23 December, Mrs Renton was woken by two loud banging noises. 'Then it was like a scuffle in the apartment upstairs and then just a dull thud on the roof of our apartment,' she later told the Queensland Supreme Court.

It was quiet for about 10 minutes, and then she heard someone running down the stairs. Mrs Renton went to the balcony and looked out. She saw two men in shorts and T-shirts come out of the security door and walk quickly away. 'I couldn't see their faces. Their heads looked like they had been bandaged like mummies or something.' She went back to bed.

Michael Webb and Linda Dark were on their way home from nearby Cavill Avenue when two men ran across Whelan Street. 'It looked suspicious, like they stole something,' Mr Webb testified. One was tall and bearded, wearing a green jacket; the other was shorter with black hair. He was holding what appeared to be a red rag to his face, added Ms Dark.

The men ran to a white Ford Fairlane parked beneath some nearby units and drove away.

About seven o'clock that morning, New South Wales holidaymakers Michael and Bernice Sharp discovered something strange in their ground-floor unit 11 at the Del Ray Apartments. Someone had slit open the flyscreen over the kitchen window and apparently climbed in from the balcony. The door to the stairwell had been unlocked but nothing else was disturbed and nothing taken.

At 9 am, not long after Mr Sharp told him of the break-in, Del Ray manager Mr John Seager was called to Wade's unit. A manhole cover in the ceiling outside the unit door had been removed; the door was wedged open by a broken piece of plaster. Two large holes had been shot through the door and there was a large hole smashed in the ceiling just inside the apartment.

Mr Seager walked to the bedroom. Then he turned and 'sort of bolted'.

Peter Wade was lying on the floor on his back, wearing only a pair of blue shorts. Maureen Ambrose was lying across him, face down to the floor, wearing only tracksuit pants. Wade had been shot three times with a .22 calibre gun. One shot went through his left shoulder and upper arm. The next tore through his upper back, lung and aorta. The last was fired through his left temple. Ms Ambrose was shot once in the face with the same gun – from almost point-blank range.

But someone else had also been shot. Police found blood and bits and pieces of teeth in the unit, two pieces of a partial dental plate near the door and a sporadic trail of blood and teeth leading away from the unit, down the stairwell and out towards Whelan Street. 'Now those teeth did not belong to Wade and Ambrose,' prosecutor Paul Rutledge told the Queensland Supreme Court in 1993.

Then detectives found palm and fingerprints on the balcony railing of unit 11. They matched those of Ronald Henry Thomas, a career criminal – but not a very good one.

Ron Thomas was born in Newtown, Sydney, in June 1949 and raised by his mother, Joy, and a series of stepfathers. He never met his real father until he was 35. He left school at 13 and, less than two years later, was locked up for the first time, for car theft. Since then he has spent 36 of his 58 years in jails or institutions.

He was 18 when he killed his first man. In July 1968, he told the court – omitting the nastier details – he was recruited to help two mates steal a safe from the Newtown postal depot. He was discovered by the night watchman and hit the man over the head with a shotgun. 'I sort of lost me block,' he explained to police. He was sentenced to life.

Thomas got out of jail on licence in March 1982, began work as a bricklayer and married the daughter of a former Newtown SP bookie. But in 1984, owing money to the National Bank, he decided to rob one of the bank's agencies in Palm Beach, Queensland, armed with a pistol. He was forced to serve out the remainder of his murder sentence in New South Wales and, in 1988, was extradited to Queensland to serve two years for the armed robbery. He was finally released in September 1991 and moved to his mother's farm at her then home at The Pocket, near Byron Bay, in northern New South Wales.

The day after Thomas got out, John Victor Bobak was released from Grafton jail and moved to Bilambil, just across the border in Queensland. Bobak, tall, heavily tattooed with a reddish-brown beard, was a lifetime criminal. He had associations with the Gypsy Jokers motorcycle gang and through them came into contact with Justin Hill, a biker and disgraced Sydney solicitor later sentenced for eight years in South Australia for amphetamine manufacturing.

One of Hill's former clients was Peter Wade. Police say that over a number of years Hill had laundered Wade's SP profits through almost $2 million in property purchases in

Sydney and the Gold Coast. But when Wade began his 'fresh start' in Surfers, he tried to fund it by selling the properties. Unfortunately, he found, they were all in the name of Justin Hill.

John Bobak and Ronnie Thomas had met in prison in the late 1970s and had not seen each other for about eight years, but they soon made up for lost time. They began fishing and scuba diving, travelled to Sydney together and, once, to Perth. On 13 December 1991, Bobak was with Thomas when he bought a secondhand white Ford Fairlane for $4500 cash from Chris's Auto on Parramatta Road, Five Dock, outside Sydney.

Thomas later said he invited Bobak and his de facto, Amanda Teasdale, to spend Christmas Day with his family at his mother's place. They never made it.

Amanda Teasdale had once been a dental nurse, she told the Supreme Court in 1993. Her training came in very handy about 2 am on Monday 23 December, when she was shaken awake by John Bobak.

'John woke me and said, "Ron's been shot. Can you help him?",' she testified. 'There was a big hole along one side of his jaw and a part of his tongue was missing. There were no teeth on that [right] side. I got out disinfectant and cleaned up his mouth and got some tweezers and tried to dig around and see if there were any bits of teeth or foreign matter.' She said she dug out two pieces of metal.

Thomas appeared to be in terrible pain. Teasdale gave him painkillers and some sleeping tablets and put him to bed. In the morning she telephoned his mother, Joy Thomas, who came and took him away.

Ron Thomas wasn't seen again for almost a month but detectives quickly knew who they were looking for. They had a positive identification on his fingerprints from unit 11, and Thomas and Bobak fitted descriptions from witnesses who saw two men running from the apartments.

At 3.30 pm that Monday, someone identifying himself as Thomas phoned a Tweed Heads smash repair shop and arranged to have his Fairlane collected from a car park south of Surfers Paradise. There was nothing mechanically wrong with the car but there was blood all over the passenger's seat and police were called.

On 7 January, a policeman found two .22 calibre cartridges by the road 1.6 kilometres from Bobak's house at Bilambil. They matched those found at the murder scene. Later, police divers searching a nearby creek discovered an ammunition box containing a .22 Ruger and silencer and a .357 Magnum Colt handgun. Tests showed the .22 was the murder weapon.

When Gold Coast investigators released his name and photograph to the media on 16 January, Ron Thomas, hiding out in a motel at Bondi Junction, Sydney, decided he'd had enough. Three days later he walked into the police station at The Rocks and began to lay out an incredible tale.

In his version, Ronnie Thomas first met Peter Wade in early December 1991 while drinking with his ex-wife in the Birdwatcher's Bar in Surfers Paradise. They discovered they'd had some mutual friends: one of Thomas' 'stepfathers' was a well-known Sydney crim from the 1960s, Chicka Reeves, and an 'aunty' was a notorious shoplifter, Jeannie Pink.

Thomas told his murder trial in 1993 that, on the afternoon of 22 December, he again bumped into Peter Wade at the Birdwatcher's. By the time he finished there, about 9 pm, he said he realised he was too 'pissed' for the three-hour drive to his mother's and decided to ask Wade if he could stay the night with him at the Del Ray. Thomas said he fell asleep on the couch in the lounge room.

'The next thing … I distinctly heard one shot coming through the door,' he said. 'I got to my feet and at the same time someone's foot started coming through the ceiling … then two legs appeared and a man dropped from the ceiling to the floor.

'I shit myself,' Thomas admitted. He said the man who fell from the ceiling jumped to his feet. 'He raised both hands, he had a gun in it and he shot me. I felt a numbing sensation to the lower part of my face. I remember a flash of light and it's hard to explain, it is an eerie feeling of something happening to your body inside you. I knew something serious had happened to me. I can recall a great deal of pain and that's the last I remember.'

When he woke one of the men was standing over him pointing a gun. Then he leaned in close, pulled Thomas' hand away from his injured face and said: 'Is that you, Ron?' He pulled off his balaclava and said his name. It was a man Thomas had done jail time with during the 1970s. He was tall and bearded but, Thomas swore, he was not John Bobak.

Another, smaller man came out of the bedroom and motioned his partner to step away. Thomas believed he was about to be executed. 'Then the bigger man said, "No, I know him. He is all right … He won't say nothing".'

Thomas said the man wrapped a piece of material around his head and helped him from the unit to his car and drove him away, south towards Coolangatta. Near the airport, the man made a phone call and 15 minutes later a woman arrived and took him to her home. He flatly denied being treated by Amanda Teasdale. He said he lived on mashed potato until his wounds began to heal. At the end of the first week of January, the tall man bought him a Kombi wagon, drove him to Sydney and told him to disappear.

In the Supreme Court, Thomas refused to name the man. It would be worth his life, he said. 'I believe that if I tell you his name something similar would happen to me or my family ... He told me that I could never tell anyone what happened or give his name to even my own mother. I was told that if these people couldn't get me they would get a member of my family.'

It was an amazing and – the jury unanimously decided – unbelievable story. They chose to believe the prosecution's version, which said that Thomas and Bobak were hired, at a price of $50,000 each, to kill Wade in a dispute over his illegal bookmaking earnings. Maureen Ambrose was simply in the wrong place at the wrong time.

Mr Rutledge suggested to Thomas that this is what happened: The original plan is for Bobak to enter the room and execute Wade while Thomas stands guard outside. But Wade hears Bobak crashing through the ceiling, arms himself with a knife and, in a struggle, is shot through the shoulder. Hearing the commotion, Thomas shoots through the door twice and starts to break into the room.

As Wade flees into his bedroom, Bobak shoots him in the back. He enters the room and shoots Ms Ambrose in the face at close range. Wade, lying on the floor, is shot once more through the left temple.

Thomas succeeds in breaking through the door but Bobak, seeing a darkened figure coming down the hallway, turns and accidentally shoots his mate in the mouth.

Rubbish, Thomas replied. 'You should be writing plays.'

In August 1993, Ron Thomas was found guilty of the murders of Peter Wade and Maureen Ambrose and sentenced to two terms of life imprisonment. His appeals were unsuccessful.

But someone apparently believed Ron Thomas' strange story. On 3 February 1997, someone claiming to be the real killer sent six letters: to Queensland Attorney-General Denver Beanland, the New South Wales Police Commissioner, criminal lawyer Andrew Boe, *The Courier-Mail* newspaper in Brisbane, the Arnott's biscuit company and 'Arnott's friend, the CJC [Criminal Justice Commission], up in Qld' alleging Thomas was framed.

The packages, carrying Sydney postmarks, also contained Arnott's Monte Carlo biscuits, the cream centres having been mixed with enough of the common pesticide Fenthion per biscuit to kill a small child.

The author or authors threatened to plant 'a rush' of similarly poisoned biscuits in stores throughout New South Wales and Queensland unless four New South Wales police who gave evidence at Thomas' murder trial were taken to Queensland and given lie detector tests. 'This is not a one-off attack. It will be a campaign of attacks until this is resolved,' said the typewritten notes.

Thomas had been in prison for five years 'serving two life sentences because of us', they said. 'We always thought Ron would never get found guilty of murder, maybe a lesser charge for not helping the police and not telling on me, but not these murders.'

In the letter to lawyer Andrew Boe – 'you sound like an honest man who could right a wrong' – they said Sydney police had 'put Ron in the picture' because he had already been given a life sentence and made an easy target, and because he would not give up the real killer. 'Ron was there. When he ran he thought he was the one we wanted, and we shot him, it was dark.'

Police and a co-operative media kept the threats secret for almost two weeks while a 50-strong team of detectives in two states conducted investigations and picked through the tangled threads of Peter Wade's murder. But when the extortion threat was revealed on 14 February, Arnott's was forced to remove its products from the shelves of 3000 supermarkets, service stations and convenience stores throughout New South Wales and Queensland. The company withdrew 800 truck loads of biscuits and dumped them, and more than 300 casual workers had to be laid off.

On the day of the announcement, Arnott's, which dominated the Australian biscuit market with a share of more than 60 per cent, requested the stock exchange to temporarily suspend trade in its shares. When trading resumed, a little over four hours later, the shares fell by 25 cents, reducing the value of the company by $35 million. Arnott's forced withdrawal of products and three weeks of lost production of all biscuit lines cost it more than $10 million before tax.

Community confidence was also badly shaken. Many people still had memories of the deadly Tylenol contamination in Chicago in 1982, in which seven people, including a newly-wed couple and a 12-year-old girl, were killed by cyanide-tainted extra-strength pain-relief capsules bought at chemists and supermarkets.

The four police alleged to have verballed Ron were never required to sit a polygraph test. Nor did Thomas have any real dispute with the accuracy of the wealth of physical and circumstantial evidence which made, according to one of the judges at his 1994 appeal, 'a compelling case that the appellant was guilty'.

A week after the letters were made public, Thomas appealed to the extortionists to withdraw their threat. He summoned his solicitor, Mr Chris Nyst, to the Sir David Longland Correctional Centre, south-west of Brisbane, and issued a short statement. 'My name is Ron Thomas,' he began. 'I was wrongly convicted of two murders and now I am serving life for them.

'I didn't ask for this and I don't want it to happen. So if you want to help me you will drop the whole thing and write to the newspapers telling them it's off. I know you are trying to help me. But this is not the way to do it.

'Innocent people could be hurt,' said Ronnie, 'and I don't want any part of that.'

For a little while investigators liked John Bobak for the extortion but soon discounted him and shifted their focus elsewhere. No poisoned biscuits were ever found on store shelves and, after six months, Queensland police announced they were scaling down the Arnott's taskforce. A New South Wales team that had been based in Queensland had already been sent home.

Then, at the end of May 1999, detectives announced they had finally made an arrest – Ron's 69-year-old mother, Joy Thomas.

*   *   *

It was a given: whenever Ronnie Thomas found himself at the centre of big trouble, the coppers would inevitably turn up knocking on his mum's door – and usually with a warrant.

They all knew Joy from way back and they knew she steadfastly stuck by her boy – even though, as one of them would later put it, Ron was 'as dumb as dogshit'. Whenever he got out of jail – on release or through escape – he would head for home. It was his mum who got the first phone call when he decided to hand himself in over the Surfers Paradise killings. Even back when he committed his first murder Joy was on hand, sitting 'cockatoo' outside the Newtown postal depot on the other end of a walkie-talkie.

She was born Joy Ellen Sharman about 1933. A daughter of Les Sharman, of the famous Jimmy Sharman boxing troupe, she spent her early childhood travelling the show circuit before settling in Sydney. There she was said to have become good friends with the likes of celebrated stick-up man and escaper Darcy Dugan and feared gangster Lennie McPherson. At one time she was the girlfriend of standover man Charles 'Chicka' Reeves, who went on to twice escape murder convictions only to be blown away in a 1979 shotgun ambush in Wollongong.

Joy was 15 when she gave birth to Ron, and she had two other children with his father, John Arthur Thomas, though Ron told his trial he never met his father until he was 35. Ever loyal, Joy was waiting in 1964 when he got out of juvenile detention on car theft charges and again in 1966 while he was in the Gosford Boys' Home for stealing offences.

By 8 July 1968, Joy had married Maxwell John Williams, a bootmaker and sometime thief. Williams, Ron would later claim, had cased the Newtown South post office and discovered that '10,000 quid or something' was kept in its safes. Ron said he was recruited to the burglary only after another man failed to turn up, and he drove to the post office depot in Iredale Street with his mother, stepfather and another man, bricklayer Danny Clark.

Ron and Clark went inside while Williams and Joy waited outside, Joy keeping watch and directing the break-and-enter by two-way radio.

'They told me that all we had to do was get the two safes out of the post office by half-past one,' Ron told police in an unsigned statement. 'If we left home at half-past 11 we would have two hours while the watchman wasn't there.'

But the information was wrong. They were interrupted by 58-year-old security guard Dudley Downton. Clark was carrying a .38 handgun and Thomas a double-barrelled shotgun. They told Downton to stay where he was, but he picked up an electric radiator and hit Thomas over the head with it.

Enraged, Ron clubbed the guard with the barrel of the shotgun, which discharged twice as they struggled. 'I sort of lost me block and hit him a couple of times until he went down,' he later told police. He radioed Joy and they fled empty-handed: 'I didn't think we killed the old bloke – he was on his feet when we left.' In fact, the father of six was horribly battered, his skull fractured in four places.

When he was arrested, Thomas said Williams had run the whole botched operation. He heatedly denied his mother was in charge. 'No, that's not right,' he said. 'All she did was sit outside in her car with a walkie-talkie and kept watch unless we got sprung.'

He refused to sign the record of interview until he saw a lawyer, adding, typically: '... and see what Mum said.'

In September 1969 the four were convicted of murder and given life sentences. Williams' conviction was later overturned on appeal. (Not wanting to look any gift horse in the mouth, he sought to have the Crown repay his legal costs – without success.)

On 6 May 1978, Ron tired of prison life and walked out of the Milson Island Centre open institution on the Hawkesbury River and disappeared for almost three months. Twenty-two days after his escape, Joy Thomas was released on parole and went to live near Byron Bay with her other son, Anthony. In late July police intercepted Ron driving a car not far from Byron Bay.

The next day two detectives from the Sydney armed holdup squad arrived at Joy's place. On 24 July mother and son appeared together in the Lismore Court of Petty Sessions: Ron charged with escaping from lawful custody and Joy with harbouring him. Anthony Thomas was also charged with harbouring.

In court it was also alleged that in June Thomas had broken into a nearby stud property and stolen goods worth $5000. But all he would admit to was using 'unseemly words' at the time of his arrest – which, given the circumstances, might seem excusable. He was fined $60, in default three days hard labour and went back to complete his sentence.

But, as ever when it came to family, Ron stayed staunch. In a statement to the court, he said: 'I am an escapee and I know that my mother and brother have been charged with harbouring me. I would just like to say I have never been to their house and they did not know where I was living. On the occasions that they did see me, they pleaded with me to give myself up.'

His plea did no good, but a group of Sydney feminists were more successful. Deciding it was dreadful that a mother should be jailed for helping her son, they started a 'Free Joy' campaign and she was released after a successful appeal. Looking back years later, one of the activists admitted to the *Sydney Morning Herald* that they may have been a little naive: 'Joy was a cunning old bugger and we fell for it a bit.'

That was in 1997, at the height of the Arnott's extortion scare. As usual, the police had quickly and repeatedly arrived at Joy Thomas' door to interview her. She told them and the media: 'We would never have thought of anything like that. It's not [Ron's] style or ours. He is from the old school – he'd rather get on a roof and protest than be involved in anything like this.'

But at least some police reckoned Joy was a lot smarter – or trickier – than she was admitting. Though not half as smart as she thought.

The tainted Monte Carlos sent out almost three years earlier had been meticulously tampered with. The cream filling of the biscuits had been scraped out, mixed with poison and a bright vegetable dye – to warn of their toxicity – then the biscuits reassembled. They were returned to their packets, which were carefully resealed. But whoever contaminated them had not been careful enough.

The cream in one of the biscuits also contained a single, fine, pale-coloured dog hair. The same type of hair was also found on tape from the packages used in the extortion. Both samples matched that of one of Joy Thomas' five pets.

When Joy fronted the Brisbane Magistrates Court on 14 December 1999, Detective Inspector John Maloney told the committal hearing that raids were conducted on her home at Billinudgel and scientific officers vacuumed animal hairs for comparison with those found in and on the boxes. He denied that the hairs could have come from investigators or those who had received the packages. 'There would be no way that they could be accidentally transferred other than when being prepared by the offenders,' he said.

The court was also told that during a raid on 1 July 1997, police found bottles containing the same pesticide detected in the biscuits. They also found the address of lawyer Andrew Boe, who had been sent one of the packages, and the names of two of the New South Wales policemen who had given evidence against Ron. In addition, they discovered letters written by Joy containing a spelling mistake similar to that made by the Arnott's extortionist – she spelled 'received' with the 'i' before the 'e': 'R-E-C-I-E-V-E-D'.

Much more damaging was the claim that police DNA testing indicated she had licked a stamp found on the letter sent to Andrew Boe. Advances in DNA testing had only recently allowed the DNA samples to be matched, police said. Prosecutor Paul Rutledge said the pattern of DNA found occurred only once in every 2900 billion: 'It is the same profile as the defendant.'

When Joy was asked how she wanted to plead she said simply, 'I had nothing to do with it.' She was committed on four charges of extortion. But, despite waiting almost two-and-a-half years, she never went to trial.

In April 2002 she walked free after the prosecution announced it was entering a *nolle prosequi*, a decision not to prosecute, and all charges were struck out.

It must have been tough for Paul Rutledge who had been involved with the Thomases since prosecuting Ronnie at the Wade–Ambrose murder trial in 1993. But, he had to admit, new revelations showed the key DNA evidence on which the prosecution relied was fatally flawed – or as he put it: 'not sufficiently strong to justify the proceedings continuing.'

That was something of an understatement. From the beginning the DNA evidence had been problematic. At the committal, the court was told stamp pulp containing the DNA had been discarded. Without it, Joy's defence team could not perform its own tests.

But in the lead-up to her trial, the Queensland Government's major scientific testing laboratory, the John Tonge Centre, managed to locate a sample of the solution containing the DNA extracted from the stamps. Thomas' legal team and scientific experts did their tests and when they compared them with those of the prosecution found evidence of a second person's DNA. This, said Mr Rutledge later, was merely 'a difference of opinion between two experts'.

It was much more than that. In a pre-trial hearing, the defence team was able to show that while the presence of a second person's DNA was indicated in a table provided by the prosecution's key forensic witness, scientist Barry Blair, it had not been mentioned in the text of his report. 'I'm not disputing the fact that there could be a weak profile present,' said Blair under cross-examination. But he said he believed the second profile was a 'stutter' – an anomaly in testing procedures.

In a further blow to the prosecution case, it was revealed the John Tonge Centre had not conducted tests for saliva, so it could not be shown if Joy Thomas had licked the stamps. It had also been discovered that two stamps taken from the extortion packages had been tested together despite national forensic best practice methods against mixing samples.

Presiding Judge Michael Shanahan said that in light of the flaws in the testing procedures he would have to warn any jury that it would be 'dangerous to convict on this material'. Mr Rutledge soon made the decision that it would not go to a jury.

Joy had never been able to explain how her DNA got on the stamps. But Rutledge had to admit: '... the presence of this second profile substantially weakens the prosecution's case that the DNA on the stamps is only reasonably and rationally explicable as a result of the accused's knowing participation in the extortion,' he said.

Joy Thomas walked free, but not without cost. After three years she owed thousands of dollars in legal bills and her house had been mortgaged to Legal Aid.

But Joy stayed true to a lifetime of form. For the Thomases, family always came first. The first thing she was going to do, she announced, was visit Ron in jail. And then she'd think about seeking compensation.

'All I want is for the mortgage to be taken off,' she said, 'so I can leave my house to my children when I die.'

CHASIN' – STORIES FROM THE HEROIN PLAGUE

2: AS LOW AS SHE CAN GO

So here she is again. Flat out on a footpath in South Melbourne, lank-haired, slack-jawed and dozy, her eyes – when she can manage to keep them open – ink-black pin pricks surrounded by emptiness. Doing her personal best to crank up the latest heroin overdose statistics. And maybe to kill herself.

When the accommodation shelter workers came running five minutes ago she was unconscious and barely breathing. But somehow they've slapped and shaken her back to the surface.

An ambulance officer tugs up a shirt sleeve to take her blood pressure and she jerks away hard. 'Fuck off,' she slurs, 'don't give me no fuckin' Narcan,' not wanting the anti-narcotic that will cancel out the overdose and, she fears, destroy her hit and leave her hanging out for more.

For 30 minutes she rages, oscillating between four-letter fury and pathetic self-pity: no-one loves her, no-one wants her, no-one cares. Then she lurches away towards the city on the arm of her male friend, walking rubber-kneed like someone on a boat in bad sea.

Helpless to do any more, the ambulance officers and the three policemen who have been called in watch her go. They suspect – they know – that it won't be long before they see her again.

Since the start of this drug-plagued week in February 1998, Metropolitan Ambulance Service paramedics have chased a spate of heroin overdoses across Melbourne: more than 50, one fatal. A purer-than-usual batch of the drug has been blamed. But in one sense, it seems, this shambling, tragic young woman shares some of the responsibility.

Just 24 and already sunk about as low as she can fall, she is a serial OD victim.

On Monday ambulance officers responded to a dozen overdose call-outs, three of them to her. On this shift, Wednesday, they'll see her three more times. 'Mate,' the friend claims, 'she's had 27 ambulances in the last two months.'

Today Steve MacKenzie gets her first. Burly and laconic, an ambulance officer for 13 years and a Mobile Intensive Care paramedic for more than four, he operates the MICA 301 Commodore from the ambulance service's central branch at St Vincent's Hospital. He's cruising Fitzroy at 4.21 pm when the call comes in. Signal One – lights and siren – to a suspected overdose near the corner of Russell and Bourke Streets.

'Mmm, yeah, that'd be it,' he says. 'The classic location.'

Four minutes later, he pulls the sedan to the kerb outside an amusement parlour in Russell. Another ambulance is already there. Its crew, Rob Paton and Paul Golz, are on their second OD call of the afternoon. 'Another sad story,' says

Paton later. 'She'd just got out of prison, it was her birthday and someone bought her a hit for a present. Some friend. We brought her out of it with Narcan.'

This time they're comforting a ragdoll-limp girl slumped near the gutter. She's in a dirty T-shirt and denim cut-offs and one of her sneakers has come off. Her face is ashen and her pupils are constricted to tiny, dark dots.

When she sees MacKenzie's car she begins to struggle. 'It's the coppers,' she says, 'the bloody coppers.' It takes the three officers and her friend to keep her down, under a withering tirade of abuse. A crowd gathers to watch the show.

'Whattaya all laughin' at,' she yells. 'Don't treat me like I'm some spastic idiot.' Then, abruptly, she quietens, becomes almost reflective. 'Yeah, I'm on heroin, I'm stoned. I'm an idiot for that. But I'm not a fuckin' fool, am I?'

The friend, doleful, lanky and crew-cut, in tracky-dacks and top, says later that they'd scored in one of the parlours, and then gone around the corner to use. Maybe five or 10 minutes later she tipped over. She won't let MacKenzie give her Narcan and under ambulance protocols he can't force the issue, but she agrees to go to St Vincent's.

As MacKenzie pulls out, he sees another young girl, probably only 16, on her haunches against the wall of one of the parlours, struggling against nodding off. 'We'll probably be back for that one soon,' he says, incorrectly as it turns out.

'You know, sometimes you feel like a vulture sitting in a tree, cruising around and waiting for someone to keel over.'

Back at the hospital, the friend is waiting. She was thrown out of her accommodation that morning, he explains, and he's worried about what she might do next. 'I'm scared she'll walk out of here with nowhere to go, no-one to look after her and she'll go score again. That's what she wants to do I reckon, she wants to kill herself, fuck up again.'

But he doesn't believe a pure batch of heroin is doing the rounds. 'People put that around so people'll buy more, you know? – "Come on down, there's pure gettin' around" … "Grouse, let's go." – It's just a load of hogwash. It's just normal gear, but some are bigger than others and that's why people drop. Maybe they've missed out a day or something and they go out and have some, they've been hangin' out and they score that big one and over they go.'

Take, for example, the young bloke in MacKenzie's next call, a 6.01 pm Signal One to an unconscious male, possible cardiac arrest, in Easey Street, Collingwood.

A six-day-a-week labourer, about 25, the mud and cement still on his boots, he was on his way home from work with a mate. They had a few beers and stopped off in Smith Street to score, says the mate. Haggled the dealer down to $20, nicked down an alley to shoot up and were driving home again when he slipped into unconsciousness. 'I shook and shook him, but I couldn't wake him up. I shit meself.'

He's come around now and is sitting in the passenger seat, scared, dopey and beaded with tiny pearls of sweat. He agrees to a small dose of Narcan.

He says it's the first time he's OD'd. 'I'm a small-time user; I don't want to get addicted. I use bugger-all: sometimes maybe three times a week then maybe not for three or four weeks at a time. I feel quite embarrassed about this, to tell the truth.'

His mate, a regular user, overdosed last September and admits he 'arced up' after being revived with Narcan. 'I took on the ambo guys. They had to call the cops and all, and it took four blokes to hold me down. I feel pretty bad about that – they saved my life and I attacked them.'

Reactions after being dosed with Narcan differ, says MacKenzie. 'The majority say thanks. The odd one wakes up, abuses you for ruining their hit and you don't know if they're going to pull a knife or come swinging at you.'

This victim is more typical. 'Hey, thanks very much for your help,' he says. Seems like a nice young bloke, though you have to wonder about the baseball bat and 25-centimetre sheath knife on the car floor.

Overdose victims often don't fit the junkie stereotype, says Mackenzie. 'They're not all scozzers. They can be professionals who use every so often; they can be people who just enjoy a beer and a shot of heroin, that's their recreation. They could be young, good-looking girls with good jobs who've used because it's trendy and ended up dying. That's the most frustrating thing. You'll go and find a young person who's dead from shooting up heroin and there's a life that had so much potential and it's gone.

'Then sometimes you might have a "save", you get a pulse and they're breathing. But they've had so little oxygen to the brain for so long they've ended up with massive brain damage. And one other thing that gets frustrating is when you go and see the same patients again and again and again. And you just wish they'd wake up and learn.'

Paramedic Rob Blaikie, 38, operating MICA 302 from the Epworth Hospital in Richmond, suffers that frustration at 7.35 pm. Bouncing from one cancelled call at Flemington to another on the Clarendon Street Bridge, he's redirected to another, just around the corner in South Melbourne. It's the girl from Russell Street again.

She had discharged herself from St Vincent's and headed back to bot some clothes at the emergency accommodation she'd been evicted from that morning. Along the way she'd had another hit and collapsed on the footpath. When shelter staff got to her she was out to it and the smack had reduced her respiratory function to two or three breaths a minute.

Awake now, alternately weeping and cursing, she claims she's 'weaning' herself off the stuff. 'I'm down to three or four caps a day. Last week it was eight. I'm so fuckin' paranoid I won't even take me Panadol.'

But less than two hours later it's all Signal One bells and whistles and 90 kmh down tram tracks from Windsor to a call at the casino. And here she is again.

She's on her back on the floor of the food court, glassy-eyed and surrounded by casino medical staff and unimpressed bouncers. The friend has surrendered to the inevitable and left her to her demons. She's quieter this time, perhaps a little frightened, perhaps simply exhausted. Again she refuses the Narcan, but asks to be taken back to hospital.

At 10.30 Blaikie's rolling again, to a report of an unconscious youth, probable overdose, possible cardiac arrest, in the toilet at Richmond Railway Station.

But as he turns into Swan Street the call is cancelled. A bystander pokes his head through the car window. 'I just rang to tell you blokes not to bother,' he says. 'He woke up and went. I've done a St John's course so I knew what to look for. He was right out of it and I rolled up his sleeve to look for tracks. Mate, there was blood running down his arm and dripping down his leg. But then he just jumped on his pushbike and took off. He's long gone.'

SO MANY BECAUSES

Matthew Wales had been working up to this moment for years – maybe for most of his life, certainly as long as he could remember – and now the rest of his life was about to change. Utterly.

He had not been sure where to hide the weapon, a piece of lumber several centimetres thick. At first, he had it in the kitchen of the two-storey townhouse he rented with his wife and infant son.

But it had bothered him there. It had not seemed right. Use it the way he intended and there'd be a shocking mess to clean up. And his wife might see what he did.

So after a few days he moved it. Indecision and uncertainty were familiar feelings to him. School had been a struggle and there was none of the academic plodder's consolation prize on the sporting fields for him. Nothing was ever quite right. He had succeeded briefly as a hairdresser, only to be undone by repetition strain so that he had to give away the trade. Even with his moderate tradesman's success, he had never felt his mother took any pride in him.

Maritza, his Chilean-born wife, wanted better anyway. A

dress shop in up-market Malvern was not quite enough, and she was planning a café, somewhere befitting their aspirations. Matthew was going along, trying to coax some working capital out of his mother, a woman with a multimillion-dollar portfolio of property and shares. Without her help, there would not be enough to start a business. Maritza's breast implants had soaked up thousands already, and her shop, Maritza's Imports, was sinking in a sea of blind ambition and inexperience. They were trying to sell it, but there had been no serious interest.

Along with his aspirations, Matthew, the runt of his litter, the slow one, the one who did not make or marry wealth, the last born who never shared the confident, take-on-the-world-at-all-costs style of his siblings, harboured a wealth of resentment.

He found a spot near the front door. Behind the box hedge. That's where he put the piece of pine. A nice and handy spot.

Matthew Wales sees the world through his own, very personal filter. Where he saw himself as a kid hard done by and justifiably hurt, his mother saw a troubling son who lacked direction, motivation and maturity.

Still others saw Matthew as a personification of Murphy's Law: that if something can go wrong, it will go wrong. He is one of those people who seem able to find failure in any possibility.

Margaret Wales liked to keep control of Matthew. A true matriarch, she kept control of the rest of her family too. But maybe in Matthew's case, the control was greater. She even tried to choose his wife for him, from one of the families that, like her, owned a beach property at Merricks, on the Mornington Peninsula south-east of Melbourne.

Matthew and his fiancée, Fleur, dated for three years, from 1993 to 1996, and were engaged for almost one week before firstly, indecision, and finally, instinct, took over and Matthew called it off.

Fleur remained Margaret's bride of choice for her youngest son. Margaret reluctantly had to accept the fact of Maritza, but she stayed in contact with Fleur.

Even as his 28-year-old fiancée, Fleur had thought Matthew seemed boyish and immature. Since he had taken up with his Chilean wife, Fleur noticed that Matthew had started calling himself Mateo. He appeared also to be acquiring an accent.

From Matthew's perspective he had been pushed into the engagement with Fleur: he had simply surrendered to pressure from his mother and her partner, Paul King. The way he saw it, it was as if – since his elder brother had moved to Sydney for work, and his sisters Sally, Prudence and Emma had married – he was the last one over which his mother had complete control.

Having failed to model him into a society husband, Margaret was now reinforcing his sense of being a failure. It was as if her remaining life's work was to exact a price for all the disappointments he had caused her.

As troubled as their relationship had been, as unwelcome as his chosen wife might be, Matthew and Maritza dined with Margaret and Paul about once a month.

Matthew Wales, 34, killed his mother with a single blow to the back of the neck. The length of pine was by the front door where he left it, hidden behind the box hedge. It was round, like a baseball bat, and he swung it like a baseballer as Margaret and Paul headed for home after a family dinner.

Paul King was walking in front of Margaret, slightly to one side, and was halfway to the car as this happened. After his mother fell face-forward, Matthew Wales stepped up to Paul King and swung again.

Before the elderly couple had arrived at Paul and Maritza's rented townhouse in Glen Iris, that evening, 4 April, had been a busy one. There was the vegetable soup – a minestrone – to prepare.

Wales crushed up Panadol Forte tablets, along with some blood pressure medication stolen from the medicine cabinet at Maritza's parents' home, and which he had read on the label could cause drowsiness. He put this cocktail in equal parts into the soup he served to Margaret and Paul.

He told police later that he had wanted to back out from killing the elderly couple, but once he drugged them he felt committed to going ahead. So even before his mother pitched forward from the first blow and he continued to strike them, there had been no turning back.

'My head was just going bananas and I just kept on hitting. I just kept on hitting,' Wales said. 'I made it as merciful as I possibly could. I first of all gave them drugs, and then I went and I hit them on the back of the neck.'

All at once, after all the thinking about it and the preparations and now the doing of it, he still couldn't believe what he had done. He walked in circles for a while, pacing and repacing the frontyard. He felt crazed, like a mad dog, he said. Then, he felt relief.

He had closed the driveway gates, shutting out the traffic on busy Burke Road, when his parents arrived. As he moved to strike them, Wales flicked off an external light to avoid being seen. But some time after, he noticed a woman opposite in a lit upstairs window. She seemed to be looking at him. Not for the last time, he panicked. But days later, when she passed him in the street without recognition, he decided she had seen nothing.

Afterwards, Wales insisted he acted alone and unaided. On this, he was emphatic, agitated even.

Maritza was upstairs putting their two-year-old son Domenik to bed. He said he went up to her: 'I said, "I've done something to Mum and Paul," and she came downstairs and she had a look and she goes, "What have you done?" And I said, "I've killed them." And she – she just went around in circles as well. She just – she didn't know what – what the hell had happened. Maritza had nothing to do with this at all. This is me. This is my emotions that went out.'

She cried, he said. She shook. She dry-retched. She retreated to her bed and hid under the covers. In a panic, Matthew was telling her: Just stay here. Don't do anything.

He went back to the bodies and dragged them, face-down, across the front lawn and laid them side by side near the side fence. He covered them with Domenik's plastic inflatable pool.

He went back upstairs. Maritza was frantic: You have to tell the police … tell what you have done, do it properly.

He told her he would fix things. He figured he could get away with it.

Soon after, wearing latex gloves Maritza had bought for cleaning, he drove his mother's Mercedes-Benz to Middle

Park. He had worn latex gloves when he started handling the bodies, and he replaced them with a clean pair for the drive. He drove with no particular destination in mind. 'I just drove,' he said later.

He pulled up in a dark street, locked the car, left it, and walked to St Kilda Esplanade where he flagged a taxi. The panic was long gone. He had the driver let him off some distance from his home, farther south down Burke Road. During the walk back home he dropped the latex gloves into a storm drain.

Anyone who knew Matthew Wales as a slow learning, rebellious, awkward kid would tell you he could not plan a double murder unaided. As he told it, there was no plan except the one he was about to create.

The bodies remained mostly undisturbed the next day, Friday, and into Saturday, except that Wales wrapped them in doona covers and swathed the heads in material so he would not have to look at their faces. He was fatalistic as he wrapped the bodies in daylight, in the frontyard: If I am going to be caught, I am going to be caught, he kept telling himself. But he was going to give himself every chance in the meantime.

He added some paint cans and a workman's sawhorse to the mound so it looked like he had a rubbish pile on one side of the front garden. Maritza was at the shop. Domenik was asleep inside. And when Domenik was awake, his daddy played with him.

From a service station in Burke Road, Wales hired a trailer and bought a trailer safety shackle. He paid $50 cash for the trailer hire, but for the security deposit he left a $20 credit card slip in his own name. He had worn latex gloves, but now he was leaving fingerprints of another sort.

From Tait Timber hardware nearby he bought five metres of galvanised chain in one-metre lengths to wrap around the bodies, and matching shackles to fasten them. At the time he was thinking of the bodies sinking. He also bought 10 metres of rope.

Next to Tait's, he picked up three concrete bricks, with central holes for feeding the chains through, to weight the bodies. At some point he bought a cleaner called Liquid Magnet, to rid the front path of bloodstains.

He manoeuvred the trailer into the frontyard, loaded the bodies onto it and then wheeled the trailer and its tragic load into the garage. Friday night he placated Maritza by telling her, yes he would go to the police, but right now he wanted to spend time with her and Domenik.

On Saturday morning, 36 hours after the murders, Maritza again went to work, although she was sick with a migraine and left early to go home. Wales telephoned his mother's home and left a voice message to provide himself some cover. And he went to a second hardware store to buy a blue tarpaulin, more rope and a mattock. He had intended to sink the bodies, but now he was thinking he might bury them.

'She loved the country,' Wales said of his mother, 'so I thought I'd take her out to the country.'

In the early afternoon Maritza was ailing and Domenik was napping, so, with the bodies under the tarp, he drove east. He headed generally towards the blue haze of the Great Dividing Range, but again he had no clear destination. Along the way, and still constructing his plan, it occurred to him to buy a crowbar, which he did from a Bunnings store on the Maroondah Highway.

It is called a highway, but for much of its length the Maroondah is a choked arterial road – one of the longest suburban shopping strips in the metropolitan area, snaking through Box Hill, Blackburn, Mitcham and Ringwood. Towing his grim cargo in the hired trailer, Wales crawled through kilometres of snarled traffic, out to Lilydale and the remoteness of the hills.

He drove for about three hours. Wales was outside Marysville and thinking to himself 'Where am I?' when he chose what he thought was a desolate spot off a dirt track, and began digging. It became dark long before he was finished. He dug until he struck what he thought was rock.

Out there in the darkness, with the mountain cold settling around his shoulders, afraid even to light the scene with his car's parking lights, his fatalism gone, those promises to Maritza to go to the police forgotten, Matthew Wales was again in a state of panic. In his words, he was scared shitless.

When he put them in the hole, his mother went in first. 'I put Mum on the bottom and Paul at the top,' he told police. 'This man loved Mum unconditionally … He did anything for her, OK … but Mum used to manipulate him all the time … I thought, if they're going to stay here at least he gets to be on top.'

His still-evolving plan took another turn: he thought he could make it look like a robbery, so he stripped his mother of her gold jewellery – a necklace, bracelet, chain and a gold ring – and later dumped it in several rubbish bins.

Two days later, he was back, towing a load of rocks bought from a nursery. Now he was worried that wild animals might unearth the bodies. By this time, the alarm had been raised. Wales' sister Sally asked him to accompany their sister Emma to their mother's house, but he begged off saying he had 'things to do'. He needed to make the grave secure.

There were five Wales children. Matthew, 34, was the youngest. He had three sisters and a brother: Sally, 43, Damian, 41, Emma, 38, and Prudence, 36.

It was Emma who first feared something was wrong. She had arranged to meet her mother for breakfast on Sunday but forgot about it until shortly before six that evening.

When her mother's landline rang out to a voice message, and her mobile reverted to the same message, Emma was instantly worried.

Paul King had always doted on Margaret Wales. Since her relationship with him precipitated the break-up of her marriage to Brian Wales in 1975, Paul seemed subordinate to her. But recently Paul had suffered a series of strokes and he was becoming an increasing burden. Margaret Wales had been indulged for many years and was finding the adjustment to becoming a carer a difficult one.

They would not be out, Emma reasoned. Because of Paul's medical condition, their mother made sure the couple was never far from help, especially at night.

When she had not raised her mother by 8.30 pm, Emma drove around to the house in Mercer Street, Armadale, and then searched the precincts to try to see their car. She rang her sisters Sally and Prue, but no-one had been in contact.

Emma checked the house the next morning. It was undisturbed but not right. An uncovered jar of pretzels and unwashed wine glasses were left out on a bench, and

Margaret's reading glasses, which she usually wore, were in the lounge room.

She reported them as missing persons and began working her way through Margaret's diary, calling her friends and later, hospitals, to find some trace of them. The affairs of the Wales-King family were about to become public property.

On Wednesday 10 April, the Wales-Kings were at police headquarters for a press conference which made public the missing couple and their missing Mercedes. The car was found that evening, in the upscale bayside suburb of Middle Park.

Full of fear, the family went down to see the car, dreading what might be in it. But it yielded nothing and the mystery disappearance deepened. Emma and Prudence spent the next day quizzing people around the site where the car was found.

Whether he knew it or not, Matthew Wales was already in the frame. His behaviour was clearly odd. He avoided the rest of the family, did not attend the press conference and tried to avoid the trip to check out the car. And there was something else.

When Sally first contacted him, on 8 April, about the disappearance, he said nothing of the fact that Margaret and Paul had been at his place for dinner four days earlier.

The bodies were found on 29 April. As it happened, the isolated spot Matthew had chosen in the dark was only a few metres from a well-used bush track. A couple of rangers noticed the disturbed ground and initially thought it was a lyre-bird nest, so they went for a closer look.

Within days, journalists were camped outside Matthew and Maritza's rented townhouse in Burke Road. It was only a matter of time before there was an arrest.

At the time of her death, Margaret Wales-King had net assets of more than $5 million, including a luxury house at Mercer Road, Armadale, the Mercedes-Benz, shares and bank accounts.

There were, as Matthew Wales put it, 'many becauses' for his actions, but his mother's queenly manner and rigorous control of her wealth were prominent among them. He was not alone in seeing how her wealth was used, but in his reaction he was wildly different in his impotent rage.

'To a certain extent I would say Mum did use her will by using her money and position in the family to dominate me and some of the other members of the family, including Matthew,' his sister, Sally Honan, said. And Angus Reed, Matthew's brother-in-law said that, 'Margaret tried to manipulate her children through the use of money. I used to tolerate her and would say that I was indifferent towards her.'

Margaret Wales-King's wealth was inherited from her father, who had established one part of his estate – a unit at Surfers Paradise – for the benefit of his grandchildren. But it was controlled by Mrs Wales-King and her sister, Sydney socialite Dianna Yeldham.

A Wales family meeting concerning the future of the Surfers Paradise unit had ended in an acrimonious dispute. Mrs Wales-King wanted the property sold and the proceeds reinvested into a Wales trust. But she was irritated that all of her children wanted to be involved in the negotiations. An agreement had finally been reached the previous February, but Matthew was angry that his mother had asked for his consent without him having an opportunity to read the relevant documents. Consequently, mother and son did not speak for a month.

Matthew told police his murderous intent towards his mother had been building 'since I was a kid' but the row over the Surfers Paradise unit had tripped fantasy into real intent.

Unlike his brother and sisters, who were financially independent of Mrs Wales-King, Matthew was still reliant upon her.

'[Margaret Wales-King] has demonstrated time and time again that she can play the hard ball when it lands in her court, which has frustrated all of her children at one time or another,' recalled James Connell, the husband of Matthew's sister, Emma, and a successful Melbourne real estate agent.

'To the best of my knowledge all of the children and their respective spouses have effectively insulated themselves from being emotionally blackmailed by Margaret. Matthew, due to his financial position, is still at her beck and call.'

Margaret Wales-King could be utterly unfair, James Connell said, and seemed to love the sense of self-importance that came with being in control.

She had allowed Matthew to keep the entire profit from the sale of a Malvern house she'd helped him buy. But instead of investing in another residential property, he and Maritza used the proceeds to open Maritza's Imports.

Matthew also blamed her – weeping during the police interview – for alienating him from the rest of the family. He saw that alienation in the form of not being invited to his brother Damian's 40th birthday celebration in Sydney, and his absence among the family photos on display in his sister Sally's house.

Damian would later dispute Matthew's account of this non-existent invitation, but he made no attempt to hide his contempt for his little brother. 'Matthew was a prick of a kid.

We were never close. He was reckless and irresponsible. His lying was a feature.'

Sally also said that Matthew was caught lying so often that she had ceased to trust him long ago.

While he cites many 'becauses', it is his alienation from the family and his mother's relentless scrutiny to which Matthew Wales returns.

Nor did Maritza feel much other than alienation from Matthew's family. Sally Honan recalled that Maritza believed Margaret Wales-King had no interest in Maritza's family as they were 'just wogs'.

Certainly, by Emma Connell's account, Maritza had not won the family over. 'The first time I met [Maritza], Mum and Paul were there and I remember thinking she was very shy and quiet, which was a total contrast to what I had learnt from Matthew.

'However, once Mum and Paul left, the façade lifted and she seemed … common [and] vulgar … I couldn't believe how much of a chameleon she was. She would say some shocking things and everything seemed to have a sexual connotation.'

Sally, too, disliked Maritza. 'She would often make sexually suggestive comments that I felt were a little out of place … I think she saw herself as a bit of a sex kitten.' Prue remembered Maritza boasting how she had Matthew 'by the balls'. Prue said she dominated Matthew and they lived way beyond their means.

A Wales family holiday at Brampton Island in 1968 let Paul King into their lives. Brian and Margaret Wales had married in 1957 and had five children.

After meeting Brian and Margaret at Brampton Island, King became a close family friend and a regular social contact. Margaret's father, the source of all her wealth, understood what was happening. He threatened to cut her out of his will if she did not stop seeing Paul King, but by the time of his death he had not made good his threat.

After Brian and Margaret split up in 1976, Paul King began an open relationship with Margaret, and some time later moved in with her and the children at their Camberwell home.

He had no children of his own but was regarded as something of a father figure to young Matthew. If Margaret Wales felt Matthew could fill some void in Paul King's life, then maybe that was true, since Paul treated her youngest as his own son.

This set Matthew apart from the others to the extent that they did not have the same sort of relationship with Paul King, and they remained closer to their biological father than did Matthew. Damian and Sally actively avoided Paul. Matthew, 'a pawn in the divorce game' according to one of his sisters, was rarely allowed to visit his father.

While his older siblings had unrestricted access to their dad, Margaret often kept Matthew at home. He lost any kind of relationship with his father, Brian Wales. Perhaps the only thing Matthew shared with his siblings was resentment towards Paul King for breaking up their family. Some said they could never forgive King for his role in their lives however much he devoted himself to their mother. 'We have all accepted it and got on with life,' Prue Reed said.

Matthew continued to be treated differently into his teenage years. While he complained of being alienated from his brother and sisters, he was regarded as a difficult child, and his siblings saw him as spoiled.

'Mum pandered to Matthew. Mum was always trying to build Matthew up and tried to be so positive,' Damian said. And Prue said her mother gave more time and money to him because she doubted his ability to cope on his own.

Of all the children, he was the sole underachiever. 'Really difficult as a young child,' Prue said. 'He had learning difficulties and he was always quite hyper and naughty. As a teenager … rebellious and not responsible … an unremarkable student and wasn't interested in working.'

In short, he was immature, isolated and marginalised. In his 20s he is remembered as subservient, to the point of being fearful of his mother: he was an extrovert with friends and an introvert in the presence of his family.

Outside observers saw him as a bit hard done by, but his siblings saw the extra financial help their mother gave this troubled runt of the litter in his early adult life. That did not win her much gratitude, since Matthew felt the money was used as a means of control over him.

When Brian and Margaret divorced, Sally was 17, Damian 15, Emma 12, Prue was 10 and Matthew, who was soon to begin treatment for behavioural problems, was seven.

This was when the children regularly stayed with their father at Sorrento, with the sole exception of Matthew, who was rarely allowed to go. But once, over summer, he joined his brother and sisters at Sorrento, and Brian Wales taught him to sail in a small boat.

He took to it quickly. By the end of summer he was entered in a race for novice sailors. Matthew was the only one to finish. 'Matthew really enjoyed the sailing but this

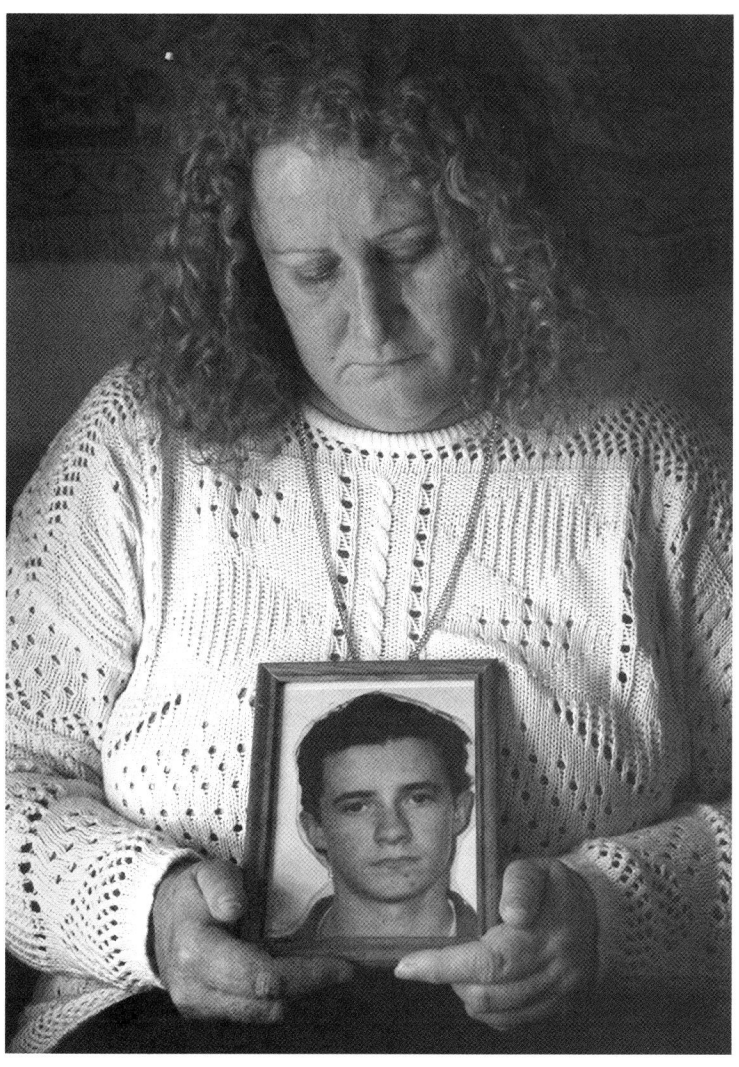

Lorraine Russell keeps a shrine to her children with candles and photos – unremarkable images, typical of any family album. In one an adolescent boy stares evenly out of the frame: Joel Russell, tortured and bashed to death under a house in Reservoir in Melbourne's northern suburbs, aged 14.

'No greater honour will ever be bestowed on an officer or a more profound duty imposed on him than when he is entrusted with the investigation of the death of a human being.' But there is a price to be paid: Greg Hough, Brian Rix and Rod Iddles of the Victorian Homicide Squad.

PICTURE BY CRAIG ABRAHAM, USED COURTESY OF *THE AGE*

Father Vincent Kiss was a man of God who defied the word of God,
breaking the eighth commandment – 'Thou shalt not steal' – to the
tune of almost $2 million. And there were other, worse, crimes.

Bonnie Melissa Clarke's body was found by her mother as she readied herself for work a few days before Christmas 1982. Bonnie was a few weeks away from her seventh birthday. She had been sexually assaulted, smothered and stabbed.

'You're in the backblocks out here. You've got to go a long, long way to catch a tram.' Tim McDonald is one of 17 circuit magistrates delivering travelling justice to country Victoria. His Worship's is a sprawling jurisdiction, spread over something like 40,000 square kilometres.

'Here's this pathetic, immature, stupid, fatuous creature ... charged with one of the worst crimes this century. I wanted to find out what's going on with this guy and how this person in front of me could possibly have committed these crimes.' Forensic psychologist Ian Joblin on Martin Bryant.

After he was punched that night in January 2004, cricketer David Hookes (pictured above right, with then Australian cricket captain Allan Border) 'hit the road hard. He didn't try to stop or break his fall at all. He fell like a plank.'

Deb Osmond, 30 years after she turned her first trick in St Kilda:
'I could be 80 and still have clients. There might be someone out
there who fancies old fanny.'

PICTURE BY SIMON SCHLUTER, USED COURTESY OF *THE AGE*

Dominatrix Mistress Saskia:
while she might be a sadist,
don't think she's cruel. 'No,
I'm soft,' she insists, a feline
glint in her eyes. 'I'm a kitten.'

PICTURE BY SIMON SCHLUTER, USED
COURTESY OF *THE AGE*

was the last time he was allowed to come to Sorrento to go sailing,' Brian Wales recalled.

Maritza Wales' first statement to police, like her husband's, had the couple waving farewell to Margaret Wales-King and Paul King after their dinner.

That was made on 9 April. According to her second statement, on 11 May after the bodies had been found and identified, she returned downstairs after putting Domenik to bed, saw the front door open and looked outside as Matthew rushed in fearing the woman opposite had seen him killing his parents. By both their accounts, she urged him to go to the police several times.

Prue's observation that the couple lived beyond their means appeared to be true. They spent at least $8000 on Maritza's breast augmentation, while taking out loans for a car and a boat. They also sank all of Matthew's money into Maritza's shop. Sometimes, Maritza admitted, they could not pay their bills.

Unlike Wales' brother and sisters, they did not own a house, but it's different, Maritza said, 'We're just starting our life.'

When she asked him on the night of the killings what would happen to them both, and to Domenik too, he told her the bodies would never be found.

When the bodies were discovered, she did not hold back, slapping and hitting him. 'I was brought up so good and I can't believe this shit is happening to me,' Maritza told police. 'I just want to die. I'm so tired. It's like a nightmare.'

She was sick of being watched, sick of being unable to take Domenik to the park. If she had a gun, she said, she'd shoot herself.

*   *   *

Matthew Wales' mental filter, that peculiar way he had of viewing the world, continued to function long after his arrest. His father, after visiting him in Port Phillip Prison, reckoned that Matthew thought he had done the family a favour by killing his mother. Matthew believed that since no-one else had the guts to do it, he should be seen as the family hero.

That was certainly not the view of the family who recognised they had privileged upbringings, Justice John Coldrey told Wales when he sentenced him in April 2003. Rather, they would never recover from what he had done.

'All the children, including you, benefited from your mother's assistance in obtaining a primary residential property ... it should not be forgotten that it was up to Mrs Wales-King to determine how she used her own money and how prudent her approach should be in retaining or distributing it.'

Sentencing Matthew Wales in April 2003, Justice Coldrey recalled how he spoke of 'utter hatred' for his victims, a hatred he bore for eight years.

Justice Coldrey referred to Matthew Wales' 'uniformly poor and below average' school results, his low–average 83 IQ, his inability to think in abstracts and his obsession with the injustices he believed he had experienced at his mother's hands.

'Since the elimination of your mother and stepfather represented the consummation of an intensely held ambition, you feel no remorse for their deaths,' Justice Coldrey said. 'Indeed, you told [psychiatrist] Dr [Lester] Walton that you felt your actions were morally justified.'

After consideration of his low intellect and his guilty plea, Wales was jailed for 30 years, with a minimum sentence of 24 years.

Maritza Wales was given a suspended two-year jail sentence for attempting to pervert the course of justice by making a false statement to police. It was a sentence that upset the Wales family.

As if unable to trust their spontaneous reactions, they expressed themselves through a prepared statement.

'We are greatly disturbed that the investigation and sentencing process has not uncovered the full facts and truth behind the horrific murders of our mother and stepfather. The confession of our brother today stands as the so-called factual account of the details and reasons behind these brutal crimes. To us, his account was self-serving and based on selfish opportunity and selfish greed.'

THE BABYSITTER

He is the birthday boy, just drunk enough to think he can dance, a little too drunk to carry it off. So every now and then he tries to find the rhythm that is moving the young blonde in the schoolgirl uniform.

He shuffles his fists in front of himself and hunches his shoulders in counterpoint. Cannot quite get it right. He tries again but gives up after a few seconds.

He shifts his heavy-lidded eyes to focus on the blonde who has shed the uniform now and has every promise of shedding a great deal more. Well, it is his birthday. Twenty-one and coming of age.

He is seated in his parents' garage on this faintly chilly, early autumn evening. Gathered with him is a leering audience of late adolescents through to middle-aged adults.

Some of the blokes are leering openly, crouching and cocking their heads for a better view. The birthday boy's dad is grinning hugely. For now, so is his mum.

But once the stripper is entirely naked those poses in front of her son will evoke a different response from her. Maybe she reckoned it would be one of those naughty-but-nice trick strips workmates use to send off the old codger retiring from accounts. That is not Cindy's go at all.

Cindy arrived in a midnight-blue sedan, safe and snug in her white-nylon 'fur' coat. A little bit of movie-star style out here on the flat river plain of Werribee, south-west of Melbourne, where the low, single-storey brick veneers grow thick on the ground.

Outside she was a little nervous. But along with her uniform she applied a personality. She actually looks like she is having fun, as if she really enjoys toying with this kid she is stripping as methodically as she strips herself.

Everyone is beaming and laughing as she leads him to lie on his back in the centre of the garage. He is left in only the underpants she soaked in baby oil with one well-aimed pressure shot from a plastic bottle.

Everyone is laughing, everyone, that is, except his mum, whose upper lip has lost shape and rests tremulously on her bottom lip while she focuses on something in the middle distance. Welcome to what the trade calls open-leg work.

Cindy exchanges the baby oil for body paints, tossing the oil deftly to a man in the audience, but not part of it. He has the orange and green paints ready and a towel for later. He was at the wheel of the midnight-blue sedan. He is the babysitter.

He is grinning too, enjoying the show. This is how he likes it. People relaxed. If they're happy, he won't have any aggravation.

Aggravation is unlikely, anyway. He is six foot three, 100 kilograms. Balding with a red goatee and the look of an older bikie about him. He looks a little frightening. Nasty. Cindy says he looks menacing, that's why she likes having him along. While she is naked in places full of strangers, he makes her feel safe.

Most dangerous of all the things that make him what he is, he lacks restraint. But when he can get a mob like this to relax and dig the show he feels good. Then the agency gets a good report about him and that makes him feel good too. There is something he can do besides break heads.

In circumstances like this, the straight working-day world meets and mingles with the underworld, briefly breathing the same atmosphere, then parting again.

He collects the money and speeds off into the night, Cindy wrapped up in her white mock fur beside him. To a pub in Collingwood for a buck's turn. Then into the eastern suburbs for a 40th birthday.

He does debt collections, too. When he was heavily wired on drugs and collecting debts he used to chainsaw his way through the front door and terrorise everyone in the joint. Impose his authority. But that was half-a-lifetime ago. He is more in control now.

Tonight is how he likes it. Money, a fast car and somewhere to go.

He will head for home as the new day breaks. For a life lived out on the edge, this is as good as it gets.

But it may not last much longer. In the next two months he has two court appearances – for cultivating and trafficking cannabis and possession of a weapon; and later, a brace of serious assault charges. And he knows how hard jail time can be.

'My main objective for babysitting is it stops the coppers looking at me driving around all night because if they pull me over I can say, "Well I work for this escort agency and I've got a girl doing a trick down there and I'm killing time until I have to pick her up."

'It's just being a security guard for them, catching their clothes, setting the props up and when I work for the escort agencies I drive the girls out to the jobs, make sure there's no dramas. If there is dramas I go in and sort them out. It's usually someone who refuses to pay or wants to try and rape them the minute they walk in the door. Some people are unbelievable, some of the things they want to get into. Mainly that's the biggest problem. Or guys refusing to pay.

'Speed and marijuana are my main sources of income. I am a consultant these days. I know that many people in the industry, people ring me and say "I've got this for sale" … If I sell a pound of dope I might take a $500 consultancy fee.

'I can't stand anyone who's prepared to sit back on the dole and do nothing. Like, there's money to be made out there, all you have got to do is use your fucking head and make it.'

Ray has been drowning since childhood. This is where he has surfaced.

When he was about 13, Ray says, one of his many stepfathers held a loaded shotgun in the boy's mouth for several hours as they sat in the lounge room of their Broadmeadows house. That was, he says, to stop him from going to a New Year's Eve party.

But that's not right, according to Ray's mum, who has a new life in Melbourne's outer-western suburbs. She says her then-husband dragged her home from the party and sat her down in the lounge room. He wrote her name – Shirley – on a shotgun cartridge, loaded the gun and pointed it at her face.

There she sat for what certainly seemed like hours. During her ordeal, Ray and his younger sister were walked home from the party by their cousins. 'I remember thinking the kids were going to get home and they'd see me, my head blown off,' she recalls. Ray certainly saw her facing the gun, she says, and ran back to the party and the police were alerted.

Memory is not a fixed thing. Ray believes it was he who fronted the loaded shotgun. Maybe his mother's ordeal has merged with some of his own.

Shirley was 16 when she fell in love with Ray's dad. Seventeen when she married and one month shy of her 18th birthday when Ray was born. She was 20 when her husband abandoned her, leaving behind one week's rent and 25 cents.

Albert, one of the men who took his place a couple of years later, was good with Ray until Shirley gave birth to a child of his own. From that time, Shirley says, Albert ignored the boy except to assign him jobs around the house, cleaning chores beyond his years. Backhanders were common, but at least once it went way past that.

That was when the boy was ordered to clean the bathroom. When Albert inspected his work he found a hair on the sink. Ray took a belting.

Mostly, the kid was ridiculed and made to feel small. On this, Shirley and Ray agree. And the man the kid became still cannot tolerate being told what to do. That's part of why he fears returning to jail. He does not trust his responses to authority.

'I've never been comfortable having to work for someone and with my attitude towards people who try to order me to do things, it just doesn't work,' Ray says now.

'You can ask me to do anything and I'll bend over backwards to do it for you, but the minute you order me to do something I'll pick up a hammer and smash you with it.'

For a time during his childhood the entire family seemed to be ostracised by their neighbours. Why that was so became clear to Shirley only when Albert was jailed for molesting a local child. One night he came home and announced he was going to court the next day. The rest of the neighbourhood had known for weeks.

As a child, Ray was overweight and often friendless, Shirley says, and although he was bright enough to do well at school he mixed with the strugglers.

'When he was about nine he started stealing money from me,' Shirley says. 'The school rang one day and said Ray's taking large amounts of money to school. It turned out he had given away all this money.

'He did not make friends easily and he was always trying to impress. Yet he was quite good at the work and if he had applied himself he would have done well. What friends he had were not good friends. He gravitated to the losers.'

Allan, her third husband who terrorised the family with the shotgun, stepped up the physical violence towards Ray. He remembers one bashing in particular that left him so bruised and sore he could not attend school for several days. Peter, the next one, told the kid he had 'a heart as big as a pea', and it seems he has been trying to prove otherwise ever since, Shirley said.

Peter used to boast of his criminal achievements, petty stuff like knocking the tyres off a truck. But it seemed to impress Ray.

'I have blocked so much out of my memory,' Ray says. 'Mum's second husband ... he'd beat you every chance he got. He was a professional gambler, but not a very good one. I saw him come back from the Cup with thousands, then two days later he blew that and a couple of service stations. He left me mum with a huge debt to Caltex.'

Because Shirley was working long hours and was often absent, she does not understand how badly Albert treated him, Ray believes. When Shirley let Albert return to the house after completing his prison sentence Ray started running away.

'I went to about 14 different primary schools,' Ray says. 'Just because Mum and Dad moved around so much, Mum and Albert, and he was in and out of jail, so I found out years later, over child-tampering with other kids.

'I was about 11 when he left. Allan was the third. He was only around for 12, 18 months until Mum worked out what a bastard he was. Mum went to work about 5.30, 6 am. I'd be left to get my two sisters ready for school. By the time I did that I had no interest in going. By morning recess I'd make enough money out of selling cigarettes to take the rest of the day off to play pool or watch a movie in the city.'

Shirley sent Ray back to his biological father in a bid to control his early-teenage stealing and habit of wagging school, but within a couple of weeks he was home again.

'He ran away from [his father],' Shirley says. 'His father said, "He's your problem, you handle it." He has never shown any interest in Ray.'

Now, Ray says: 'I don't have any feelings towards him. I saw him at his brother's funeral last year. He looked like a bum. He was wearing dirty jeans and a dirty T-shirt. You know everyone else in the family was respectful and whatnot and he was just an absolute shitkicker.'

So after Ray's fathers had taught him about rejection and abandonment, about worthlessness and dishonesty, Shirley sent him to live with her brother in Perth.

He is late for court. Ray arrives flustered, in a denim shirt stretched tight over the beginnings of a pot belly, black jeans and sneakers, and carrying a bottle of mineral water. This is the first of his two big hurdles this year.

It goes back to him being pulled over by police while carting skunk weed – potent smelling, whole marijuana plants – and some cured dope as well, in the boot of his car. He says it was repayment of a debt. He didn't want the dope, he says, but he took it instead of cash. After they stopped him, the cops told him they could smell the stuff from 10 metres away. He is a mug in a game for smarties.

He is facing charges of possession and cultivation of cannabis and amphetamines, also possessing a weapon – in this instance a carving knife, and a lump of four-by-two which was in the back seat.

His lawyer, criminal specialist Tony Hannebery, has good news. The police have dropped the charge of cultivation. Ray is not particularly grateful. 'How can you cultivate in the boot of a car?' he wants to know.

It still does not leave Hannebery many feathers to fly with. Ray is guilty and has a long, long record. Hannebery has a psychologist's report paid for by Legal Aid urging a tolerant approach to Ray's lifestyle. Essentially it says this man lives on the line and drugs are an integral part of his lifestyle. The possession charges reflect a way of life. He is trying to stay out of police trouble, he is coping, in his fashion, and he knows no other way. Whatever happens he will continue to live on the line. Jail will do nothing for him.

Not every magistrate will buy this. Is today's the right one, or should they seek a stay of the hearing? Hannebery leaves the final call to Ray. He is edgy and his instinct tells him to go for a stay, hope for better prospects another day.

So he will be back here in a month, and again three weeks after that for a committal on an aggravated burglary with its cluster of assault-causing-serious-injury charges arising from an incident involving one of his former stepfathers.

Growing up in Broadmeadows introduced Ray to one of the constants in his life. In the same street was an amphetamine dealer and Ray says he has been a daily user since he was 13. He also learnt that selling speed was a lot more lucrative than flogging his mum's cigarettes to his classmates.

'I can now use 10 grams of speed a day and not get off on it. I use it like a medicine these days, it keeps me clear-headed so I can concentrate on one thing without going off my head … The speed's a big issue in my life. It keeps me on a level playing field, keeps me calm like this. If I didn't have a taste this morning I would be climbing the walls. I can give it up but I can't live the lifestyle I've become accustomed to [without dealing].

'I drink every day, sometimes only a couple of stubbies to try and stop the shakes, settle my stomach. The booze I have got under control – all my drug habits I have got under control – that's why I have kept myself out of trouble since I have been out.'

Moving her increasingly difficult son to Western Australia

was his mum's last throw of the dice. At 15 he was in Turana Boys' Home. When he was discharged he refused to return home, where the fifth of his mum's husbands – and the most abusive of the lot – now ruled, and he was placed in a youth hostel.

So she hoped her brother Bob, 10 years younger than herself, might connect with or control him. It did not work. Her brother had a property south of Perth and talked Ray into a welding job, but soon the kid was spending weekends in the city and his wage was not going far.

Within six months his uncle had lost contact with him. Ray had found in Perth a market for the amphetamines he knew he could locate in Melbourne, so he began flying to Victoria for stock and dealing speed in the west. He sold cannabis too, buying it wholesale then retailing it.

He rode a motorbike for a while, a 1000cc Kawasaki. Big bore 'Kwakas' were then the bad boys' bike of choice. But a savage bashing over a drug dispute left him hospitalised with serious head injuries and untrusting of his balance and co-ordination, so he gave motorbikes away. One of the biker brothers had taken to him with a brick.

By age 21 he retired from anything like the straight world would call employment. 'I'd had little shitty jobs, like working for scrap-metal dealers. Mainly what I concentrated on was dealing. I enjoyed the lifestyle, the drugs, the fact I did not have to answer to anyone, always had money for rent, for a nice car, always had plenty of young girls hanging off me.'

Dealing amphetamines led him into the sex industry and working as a minder, but it is a precarious existence, not much removed from the criminal milieu. He had served one month in Pentridge as a 17-year-old and continued building a record.

His record shows lots of dumb stuff, like multiple counts of speeding offences, drink-driving, failing to keep left, failing to wear a seat belt, failing to display 'P' plates. But also firearms offences and theft.

Then the big one. Assault. According to Western Australia court records, assault with a monkey wrench. He had been ripped off, cleaned out, and went on a drug-fuelled rampage. His victim, a motorist stopped at a red light, suffered a broken jaw and a suspected fractured vertebra and went into months of counselling.

Ray went into prison for almost four years. Much of the time he was in solitary confinement and suicidal. Check the records, he says, virtually no visitors the whole time.

A psychiatrist had him write down his thoughts: 'Im sick but everybody tells me it's because of the drugs. It's not. There the only thing that keeps it out – they dont let it take hold of me – they keep me safe I dont want to be like this … it wants me to take a life … I dont know how to talk to people. Thats why I had to write it all down.' (sic)

And during another session he wrote: 'Hatred is eating me. Every day it gets worse. I am losing control of the desire to kill.'

They installed him in an anger-management program, and it worked, up to a point.

It is another day in the Melbourne Magistrates Court. Now there is no turning back. The drug charges will not be stayed again.

Ray knows this. He has scrubbed up, the denim shirt and jeans giving way to a sports jacket and slacks.

As well, he is off the dope, he says. And being off the dope means not dealing it either. You have to get right away to stay clean.

He is desperate to avoid prison. That time when he was in Pentridge as a 17-year-old still haunts him. You can't ever relax in there, can't ever turn your back.

So he is clear-eyed, but broke as well. Still babysitting for strippers and hookers but looking for other work, sometimes finding the 'little shitty jobs'.

Today, he is in luck. The magistrate knows Hannebery and welcomes him warmly.

Hannebery is faintly apologetic: 'My client today is no cleanskin, Your Honour …'

To which the beak responds: 'If he were then you wouldn't be here, Mr Hannebery.'

Hannebery hands up the psychologist's report and the beak talks about an intensive corrections order, but Hannebery says a good behaviour bond coupled with a suspended sentence would better throw responsibility Ray's way. And that is how it goes: a suspended sentence and a bond.

A month later it is mid-winter and Ray is keeping his car on the road and finding bits of work to top up his babysitting. Legal Aid will not finance his defence on the assault charges for a full trial so he waives his right to a committal hearing. It means his trial will be sooner rather than later, but for now he is out of jail. He has 'lots of mates' and shares a house, but strictly speaking he lives alone.

'I don't have relationships,' he says. 'I have tried it before and it doesn't work.

'I don't trust myself. I have very strict guidelines that I live by and I am fanatical about hygiene and unless somebody's hygienic,' he does not finish the thought, but continues, 'and I don't like picking up after people.

'I'd love to settle down in a relationship, have some kids, be Joe Citizen. I don't know if it will ever happen. Why not keep striving to be the person I want to be?'

He is, he says, 'a nice easy-going bloke'. An easy-going bloke who breaks legs.

'These days, I wouldn't class myself as an aggressive or violent person – specifically – unless I need to be. I found years ago that by being able to channel my fear in any circumstance I could put myself in a controlled anger situation. Instantly adopting an aggressive mentality. In controlling the situation you can achieve anything.'

But within weeks the old familiar pattern is back. The midnight-blue car is bingled and he has not made any of the payments. If the finance company can find him, the car will be gone.

And he will be arraigned on the assault charges late this year. The trial, and the possibility of more jail time, is still maybe six months away.

In six months, anything can happen.

THE WAR WITHIN

P erhaps it all started going wrong for Al Wilbur that day back in '65 when he found the horror in a clearing of jungle and elephant grass in the murderous Ia Drang Valley of central South Vietnam.

Then again, as the last of his friends said, perhaps he was always an adrenalin junkie and the buzz and the lure of a big score from running marijuana was enough.

Whatever the reason, Alfred Wayne Wilbur's crash-landing was swift and hard; a sudden, spiralling fall from much-decorated Vietnam veteran, CIA flier, Victoria Police air wing sergeant, National Safety Council helicopter pilot, bushfire fighter and lifesaver to convicted drug trafficker – his life, his marriage and his reputation in ruins.

In June 1995, Wilbur, 51, by then a failed businessman, was jailed for 18 months after pleading guilty to two charges of trafficking in marijuana. When the father of two was arrested the previous November police found more than four kilograms of leaf cannabis in his possession.

But he couldn't stay away from the stuff. In February, while on bail, he was arrested again with an interstate truck driver who had just handed over a further 2.4 kilograms, and police confiscated almost $28,000 in cash they found hidden in his home.

In a plea to the Victorian County Court, Wilbur's barrister, Mr George Henderson, read from a long list of Wilbur's achievements 'on behalf of society', including saving lives in war and in peace. He had turned to dope dealing only after three businesses had failed and was now 'all alone in the world' after all but one of his friends had wiped their hands of him and his 28-year marriage had ended.

His one remaining friend, a fellow Vietnam veteran and police pilot, Mr John Sonneveld, suspects the genesis of Wilbur's problems lies in his Vietnam experiences and the post-traumatic stress he has suffered since. 'I reckon the guy at the moment – sure he's broken the law and you've got to pay the penalty – but he's sick,' he said after the trial. 'He needs more psychological help than locking away.'

The Court of Appeal did not agree. In September 1995 it dismissed Al Wilbur's appeal and sent him to Pentridge.

In November 1965, Alfred Wayne Wilbur was a United States Army pilot flying helicopter gunship, troop carrier and medivac 'dust-off' missions for General George Custer's old unit, the Seventh Cavalry, hunting three regiments of the North Vietnamese Army in the Ia Drang Valley. It was brutal and bloody and the body count was high.

One day two Bell Iroquois 'Huey' gunship pilots had been caught on the ground by the enemy and Wilbur and his co-pilot were sent to rescue them. What they found apparently damaged Wilbur deeply and lastingly.

Chickenhawk, the best-selling 1983 book by Robert Mason on the helicopter war in Vietnam, recounts the incident, using pseudonyms. Wilbur was almost in tears as he told Mason of what happened to their colleagues: 'Typical gunship pilots. Somehow they think their flex guns make them invulnerable.'

The other chopper crew had found some Viet Cong or NVA regulars and decided to attack. Wilbur said he didn't know how long the fight lasted because they called after they got hit.

He said he and his partner 'Kaiser' were there within 10 minutes, and the other Huey had touched down in a clearing and seemed undamaged. Two other gunships in the rescue flight circled the scene but attracted no fire, so he and Kaiser went in behind the grounded chopper.

He told Mason that when they landed, 'I saw a red mass of meat hanging off a tree branch. It turned out to be Paster, hanging by his feet with his skin ripped off … I got out, Kaiser stayed with the ship. The medic jumped out and ran with me. Paster's skin hung down in sheets and covered his head …

'They must have just started on Richards, because we found him lying half-naked about 100 feet away in the elephant grass. His head was almost off.'

Years later, when he was working with Wilbur in the National Safety Council, John Sonneveld read *Chickenhawk*.

'I've seen a lot of rubbish on television about Vietnam, but this book was fairly accurate,' he told the court. 'I said to my wife, "You could change the name of the lead character in this to Al Wilbur".'

The next day at work he mentioned the book to Wilbur and suggested that he must have gone through similar experiences.

'He said, "Would you believe the fella who was skinned alive, I actually retrieved his body",' Mr Sonneveld said after the trial. 'It knocked the shit out of him, upset him something dreadful.'

He said he believed that and other terrors Wilbur experienced in the war were at least partly responsible for his current problems. 'There's a pattern of people like him in the States who end up in jail or on the wrong side of the law, far too many. The other side of it is that too many of them top themselves as well. There's a pattern there and I think he fits in that pattern and it worries me a bit.'

Mr Sonneveld said Wilbur's war experience 'does play on his mind ... It's a never-forgotten experience. My wife tells me I am [also affected by it].'

Mr Sonneveld, an air safety investigator, said he had attended about 35 fatal air crashes in the past 10 years. 'I've seen people – without making it frivolous – burnt, buckled, broken, burst ...' but he believed that Wilbur had 'seen as bad, if not worse, than I've seen ... and at a much more impressionable age. He's seen more atrocities than I did and, yes, I think it does play on his mind.'

He said Wilbur suffered terribly from the skin disease psoriasis, with blotches the size of his hand all over his chest. Mr Sonneveld said he believed the condition was also a result of his war experiences.

'This guy, I reckon he's really screwed up, needs a lot of help.'

Al Wilbur was born in New York State in 1944. In May 1963, he dropped out of college where he was studying machine-tool design and metallurgy. According to a brief history he prepared for his solicitor Brian Cash, he enlisted in the US

Army at Fort Dix, New Jersey, and was trained in helicopters at Army aviation schools in Texas and Alabama.

He graduated as a warrant officer in April 1964 and was assigned to Germany, flying training, reconnaissance and border patrol missions. In March 1965 he was nominated for the US Air Medal for his part in a rescue operation in which his crew was credited with saving three skiers and transferring 22 others to hospital after an avalanche near Garmisch-Partenkirchen in the Bavarian Alps.

In September 1965 his company was sent to Vietnam. From then until January 1967, 'I flew gunships, slicks [troop carriers] and dust-off medivac operations,' he wrote. 'During that period I had flown in excess of 1200 combat hours on more than 525 combat missions. I was awarded two Army Commendation Medals for valor and 22 US Army Air Medals.'

On one occasion, according to *Chickenhawk*, Wilbur's Huey was shot down and he had to make an emergency autorotation landing. It was not a particularly traumatic event for Wilbur and his partner – except that the chopper had been making the camp's beer run and they lost 100 cases.

In February 1967 he came to Australia to marry Patricia Oxley, whom he had met in Europe. He worked for Ansett's helicopter division until April 1968, and then returned to the US where he obtained his fixed-wing pilot's licence.

But the allure of the jungle and the war called Wilbur back to Indochina. Between late 1970 and early 1974 he accepted a job flying choppers for what his barrister Mr Henderson described as 'the somewhat mythical' Air America, the shadowy Central Intelligence Agency airline in South-East Asia, whose existence has long been denied by the US Government. Flying missions in Laos, Cambodia and Vietnam he was cited for search and rescue operations in locations he said were 'far from safe, friendly and down-rite [sic] bad news'. One mission into the Plain of Jars in Laos failed, but he rescued 14 operatives from the jungle at Pakse, Laos.

In 1973 he acted as a pilot for the International Commission for Control and Supervision set up under the Paris Peace Talks.

In January 1974, Wilbur returned to Australia and, after flying here, in Singapore, Indonesia and Abu Dhabi, joined the Victoria Police air wing in 1979, training at the police academy. He was one of the first three pilots endorsed to fly the force's new $1.5 million Dauphin helicopter. He was an excellent pilot, hyperactive and a workaholic, said Mr Sonneveld, who joined soon after. 'He was very keen to see helicopters work for the benefit of the community. He'd seen how they were used to save lives in Vietnam; he'd seen what they could do.'

But Wilbur resigned in September 1980 after the Dauphin was grounded for a month following a minor crash. Wilbur blamed the 'bureaucratic system' for the aircraft's frequent spells out of service, saying: 'It is very frustrating for pilots when they can't get out and fly.'

'I mean he and I were in a sense adrenalin junkies,' said Mr Sonneveld, a former Australian chopper pilot in Vietnam, who also resigned in frustration from the air wing. 'We were out doing all sorts of horrendous things with helicopters [in Vietnam] and it was great, like riding flying motorcycles.'

Wilbur set up a sheet metal business in South Melbourne but continued flying helicopters part-time for the National

Safety Council until its ignominious demise in 1989. He flew search and rescue, air ambulance and bushfire missions – and pioneered water bombing of fires.

Mr Sonneveld said Wilbur worked hard but 'slowly but surely the recession overtook him'. Mr Henderson told the County Court that Wilbur's sheet metal and then helicopter and pizza shop businesses all failed and he turned to marijuana trafficking.

On Thursday 3 November 1994, staff at the Greyhound Pioneer Bus freight terminal in Franklin Street became suspicious of two parcels sent from Adelaide. The packages, someone pointed out, had the faint, sweet smell of cannabis.

Plainclothes police were scattered through the terminal when Wilbur arrived that afternoon to collect the parcels, which were addressed to Dave Powell and Wayne Allen. Telling two policemen masquerading as freight clerks that he was a courier, he took the packages outside to his yellow utility and was arrested. The parcels contained 3.227 kilograms of leaf cannabis, and a search of his car uncovered a further 280 grams of marijuana in 10 plastic bags. When staff told police of invoices showing previous deliveries sent to the terminal, Wilbur admitted receiving 1.19 kilograms of marijuana by the same method.

Interviewed that night at Flemington CIB, Wilbur said he had turned to drug dealing after his business became 'very rocky'. He had avoided receivership by selling his machinery. '[He said] he had got into the cannabis trade essentially to provide himself with a cashflow for his own personal expenses,' the prosecutor, Damian Elwood, told Judge Alan Dixon later.

Cash from the sales went on 'food, household and electric', Wilbur told the detectives. 'I thought this was a way to recoup a little bit of money until such time as I could establish myself in employment elsewhere.'

He said he was buying the marijuana for $300 an ounce and selling it at only a small profit. But he also admitted that he was hoping to find customers for larger quantities that he could sell for a commission or finder's fee. Ever the hopeful businessman, he said: 'I was just trying to establish a market over here.'

Wilbur was charged and bailed, but on 2 February 1995 was arrested again after a South Australian truck driver delivered a further 2.45 kilograms of marijuana. At his home, police found 11 grams and $27,720 in cash, hidden in an ammunition box in his bedroom wardrobe.

Mr Henderson told the County Court in June 1995 that Wilbur had received threats from associates in the drug trafficking operation. His marriage broke down and the second offence, in February, occurred because he had been threatened by people he owed money to over the November delivery. One, a South Australian Vietnamese named Le, 'threatened on a number of occasions to mutilate his family'.

Mr Henderson asked Judge Dixon to give Wilbur, who had no prior convictions, a lengthy suspended jail sentence. 'It can't be said that Mr Wilbur comes before Your Honour as a malingerer, a bludger, a person that's relied on society. Mr Wilbur is a person who has put an enormous amount into society. He's saved lives. He's flown many, many missions. He's protected people, he's risked his own life,' he said.

'He's gone from being a successful businessman to a convicted trafficker. He's lost his house, he's lost his wife, he's lost his family. He's all alone in the world now. The only person that's here today is a very, very old friend. Everyone else in his life has just wiped their hands of him.

'He's 51 and now has to realign his life,' Mr Henderson said. 'This was not pure greed. He was motivated by his own lack of [business] success.'

Judge Dixon told Wilbur he committed the offences to 'retrieve your fallen financial fortunes' and the scale and organisation of the operation 'leaves me little option but to send you to jail'.

'Cannabis plays a significant part in corrupting our young people. They start by experimenting with cannabis and go on to hard drugs and the destruction of their mental and physical health,' he said.

Judge Dixon said he took into account Wilbur's age, early guilty plea, previous good character and the effect his war service and post-war activities 'must have had on you and your misfortunes in recent years'. He ordered that Wilbur serve a minimum of one year before being eligible for parole.

Wilbur's solicitor, Brian Cash, lodged an appeal against the sentence on the grounds that the penalty was excessive and that Judge Dixon failed to give adequate consideration to the matters raised in mitigation and/or sufficient weight to the early guilty plea.

But that September the Court of Appeal – the president, Justice John Winneke, Justice William Ormiston and Justice Ken Hayne – took less than two hours to dismiss the appeal. So for a year Al Wilbur languished in prison with his memories – and his nightmares.

With Steve Butcher

WHEN THE JOB IS MURDER

There is a paragraph: two sentences in elegant typeface. It can be found in squad rooms across the English-speaking world, on blotters and bulletin boards. Here, it is pinned to a conference room wall and sticky-taped to glass doors in the sprawling ninth-floor office of the homicide squad.

Titled 'The Homicide Investigator', it is affirmation and reminder, a statement not only of mission but pride. It's all about The Job.

'No greater honour will ever be bestowed on an officer or a more profound duty imposed on him than when he is entrusted with the investigation of the death of a human being. It is his duty to find the facts, regardless of colour or creed, without prejudice, and to let no power on earth deter him from presenting these facts to the court without regard to personality.'

But it doesn't say this: There is a price to be paid.

There's a beautiful view from here: out across Melbourne's Albert Park and the lake to the bay and the blue horizon. Ron Iddles has been gazing at it for close to a minute now, but seeing none of it. Lost instead in regret and a kind of guilt.

It had seemed a straightforward question. We were talking about the things he has seen in 10 years, on and off, in homicide. About the blood, the loss and grief and the mean, dumb ugliness. I wanted to know how could you avoid dragging a little of that home, like the stink on your clothes.

'What effect has it had on your family?'

'I've been married 26 years,' he answers, 'and she's been with me the whole time. She used to talk about me being married to the job.' Then he goes on, voice faltering: 'But now my first daughter I'm not all that close to.'

He drags in a deep, rattling sigh and turns to the window. Lingers there that long time. When finally he turns back there are tears down his cheeks.

'Well,' he says, 'there's your answer.'

Iddles is a big man with a gentle, considered disposition and high principles. A detective senior sergeant, with 24 years in the job, he is one of Victoria's best, and best regarded, investigators. In this stint, he's been with the homicide squad six years, but he first came here in 1980, when Joanne, the first of his three kids, was just four.

Other coppers might tell you that the homicide crews are the elite, but the detectives themselves steer away from such conceit. Iddles simply says that it can be seen as 'the pinnacle of investigation'. Back then though, he allows, he may have thought – and certainly acted – differently.

'Well, when you're young, 1980, you come into the job and it's all excitement and glamour. You're in the homicide squad and going out there to solve every job, and you get to the stage where you work and work and work. I work bloody hard now, but in the early days I'd come home and Joanne'd be gone to bed and I'd go to work again before she got up.'

It's the nature of the beast and it never lets up. Even now he might get home – doesn't matter if it's six, seven or eight o'clock – and he's been there five minutes before the phone rings. Or it's in the lonely hours: another killing, another call-out where he dresses in the dark and is gone. And stays gone, for weeks of 15- and 18-hour days. 'Sometimes in here,' he says, 'you can forget what you have at home.'

Iddles says he's 'refocused', and now tries to make up for all he missed then with his two younger kids, Matthew, 12, and Shae, nine: the little important things like a fishing trip or a game of putt-putt golf.

But he never got to Joanne's 21st birthday. One of those calls the night before took him to a murder in Swan Hill. The night of her engagement party they had a limo booked for six o'clock. The call came at five-to: a shooting in King Street. This time he told them no, and sent the rest of the crew. Still they came to see him twice at the party to pick his brain. He got home at 2 am, had a shower, and went straight to work.

Things like that, the long list of them, you can never give back. It's why she's told him, more than once: 'You were never there.'

It is 1881. In an adobe stable turned temporary courtroom in Taos, New Mexico, a US Federal District Court judge looks down on a convicted murderer.

'Jose Manuel Miguel Xavier Gonzales, in a few short weeks it will be spring, the snows of winter will flee away, the ice will vanish and the air will become soft and balmy. In short, Jose Manuel Miguel Xavier Gonzales, the annual miracle of the years will awaken and come to pass. But you won't be there.'

He waxes poetic for two more paragraphs, lyricising on timid desert flowers and wild wood songsters, sporting butterflies and breeze-teased tassels of wild grasses. All these will come but Gonzales will never see them, because the sheriff is commanded to lead him to a remote spot and swing him by the neck from a knotting bough of some sturdy oak.

'And then, Jose Manuel Miguel Xavier Gonzales, I further command that such officer or officers retire quickly from your dangling corpse that vultures may descend from the heavens upon your filthy body until nothing shall remain but bare bleached bones of a cold-blooded, copper-coloured, bloodthirsty, throat-cutting, chile-eating, sheep-herding, murdering son-of-a-bitch.'

Brian Rix grins as he reads the transcript, now laminated and pinned to a conference room wall. Homicide coppers celebrate the anonymous judge's words, not just for the black sting in their tail or their sense of unblinking justice, but as a reminder of where their own duty and allegiance lies. With the victims. Those gone and those left behind.

I remember a misty Saturday morning in May 1996. It is six days after the Port Arthur massacre, and the tragic penal colony is being re-opened to the public for the first time. Management calls it a 'soft opening'. But it's not soft. It's hard.

Down beside the Broad Arrow Café, its windows painted over, waits Salvation Army Major Don Woodland. All morning, men and women come up, and he wraps them in his hug. Others hold his hands and pray. They wet his broad shoulders with tears. And it strikes me that this is his terrible, heroic job: to soak into himself a piece of each one's misery and pain.

Being in homicide must be a little like that.

It might be comfortable to imagine homicide crews as types from bad TV: hard-nosed, methodical, just-the-facts-ma'am investigators, clinically working their way from bloodstain and powder-burn through tip-off to solution. But that ignores the scenes into which they routinely step: the brutal, futile stupidity of the killing, and the waves of misery and anger that ripple out from it, swamping family and friends. Some of that must seep in.

The job description for a homicide detective no longer simply calls for skilled investigator. In a time when it is increasingly recognised that the dead are not the only victims of murder, you need to be confessor and late-night counsellor, sounding-board and shoulder to cry on, sometimes surrogate family member. It takes a certain type.

'There's no doubt that's part of the hidden criteria,' says Inspector Brian Rix, the lean, gregarious head of the 62-member squad. 'It's not written down anywhere but you're looking for people who have that strength of character to be able to carry on through very, very devastating circumstances. Blokes are out there dealing face-to-face with families all the time, and at times it can be a little difficult. It's draining. But then again, it can really focus you on what it's all about.'

What it's about, says Acting Inspector Greg Hough, is the very worst of crimes. Hough has been in homicide for six of 25 years in a career including long stints in CIB, the Delta Taskforce into child exploitation, and surveillance units, but has always wanted this. Partly for the rigor and challenge of the investigation, but more than that. 'I've never liked the fact that anyone, at any time, can choose to take someone else's life,' he says. 'A life taken away. It's the one thing that can never be replaced.'

But Hough says he never realised the level of involvement, in terms of both time and emotion, that he would have with victims' families. 'From the time you have to break the news to the relatives, you then spend the next two to three years with them.'

It is the beginning of an often intense bond. In a sense, the homicide detective becomes not only someone to lean on and a link with their loved one, but personification of the possibility of light at the end of their awful tunnel. In many cases the relationship lasts years after a case is solved.

Neither the intensity nor level of dependency should surprise, says Garry Thomson, former senior police psychologist and now head of counselling at Melbourne University. 'Think of it from the family's perspective,' he says, 'where they are in a time of real crisis, where it's like there's no anchor point in their life. Into that life walks a number of people who are competent, professional, clear, know the system and are curious to find out what's gone on, both professionally and personally. And that starts the bond.'

But how do you base a relationship on beginnings like this?

On Oaks Day, 6 November 1997, Jane Thurgood-Dove is murdered, shot in the head in front of her three terrified children. Late that evening Ron Iddles walks up the driveway of a house in suburban Niddrie to where her husband, Mark, and her father, John Magill, are waiting. Both men are in shock.

Iddles approaches Mark Thurgood-Dove. He says: 'I know you were at work today, Mark, and you couldn't have pulled the trigger. But you're my first suspect. Until I eliminate you from this inquiry I don't move forward.'

John Magill is horrified. 'I think you're being a bit harsh,' he tells the detective.

'No, I'm not,' replies Iddles, turning to him. 'And you're also a suspect.'

There's a grim statistical side of murder, Iddles explains now, and the statistics will tell you this: about nine in every 10 killings are committed by someone known to the victim, and about 50 per cent are direct family members. 'So basically I work from that circle outwards.

'It's a bit hard and a bit callous,' he admits. 'Here's a man grieving the loss of his wife, but I also want to look at him and see is that false and put on, did he really set up the murder of his wife?'

Clearly not, Iddles quickly came to realise. And hopefully, he adds, Mark now understands and doesn't resent the initial apparent cruelty. Relatives come to see the necessity and logic of the approach, and you can move on and build a relationship. It has happened with Iddles and Jane Thurgood-Dove's loved ones, particularly John and Helen Magill. It happened with Hough and the parents of Mersina Halvagis whose 25-year-old daughter was stabbed to death in Fawkner Cemetery in 1997. But at the beginning, the detective owes first duty to someone more important – the dead.

Brian Rix puts it this way: 'I think most people here would concede that you are the eyes and ears of that person who's been killed. You are there to solve the mystery of what happened to them. In a sense, you're their proxy.'

That relationship can also be profound and lasting. Senior Detective Carl Stella spent days combing through the life of Nicole Patterson, murdered by the predatory Peter Dupas in April 1999. 'I never knew her, but each document that comes into your possession – diaries, letters or whatever – you're opening a page of that person's life,' he says. 'And at the end of it I felt as if I'd known her for years. And I guess I always will.'

But no-one, says Iddles, pretends to know the depth of suffering felt by the family. 'It never goes away. Go and talk to any family member and I don't reckon there's a day goes by when they don't think about it.'

He has watched it obsess and consume the Magills. It's why he made a point of giving them, like every family member in every murder, his mobile phone number, telling them to ring, 24 hours a day, seven days a week. Sometimes they'll wake in the middle of the night with a theory or a fear and want to talk, and sometimes he'll get out of bed and drive out to see them. He has visited at least once a month for the past three years, and phones every couple of weeks, even if there's nothing new to report. It's why last year he took Jane Thurgood-Dove's son Scott camping with his own son Matthew.

He speaks to Mark and to Jane's sisters whenever they need him, and took the Magills to the squad offices to show them how an investigation works, how information is collated and recorded, how suspects are eliminated. Still, the day after every leave, John Magill is on the phone, checking that he's still chasing.

Iddles understands. For every family, this is the biggest and worst thing that's ever happened and it will dominate the rest of their lives. What they want is an answer and they see him as the man who will find it.

'But what I've said to John is: "Don't make yourself the victim. You'll always remember Jane. You'll always remember the good times. You'll never forget how tragically her life was taken, but if you become so obsessed with it, you yourself become the victim."

'There's times I've shed tears for them. You don't become emotionally involved because if you do, your judgement becomes clouded. But it's hard …' he says. 'It's pretty hard when you've got all the family there, all teary-eyed and saying, "Ron, you're going to solve this".'

There are times when he's just held them while they cried: 'Policemen are meant to be, or at least are perceived to be, tough and strong. There's many blokes who'd find it hard to put their arm around someone in a time of real grief. I suppose it comes down to a personal thing; I don't mind, I put my arm around them and give them a tissue.

'It's just a human thing.'

A final cautionary quotation pinned to the homicide conference room wall: 'One of the most terrible things about an unsolved murder is the taint of uncertainty it casts on everyone around it. If one person in our midst is capable of violently taking someone's life then any of us may be capable and may be scrutinised with that possibility in mind. Suddenly the most innocent actions may be viewed in the most sinister light.'

This isn't the one about honour, duty or pride. This is the one about the price to be paid. Or one of the prices.

This is the job: to go where the worst things are. Brian Rix remembers Queen Street, where the laughing Frank Vitkovic ran wild in December, 1987, shooting eight people dead before leaping from a window to his own end. The extent of the blood and gore was horrific, but in its midst was a young girl, with a single, small wound in her throat, lying there as if asleep. That's the sight that stays in his mind.

You go to the job with the armour of professional detachment. 'You're looking at a dead body,' says Rix, 'but quite often the thing that's in your mind is that this is the greatest piece of evidence you've got. If you think about it on those lines you can deal with the horror.'

Iddles suggests the body is the central and most important part of a jigsaw puzzle. Sometimes you have 900 pieces of a 1000-piece set, perhaps even 999. It's all about finding that one lost piece.

But there must be tiny pieces that stick, a little stain from every terrible scene, the peaceful dead girls that stay with you forever. Police call up psychological defences to do their job, says Garry Thomson, but it's later, perhaps when they're tired or winding down, that the emotional repercussions can set in.

'You can't inure yourself permanently. I think they're all cumulative, bits that are left behind from every event, and some people find they add up over the years, and they say I can't do this any more. Others have a tolerance and they just block it for longer.'

Anyone who says some cases don't affect them more than others are kidding themselves, adds Greg Hough. You reflect on them, in the car driving home or when you're with your family, and you look at your own kids and think, "Well, I'm thankful for the life we have."

'I don't really think it's had an impact to the extent that I go away and shed a tear; I don't go away and really dwell on it. But there are certain little things, just an image of some scenes. And tragedy is the only word you can use.'

It also pollutes your view of the world, he says, painting everything in that sinister light. He notes, darkly, that there are people out there who know someone who has killed, but who say 'So what?' Iddles has felt it, too. There was a stage where he came to believe everything was bad, that there were no good people in the world.

'I've been through all that, but I've refocused,' he says. 'You'd say to your wife or your kids, "You're not going up to the local shop," because everything you deal with is so negative you get to thinking there could be a bloke around the corner that's going to abduct them, or whatever. You just have to find that balance and come through the other side.'

And the lasting cost? You try not to think it has a toll, but it has to. You're dealing with death every day; you're dealing with grieving families nearly every day.

'So you'd be fooling yourself if you said it didn't have any effect on you. What it is, I don't know. But because it's all about death – it's a fair old burden to carry.'

FALL FROM GRACE

F ather Vincent Keirin Kiss was a man of truly catholic tastes and contradictions. On the surface, most of his 61 years had been devoted to his God, his church, and charity for the needy. But at the same time he had delighted in worldly temptations – the heady thrill of high finance, the swirl and glitter of society and life in a credit card comfort zone.

Father Kiss was a pastor more at home in tuxedo and tie than clerical collar; better cared for by a Filipino houseboy than a spinster housekeeper; happier in a spa-bathed and Spanish Mission-style terrace home than a priestly presbytery.

He was also a man of God who defied the word of God, breaking the eighth commandment – 'Thou shalt not steal' – to the tune of almost $2 million. It was, a judge of the Victorian County Court noted in August 1993, 'a gigantic theft'.

So, broken and humiliated, Father Kiss was left to meditate in what some might say were more fittingly monastic surrounds than he had grown accustomed to – a bluestone Pentridge prison cell.

After being convicted on seven charges of stealing $1.8 million from a charitable trust he had been employed to administer, he would spend the next seven years in Pentridge and other Victorian jails. And while he did, other demons from his past would begin surfacing to ensure it was the type of environment he would return to.

The fall from grace of Vincent Kiss began with an ungodly swindle. After he pleaded guilty to the theft charges, Judge Paul Mullaly heard how, between June 1984 and November 1990, Kiss had devised what was, on the face of it, a deceptively simple scheme to cheat the ANZ Executors and Trustees Company and four Victorian charities to finance 'an orgy of spending' and 'a public, extravagant and obvious lifestyle … [among] the rich and famous'.

Seconded by the diocese of Wagga Wagga to private enterprise as manager of the Charitable Trusts Department of ANZE&T, on a $52,662 salary, Kiss had discretion 'off his own bat' to distribute up to $100,000 to various charities. To a large extent that is what he did. But he also diverted $2.5 million from four Victorian charities – the Fitzroy Community Youth Centre, Lions International, International Social Services and the Open Family Foundation – into the Vanuatu Development Project, a charity that simply did not exist.

All that the Vanuatu Development Project consisted of was a single Westpac bank account – number 550527 – with Father Vincent Kiss the sole signatory and beneficiary.

'Effectively, that bank account is the key to this whole matter,' Crown Prosecutor Kevin Silbert told the court. '[Kiss] engineered the distribution of funds from various wills under his control or subject to his influence into four well-known and respected charities … Trading on his position, he persuaded each charity to remit monies by cheques payable to the Vanuatu Development Project.'

Beginning with small amounts before graduating to more than $50,000, he used the four charities as a 'conduit'. He would approve a donation to, say, the Open Family Foundation, which would bank that cheque and then draw another for the same amount to be paid into the VDP account.

'The matter became so mechanical over such a period of time that there were cheques going from the ANZ to the charity and then straight to the VDP,' Mr Silbert said. 'If [Kiss] needed money for a house purchase or for some form of expenditure then there was a very quick flow of funds into the VDP to source his expenditure.'

It is the extravagance of that expenditure and the ostentatious flaunting of the lifestyle that it purchased that is so intriguing. There was scarcely a society charity 'do' that Vincent Kiss did not swirl through, usually as a so-called 'walker' – the safe and unattached escort – of society mainstays such as Mrs Lillian Frank, Mrs Jeanne Pratt or Lady Primrose Potter.

(It was Kiss who was flown to Venice in 1990 to officiate in St Mark's at the marriage of Lady Potter's daughter, Primrose Dunlop, to Prince Giustiniani, Count of the Phanaar and Knight of St Sophia, also known as airline steward Mr Lorenzo Montesini. This was an occasion to be remembered – for all the wrong reasons. In a fairy story made for the tabloids, the beautiful Australian heiress was jilted on the eve of her wedding when the groom ran away with the best man, his lover, Robert Straub. 'Everybody knew he was not the marrying kind,' socialite Sheila Scotter somewhat redundantly said later.)

Kiss also ate in the best restaurants, had a well-stocked wine cellar, donated more than $19,000 to the Carlton Football Club where he was president of the Blue Boys Coterie, and travelled frequently – enjoying 17 overseas trips in five years.

He was also 'upwardly mobile' in real estate. Between 1982 and 1987 he bought three houses: a $45,000 property in East Brunswick, an $83,000 home in Prahran (which he later sold for $135,000), and a $197,000 place in Cecil Street, South Melbourne. Over four years he spent more than $150,000 on renovations – including a $16,745 spa bath.

He also owned property worth $4.85 million pesos ($A285,000) in the Philippines, including Casa Bianca – a luxury villa with swimming pool and tennis court at Cuba Laguna, 95 kilometres south of Manila – to which he was making plans to retire when arrested. A police search of his briefcase found application forms from the Philippines Retirement Authority.

He had already paid for two Great Danes and two windsurfing boards to be flown to Casa Bianca in preparation for his retirement. He had also introduced others to the attractions of his seachange option, once funding five members of the Australian Ballet on a tour of the Philippines.

At his committal hearing in 1992, the prosecution read out a letter, allegedly to then Human Rights Commissioner Brian Burdekin, telling him of the villa and saying: 'Feel free to stay as long as you want.' (Casa Bianca, it would turn out later, would not be the sort of place a human rights advocate would want to go anywhere near.)

Kiss carried 11 credit cards on which he charged almost $416,000 between 1984 and 1990. On American Express alone he was spending more than $1000 a week. From 1986, he withdrew $565,980 in cash and cheques from the VDP account.

Between 1987 and 1990 he spent $8456 on chauffeured limousines and in one six-month period utilised them on 66 separate occasions, usually for the use of friends such as Mrs Frank, Lady Potter and former Victorian Government Minister Mrs Caroline Hogg.

It was, said Mr Silbert, 'clearly a jet-set lifestyle'. Yet no-one seemed to see the contradictions. Perhaps, as Mr Silbert put it, 'their manner of lifestyle was such that … they just assume others are able to live that lifestyle without anything suspicious arising'.

Certainly arts patron Mrs Pratt had no suspicions. She once described Kiss as 'like Jesus Christ. He is not priestly, he is saintly.'

Sheila Scotter said after his conviction that she had found Kiss 'an utterly charming man'. He could always be counted on to take at least one table at functions she organised to support the Victorian State Opera and the Melbourne Spoleto Festival, and 'never, ever kept you waiting for the cheque'.

'I got an awful shock when I heard about his arrest – he must have been something of a split personality to be like that.'

Even cynical politicians admit to being fooled. One, formerly at the highest levels of government, said: 'It seemed there was no function of much consequence at which he did not appear. I think everyone had the impression that he was a man of independent means who hadn't embraced a vow of poverty with much enthusiasm.'

*   *   *

Yet Vincent Kiss had humble beginnings. He was born in the Sydney suburb of Randwick on 1 June 1932, into a devout Catholic, working-class family. His father was a clerk in the railways who fought overseas from 1939 to 1945, returning with a number of injuries. His mother was for many years housekeeper to the local parish priest. Two of his sisters became nuns in the order of St Joseph.

Educated by the Marist Brothers in Sydney, Kiss worked for three years, from the age of 17, at the Rural Bank in Junee, near Wagga Wagga, but had always felt a calling to the church and, in 1955, joined the Divine Word Missionaries in Sydney – as a fundraiser.

In 1957 he entered the Springwood Seminary to study for the priesthood. Kiss was a fit and keen sportsman but while playing rugby league for a seminary team in 1962, he broke his neck and had to give the game away. He was ordained in mid-1964. He went to the North Albury parish as a curate and remained there until 1969 when he was appointed director of students and mission societies for the Wagga Diocese.

The job involved him travelling up to 1600 kilometres each week, forming youth groups, such as the Young Christian Students, and attending to youth issues, which he said at the time ranged from shoplifting to underage drinking, sex and drugs.

In an interview with the Albury *Border Mail* in 1972, he described himself as a stirrer. 'I am basically stirring in Christ's name. If there's no stirring, it's not worthwhile ... all the silt or good qualities of a person sinks to the bottom.'

Kiss seemed a thoroughly modern minister to much of Albury – leading his YCS members in·a peace march – and was proud, even a little cocky about it: '[People] must realise that priests are not jelly moulds – each has his own individuality and personality.'

And his was a personality that had immediate impact in the dry surrounds of his diocese. A Wagga real estate agent said the young priest who arrived in the area was a very different Vincent Kiss to the one who would be uncloaked later. 'I remember him as having little time for people inclined to play up their wealth, little time for the trappings of society,' he said.

But by the time he was working with the YCS he was said to be a flashy dresser, good looking, with a penchant for fast, late-model cars, including a Holden Torana GTR, Jensen Healey and a blue Valiant Pacer – the sort of rides his young followers aspired to own.

'I remember parents thinking it was great having a "with-it" priest in our area,' said one local. Another later recalled him as 'tall, blond and charming, full of life, a fantastic young man and always out to help people. He was a very charitable person and very popular with the young ones.'

At the same time, he wasn't about to put up with the young ones' shenanigans. In January 1972, according to the *Border Mail*, he gave a sermon at St Patrick's Church in Albury, chastising parents for letting their teenagers get away with drinking liquor while camping at the Lake Hume caravan park.

'It will be a sad chain of events if something that is there to be used for the benefit of all people becomes a haven for the person who sees life has no more to offer than unbridled sex and undisciplined drinking,' he thundered.

In those times, suggested the paper, it was a frank pronouncement for a priest. In fact, it was far from frank.

As later events would reveal, it was a monumental and appalling piece of hypocrisy. But by the time most of his parishioners would realise that, Kiss would be long gone from Albury and Wagga.

In the mid-1970s he began looking for greener pastures. As his counsel Leonard Hartnett would later put it, 'He felt that he wished to diversify into a vocational area which would allow him some satisfaction ... of the skills he had. He sought an area which would allow him to unite his spiritual background and faith with a commercial vocation.'

It was his first dip into the world of high finance but it was not auspicious. He applied for and was given a position in personal consulting and counselling with a company in Melbourne but was dissatisfied and soon quit, returning to priestly duties in Wagga and a stint as a missionary – in Vanuatu.

That episode was also short lived. Vanuatu Bishop Francis Lambert later recalled it this way: 'Yes, we remember Vincent Kiss. He did a lot of work with the young. And then he left ... yes, in a bit of a hurry.'

In 1979 he took a position as executive director of the Youth Affairs Council of Victoria and the following year was made manager of charitable trusts for Trustee Executors. When that company crashed in 1983, he commenced his position with ANZT, which took over the failed company's trusts.

It was a position he seemed born to, that of professional fundraiser. At his committal in 1992, an ANZ senior manager, Mr Arthur Hubbard, outlined the method employed by such people: they would mix with high-fliers and the rich and famous, gain their confidence, interest them in charities, and then 'put the bite' on them.

But eventually society bit back and Kiss suffered his punishment – of this world at least. He sat out a lonely, humiliating – perhaps even humbling – seven-year jail sentence. His society friends, no doubt also feeling cheated, left him. He even briefly considered – and rejected – that other mortal sin of suicide.

But at least his church had not abandoned him. When he left jail, Father Kevin Flanagan of the Sacred Heart Church, North Albury, told the court Kiss would be given a home in his old diocese and perhaps be permitted a small clerical role, maybe as a chaplain in an elderly persons' home.

'It is a place where his bishop resides and people he has known and shared so much of his life with,' Father Flanagan said. 'I would hope they would welcome him back because the essence of Christianity is forgiveness.'

But there was so much more about Vincent Kiss that would prove so much harder to forgive.

Two years into his incarceration a whiff of further shame began to gather round him. In the Philippines, Senator Ernesto Herrera, a crusader against child sex in his country, claimed an Australian syndicate was involved in the sale of children to foreign pedophiles.

A crackdown by Philippines police in 1988 had exposed a sophisticated network of child molesters operating out of Pagsanjan, the province where Kiss had built his villa, Casa Bianca. American pedophile Andrew Mark Harvey and 21 other foreigners were arrested and hundreds of compromising photographs and videos seized. In 1993 some of the pictures, of Harvey having sex with boys and girls from Pagsanjan, were shown to visiting Australian officials, including then Justice Minister Duncan Kerr. They were so upsetting that one of the Australians became physically ill.

Several children, many of them naked, had also been found in hotels and houses used by the ring. It was in such places, police suspected, that members of the syndicate had treated child prostitutes as virtual slaves. One of the guesthouses linked to the syndicate by Senator Herrera and local social worker Dr Sonia Zaide was Casa Bianca.

In 1995, when the Filipinos were raising their concerns about him, two men who had been youths under the care of Vincent Kiss in the late 1960s and early '70s got together and began swapping memories of the young priest they had known. They found they had much in common and decided to share it with the police.

By the time Kiss was released from Ararat Prison in 1999 more of his former charges had come forward to tell similar tales. For at least seven years while he ministered to the people of Albury and Wagga, Kiss had been sexually assaulting their children. At the time he was berating teenagers for drinking liquor on the shores of Lake Hume, he was using a holiday cabin there as one of his bases for molesting them.

One of the boys he took there later recalled that the cabin was much more luxurious than the usual weekender. One wall was covered in mirror tiles and the living room was equipped with a new stereo system. It had a bar that, with the application of an appropriately-patterned table cloth, could be transformed into an altar but also contained a well-stocked mini-fridge.

There was a speedboat outside – Kiss apparently enjoyed teaching visitors, including a few of the Albury nuns, how to water ski.

The teenager, a student at Aquinas College, had been disruptive at school and Kiss had been asked to counsel him. Later he invited him to the cabin for another chat, spinning the old line when they got there that the kid should have known better because he was more intelligent than other boys: 'Buttering me up.'

Later he suggested they have a swim and after that suggested a nap. 'I thought it was a bit strange. He went to his bedroom but then came out and started telling me about the priesthood and how lonely he was. He had his chest on mine, but then he backed off.'

The boy didn't tell anyone. No-one would have believed him, he told Nick Higgins of the *Border Mail* in 2002. 'You just didn't back then … this is the main man, this is a priest. You think about it later and realise it's all just a scam – and a good one too, because he was king of the kids.'

Kiss played to the role. The boys admired his hot cars, like the two-door Torana coupe and the canary-yellow Falcon 500, his sportiness, his flamboyance and his generosity – particularly with alcohol. He would take them on trips, not just to the lake but to Sydney and the Gold Coast. In Sydney they'd stay at the Boulevarde Hotel in Kings Cross, where he'd ply them with sweet Black Tower wine. At the Gold Coast, as one commentator later put it, 'they combined putt-putt golf and mutual masturbation'.

'He displayed calculated premeditation in his conduct towards the youths, engaging them with his apparent sophistication,' said Judge Penny Hock of the Sydney District Court. '[Then] he corrupted their youth.'

That was in September 2002, after Kiss had pleaded guilty to 10 charges of indecent assault and three of 'the abominable act of buggery' on four youths aged 13 to 17. All four victims were members of the Young Christian Students and the offences had taken place between 1966 and 1973 at YCS camps and meetings in Albury, Yass and Sydney.

Judge Hock said that in his positions with the YCS and as priest at the Sacred Heart Church in North Albury, school chaplain and athletics coach, he had abused both the bodies and the minds of boys in his care.

One of his victims had been asked to attend athletics and join Kiss for a 'steam bath and massage'. After four or five such visits, he received permission from the boy's parents to take him sailing. They drove to Lake Hume where Kiss sexually assaulted the boy in his car. Later assaults took place in the boy's bedroom at the family home.

Another boy was given cans of beer to drink before being molested. He told police he initially resisted but felt too drunk. Another assault occurred after Kiss gave his victim wine left over from a service club meeting.

No piece of manipulation was beneath him. As two of the boys grew older and began seeing girls, they wanted to end their relationships with the priest. Kiss spun them a tragic story about how he was dying from leukemia. He wasn't, but for a time he won back their sympathy.

He got little of that from Judge Hock, despite the best efforts of his counsel, Bruce Stratton, QC. She rejected his submission that the buggery offences were no worse than the indecent assaults, but conceded that they were not at the most serious end of the scale because Kiss had not sexually penetrated the boys – rather he had incited them to penetrate him.

Mr Stratton argued that the delay between the police first

interviewing the ex-priest, in 1995 when he was still in jail, and the trial was 'utterly inexcusable'. As a result his client, then aged 70, had become severely depressed and frightened, suffered from feelings of helplessness and worthlessness and was suicidal. Kiss, he said, had expressed 'genuine and sincere' remorse for his actions and had undergone considerable rehabilitation: 'Outside of these matters, it appears he has been a person of good character, he has done a lot of work for the community.'

The judge was unconvinced. Until he was interviewed, she said, Kiss seemed to have been untroubled by his crimes, lacking remorse and feeling confident they would never come to light.

Perhaps she had been swayed by some more of his wanderings, which until then had never been publicly revealed. When Vanuatu's Bishop Lambert made wry mention of him leaving that island in 1979 'in a bit of a hurry', it was shorthand for another collision with the law Kiss had there. He had been guilty in Port Vila of five counts of gross indecency, for which he received a suspended sentence and was quickly but quietly deported.

As Crown Prosecutor Trevor Bailey had pointed out: 'Since 1973 just on that information alone, Vincent Kiss went on being greedy, selfish and self-satisfying.'

So once again Vincent Kiss went back to prison. He was sentenced to 10 years and six months with a minimum of seven years. If he is paroled he will still be nearly 78 when he walks free, but this time there is no talk of welcoming him back to his old diocese to be close to his bishop.

In 2002 the Bishop of Wagga was the Most Reverend Gerard Hanna. The best hope he could offer Kiss was that local Catholics would be asked to pray for his victims – and in a spirit of reconciliation, for the former man of God as well.

All he could offer about the man himself was damnation with faint praise: 'We don't brand him as *worthless*,' he said.

THE BIG STEAL

He used to lie in bed some mornings and dream of houses just like this. Little white single-fronted cottage, picket fence, wrought iron around the veranda, pretty pocket-handkerchief garden. A laneway out the back, an extension in glass and timber bathing a sunroom in natural light. The sort of place into which people had put a lot of work and pride and money.

And then he'd go and rob it.

Lie back, shut his eyes and he could picture the place perfectly: seeing the way in through the alley, the fence high enough for cover but not too high to climb, the very window he was going to pop. Imagining all the good gear inside.

He'd lie there for half an hour or so, thinking it through, getting comfortable with it. Then he'd get up, get dressed – gloves in one pocket, screwdriver in the other – and walk straight out and do it.

But this particular joint, which he and a mate knocked off four, maybe five years ago, was more of a happy accident.

They'd come out to do a rip from a place down the lane. A year earlier they'd thieved a big marijuana plant, thick and heavy with heads, and now they'd come back for another dip. Coming up empty, they began scouting the other backyards for plants, poking their heads over fences on each side of the lane.

And here it was. A place just too good to pass up: yuppie dream with a big new sunroom extension, plate glass from floor to cathedral ceiling. You could look straight in and see everything they owned. Like a smorgasbord. The real laugh was the idiots hadn't even locked the doors.

They were in and out in five minutes. Got a TV, stereo, mobile phone, a bit of jewellery and a couple of hundred in cash from the bedroom. Another nice little earn.

Did a lot of places around here in those days. Did that one over the road, the green one up the street, and the place three houses along. Knocked over the milk bar up the corner one night when he was just a kid. Robbed that one and ripped their dope plants as well. In three or four years he probably robbed a couple of hundred houses all around Port Melbourne and South Melbourne.

That was the thing he used to do. He was a burglar. Only job he'd really ever had.

'Mate, I've been getting into other people's houses since I was 11 years old. I was a little larrikin. Me and all the boys round the Graham Street flats.

'I remember me first. This was when Dad was still alive. It wasn't a burglary, just a break-in. It looked like a dump, a run-down old house, and there was an old man that lived there, he collected junk and that. We ended up getting in and trashing the place, throwing things everywhere.

'The police ended up coming and they caught me. They

said, "Where's your father?" and I told them he was probably down the pub.

'We walked into the pub and there's me old man and I could just see his evil eyes looking at me, this little kid with two big ugly jacks standing beside me.

'He made me sit in the corner in the pub all afternoon. All me dad's friends are coming up, trying to give me chips and drinks and money and he's saying, "No, don't give him nothin'." When I got home I copped a spanking and got grounded. It never stopped me but.'

Call him Mick, but only because it's not his name. He hasn't done an earn in a couple of years now, not since he got pinched and sent to Pentridge and decided to give the whole game away as a bad joke. But there's no point sticking your neck out.

In four or five solid years of thieving, he never went down for a single burglary. What got him sent away in the end was a couple of nasty street brawls, fuelled by pills and alcohol. He was locked down in B Division on the day his son was born, the most important day of his life, and reckons that was his wake-up call.

Now, just 23, he's doing time in a dead-end caravan park, jammed between the scotch thistles and freight tracks out on Sunshine Road, Sunshine, in Melbourne's rust belt western suburbs, picking up the dole and the odd job, looking after his little boy on weekends and trying hard to stay out of trouble.

Of course he's tempted. It'd take only one day, one score, to get out of this dump. Just enough to pay the bond on a decent flat. And he could rationalise it, tell himself he's doing it for the boy. But it'd just be an excuse, wouldn't it?

And that one day could mean another 12 months away from the boy, and he couldn't handle that. Because it's true what they say: If you can't do the time, don't do the crime.

Doing the crime's the easy part. Always has been.

'When me dad was in the picture and he was strict on us, I was a little goody two-shoes. But when Dad passed away, a couple of days before my 12th birthday, I just turned into a renegade.

'I was about 13 when I first started getting in trouble with the coppers: doing break-and-enters, breaking into factories just to play in there. Then, probably about form one, I started shoplifting, stealing lollies, chocolates and stuff. Then it got worse and worse.

'Probably from 14 and upwards I was doing burglaries, actually doing factories, houses, warehouses, anything. Shops, milk bars. I can't really remember the first one because they weren't that serious, they were just a piece of cake. It was so easy just to get into someone's house and take what you need, within five minutes. There's been that many houses I can't remember the first.

'But I do remember me first shop, me first milk bar. A couple of mates told me, "That joint's got a lot of money in there," and I said, "It's pretty dangerous doing shops, isn't it, with alarms and everything?" But they said, "Nah, this one's got nothing, they're stupid."

'So we climbed up on their roof and took one of their skylights off. They had bars across and I thought, "So, they're not that stupid." But we only needed to cut one bar and because we were so small, we could squeeze through.

'We got in, pinched all the smokes, the money – got about 500 in cash, five- and 10-dollar notes. And heaps of lollies – lollies and ice-creams. We left a trail of chocolate and ice-cream wrappers all the way back to the flats.

'From then on, basically I made a career of it.

'Come 16- or 17-years-old I was a really full-on dopehead, full-on bonghead and a semi-alcoholic, and that's when I got introduced to the pills: Serapax, Rohypnols – a lot of serras and rowies. And that's what it all went on – drugs and alcohol.

'I wouldn't be greedy and have a big bundle. Once I got a hundred bucks in my kick, I'd buy booze and drugs and that. Plus if I've got a hundred, all my mates have got a hundred – what we get we split. Say we make a thousand in a couple of days and it's got to be split and then it all goes on piss and drugs and munchies. Then you go out and do another.

'But by the time I was 18 and 19, that's when I was full-on into burgs. I was popping pills and I always had cash, rolls of cash inside my mattress. 'Cos I was doing rips as well, pinching marijuana plants from people's backyards and selling it to all the boys around Port and South. That was another good one.

'But if I didn't have a rip and I'd run out of cash, I'd go do an earn.'

He was always on the lookout. Keeping an eye out for a nice, fancy house, something clean, tidy and well-kept. He'd go for a house with style – the sort of place that looked like rich suckers lived there: a place where you'd expect the people to have big TVs and flashy stereos, a bit of designer gear in the walk-in robes. Something with all the mod cons – for the taking.

Plus, of course, he'd be looking at what kind of windows they had, what sort of locks, and whether they had any dirty big dogs or alarms. Nice big letterboxes where the mail sat all day. Rear access was always handy and he used to love those houses with the high walls out front, where you could just walk in, shut the gate and enjoy the privacy. Away from the prying eyes of the neighbours.

And he knew his little patch of Port and South Melbourne and Garden City so well he could picture every street, every back lane and every narrow, one-man alley sneaking off them. Never really had to case a joint, he'd simply be out there every day, walking down the street to the milk bar or just wandering, taking the shortcuts, and that's when he'd see a place he liked.

And he'd say to himself: 'That looks like a nice house to rob, I'll keep that in mind.' And a week or so later he'd go back and do it over.

'I used to pop pills, heaps at night, and I'd still wake up in the morning, pilled off me head, and I'd just lay there thinking, "Who can I rob today?"

'Most of the time I'd picture a house before I got out of bed. I used to lie in bed for half an hour before I got up, picture a house I'm going to rob, then go do it.

'This is when I was doin' earns by myself. I'd go in there, pop open a window with a screwdriver, get into the house, and I'd go straight to the lounge room: the TV, video, stereo, straight to the electrical goods. Get all that set up, put it on the side, only take what I can carry. And always I can carry a TV and video, always, no matter what.

'A stereo: I'd always get the little portable ones, the latest ones, 'cos they're so light but they're worth a lot of money. A lot of times I'd leave the speakers behind because it's too much for me to carry.

'And you get your exit happening, know how you're getting out. And a bit of safety: you flick the lock on the front door from the inside. Anyone turns up they can't get in, you hear the key wiggling in the lock and, boom, you're straight out the back. It's happened a few times.

'Next, I'd hit the bedrooms. Go for the drawers. Straight away – top drawers in the bedrooms. Open them up, in under all the socks and jocks and that's where the cash is, you know? Or down the bottom drawer, you pull it right out and you've got the inside of the cupboard and that's where there was a lot of money stashed. All that space underneath and you've got money boxes sitting there, little tins and cash boxes, stuff like that, lot of valuables, little jewellery boxes.

'The main objective, the main thing I'd be looking for, would be cash, quick-earn cash. That was the whole idea, to make money. If you were greedy you'd take the electrical stuff. But I'd take the cash and fuck off, because I'm not a junkie. A junkie takes the cash, the electrical goods, the lot. And he'll trash the whole house.

'There was one place I robbed and I got $1200 cash. They had a grouse TV, video, stereo, and I said, "Nah, I don't want that, I've got what I want, I've got me cash." You know what I mean? I wouldn't risk me arse to carry that to where I've got to go and get pinched for it, when I've got the cash in my pocket.

'You'd always look for a case or something to haul the stuff home in. I'd walk down the street with a suitcase on each arm, full of hot goods, sweat pouring off me; I really want to get to me place so I'm sweet and can get rid of all this gear. Me heart's pumping and it's like you can carry a ton and walk 50 yards, you just had to get there. Find a shopping trolley and you think, "You beauty."

'You used to be able to get rid of some stuff in pawn shops, but it's tough. A couple of times I even grabbed people's own ID and used that. A couple of things with their names and addresses, receipts, telephone bills or something like that.

'A lot of times the videos, stereos and that used to go around the flats. A quick 80 or 100 bucks and people jump on them, especially the drug dealers. They sit there and wait, let everything come to them. Like me, I'm out there doing it and I bring it to them, they give me money and they go sell it for more. I'm happy with that.

'Sometimes I used to ask them "What do you need? A video, stereo, what? Clothes? Jag, Country Road, what?" Stealing to order.

'Never used to go for home computers much, just couldn't sell them. There was one bloke, bought maybe three off us. He was a wog, smart suit, had his own business. But none of the local boys used to buy them. Too fuckin' dumb.

'But it was money you really wanted. Cash. I always used to think I'm going to come across a big earn – a nice house with 10 grand. That was always on my mind: "Which house am I gunna hit, which house am I gunna hit?" I always wanted that big earn, eight thousand, 10 thousand cash and I'd be laughing.'

*   *   *

So now he returns to the scene of the crimes. Slinking down back alleys and chinning himself over grey and broken paling fences, pointing out windows he's broken, back doors he's jemmied, house after house that he's been in uninvited. Seeing if they've learnt anything from having him around.

That lovely little white cottage on the corner is as tempting as it was the first time, but the blinds of the side windows are drawn down tight and there are deadlocks on the windows and doors. Peep out the back, though, and all that glass on the sunroom is still wide open. You can take inventory of everything they own.

The place he ripped the dope plants from might be producing again but he can't be sure: the fence is a couple of metres higher and topped with barbed wire. That one down the lane has invested in a yappy dog. But most are wide open and welcoming because, well, because people are stupid.

He used to see that actress, the cute little policewoman from the TV drama 'Blue Heelers', doing ads on the telly telling you how to avoid getting burgled by blokes like him. You might reckon she came across as a bit of a goose, but what she says was spot-on.

But take it from a bloke who knows. All that's required is just a bit of common sense. Like never leaving your letterbox chock-a-block with junk mail. Don't leave the curtains wide open, advertising all your nice possessions. Leave a radio or a TV on, because if a house is dead silent you always know no-one's home.

Know your neighbours, those on both sides and the people opposite. Let them know your routine and get to know theirs. Take an interest. Join Neighbourhood Watch. Fix up your back fence to make it more secure and add on a trellis too high and wobbly for anyone to easily climb.

Don't kid yourself that you can hide your money. Under the mattresses, under beds and in boxes, taped to the bottoms of drawers, stashed in the freezer. That's all old news.

Get those sensor lights that switch on when anyone comes near and invest in an alarm system: they were always a must to avoid. He'd been told you only had to snip the wires, but getting at them meant you were red-lighting yourself and there's no profit in that. He just wouldn't take the risk. There are thousands of homes in South and Port, and he'd just move down the street to another one.

Stick bars on your windows if you really want to be sure, he reckons. Citizens work hard day after day, slaving for a boss, so they can get all that nice stuff, but other people want it too. And they don't have to put in half the effort.

'There are burglars out there who do it for a job, day in, day out. Even if they've got money in their kick they still do it. Every day they clock on. The professionals, they've got a lot of contacts, soon as they've got their gear it's gone. There's a few people out there making a real good living off it. They own their houses out of burgling other people's.

'But mostly it's all young kids now – and junkies of course. A lot of people who do burgs now are supporting their drug habit. That's the majority: probably 95 per cent.

'The kids, it's for pocket money, booze, maybe a choof. They're 15 or 16 and they've got money in their pocket, to show off for all the girls, buy booze, be a big man for a while.

'But the junkies, they're right into it. They've got a lot of dash but they're stupid cunts, they're just completely dumb, they don't think. They go in to do a house and they wouldn't even check for an alarm. They wouldn't even go around and check for an alleyway where you could get in from the back – they'll go right in the front. Get a screwdriver and go bang, flip the window up and they're up and in and you've got people across the road looking through their curtains.

'A good thief, you can do the same thing out the back and no-one's seeing you. You're squared off behind the fence. But, these pricks, they're really clumsy. That's why a lot of them get pinched: they're hanging out so bad for their whack, they just get in there so they can hurry up and get to their dealers. And that means they're dangerous, you don't want to come home when one of them's in your house.

'Me, when I was doing earns on me own, when I was greedy, most times I was pilled off me head and you've got more front than Myers when you're on pills. But if someone came in I'd do the bolt, I'd try and run. But if he had've got hold of me, you'd do anything to get away because you don't want the jacks to get you.

'It never happened, I've never had a fight in someone's house. That's a bad charge, it's aggravated burglary.

'Hardly ever would I do an earn when I was straight, because I'd have too much remorse for the people. Every time I'd do the earn I'd feel sorry for them – not at the time, right? But after.

'When I'm stealing, I don't feel nothing. But when I get home and I've sold the goods, I can picture everything in that house: the family photos, everything, and I think these people worked hard for their gear and you've got cunts like me coming in and pinching it.

'But I didn't care at the time. This is after I've got the gear, I've sold it, I've had a choof, I've come down off the pills – and when you've come down off the pills that's when you feel guilty. I used to feel real guilty.

'And I used to think to myself, "If I ever win Tattslotto, I'll go to every place I've robbed and give them everything back, write 'em out a cheque." Then I'd have a few more pills and that's when all that remorse just goes out the door. Something like evil comes in and all that goes out.

'I should've stayed at school. People told me stick it out, stop wagging and I just said, "Nah." If I'd kept at school I could've had a trade, I could've been smarter up top. I'm not that good at reading and writing, so there goes an office job, any business, any job with a lot of paperwork. I can't do that. All I can do is labour – hard labour.

'Looking back now I curse myself. I'm 23 and I've done nothin', I've got nothin'. Just a beautiful little boy who better not grow up like his daddy.'

THE LONGEST REACH

By February 2001, Tim Day had finally arrived right where he wanted to be: Victoria's homicide squad. Working homicide was the reason he had become a cop, and the only reason he would willingly leave it would be to progress through the ranks.

The way Victoria's police hand out their promotions, you have to leave a detective role and return to uniform to gain a higher rank. Even if it came to that, he would always be aiming to come back here. Not that having arrived there was any time for self-satisfaction or elation, because life just goes on testing you.

What Day lacked in experience he would try to make up in enthusiasm. Yet his first case – thrown to him by Senior Sergeant Ron Iddles, head of the cold case squad – could hardly have looked less promising. Almost 20 years earlier, while Day himself had still been in primary school, a girl young enough to have been one of his classmates was murdered in her bed.

And he was not even the first young and serious try-hard homicide novice to be handed the box of shadows that comprised the case file. Bonnie Melissa Clarke's body was found by her mother as she readied herself for work a few days before Christmas 1982. Bonnie was a few weeks away from her seventh birthday. She had been sexually assaulted, smothered and stabbed.

In the years since the murder, Bonnie's mother, Marion, had been contacted several times by callers identifying themselves as police reworking the old case. But the truth was, according to the cop who led that investigation in the summer of 1982–83, she was the prime suspect. Within hours of Marion finding Bonnie's body, the cops were accusing her of killing the girl.

When police rang her over the years she reckoned that was just their way of letting her know they still had her in their sights. Marion Clarke – who had since remarried and was now Marion Wishart – would be unimpressed to hear another novice was being tested on the old file.

At first, Day left her alone. She was still officially the prime suspect.

One thing had changed from the early file that Iddles handed him. A newspaper article about unsolved murders had prompted a woman, Kylie Ward, to ring the cold case unit.

Ward had been a school friend of Bonnie's and used to visit her home in Westbourne Grove, in inner-city Northcote. Ward told police of a boarder who lived with Bonnie and her mum about the time Bonnie was killed. He hung around the two girls, gave them unwanted piggyback rides and talked about sex. He gave Ward the creeps then, and still did now, in the remembering of it.

'I can recall one time Bonnie told me that she woke up in the middle of the night and found this man in her bedroom. Just standing there,' Ward told police.

Day began by hunting down records from the crime department and homicide archives, boxes of papers from the time of his own early school reports. If the law truly had a long arm, then Day would need its longest reach.

Still, put with something from the file, Kylie Ward's account was no small thing. Another frequent visitor to the house, a male friend of Marion's who had gone to school with her, had also recalled a boarder who remarked how he 'liked kids' while Bonnie, fresh out of the bath, dried herself in front of a heater. The statement had clear sexual connotations, according to the witness.

Otherwise, all that Day had to go on was an incomplete record of the inconclusive investigation into the six-year-old's murder in Northcote 19 years before.

The name 'Mal' turned up for the boarder and after two months of sifting through old records, Day had a fuller name for him: 'Mal Clarke'. He still was reluctant to go to Marion, Bonnie's mother. Unlike the original investigators, he did not think she was responsible for Bonnie's murder, but she was technically still a suspect, and there had to be some reason the earlier investigation targeted her.

He ran the name Mal Clarke, with and without an 'e', through the LEAP police files computer. Nothing turned up. The name did not correspond with anyone of the right age and history to consider seriously as a suspect. The one thing he knew about Mal Clarke was that Marion had described him as a movie projectionist, with Greater Union Cinemas in central Melbourne, at the time he lived at Westbourne Grove.

It was unclear to Day whether the mystery boarder, Mal Clarke, had ever been eliminated from the investigation.

There was simply no note of it. It appeared that of 15 witnesses, some were eliminated, others not.

At least one witness, John Hawker, Marion's student friend who reported Mal Clarke's comments about Bonnie as she dried herself in front of the heater, had suggested Clarke be looked at for the crime. That was in September 1983.

The lead investigator from the first inquiry, Eric Lilley, had since died but Day tracked down another of the crew who could not recall if a Mal Clarke had ever been considered a suspect. In a progress report in March 2001, Day noted that Mal Clarke 'was either overlooked or not adequately eliminated from the initial inquiry'.

Day headed off to the Criminal Records Branch to laboriously sift through hundreds of criminal dockets to find anything on Mal Clarke. The breakthrough came late at night.

'While sitting up there one night and going through hundreds of these old dockets I came across a Joe Clarke. The link was made when I saw the words "assistant projectionist",' Day later recalled.

'At that stage I knew that "Mal" was an assistant projectionist. Marion had said that Mal Clarke was a projectionist at a city theatre. Then I started looking at Joe Clarke.'

Through his old criminal dockets Joe Clarke stepped out of the shadows and into the light: a socially awkward, overweight slob with a distinctive, untamed head of thick, coarse hair.

Day found a conviction for rape of a woman, a young mother who lived next to a Joe Clarke in West Brunswick, an inner northern suburb close to Northcote. The rape was at knifepoint. This Joe Clarke had crept into the woman's house as she slept, and while her husband was on a night shift. He knew the husband, knew his routine, and knew the house since his flat overlooked it.

He stabbed the woman in the leg and threatened to kill her five-year-old daughter if she resisted him. He raped and tormented her over hours. She stayed strong enough to endure him, and in the darkness made mental notes of her attacker.

Day reported what he had found to Iddles, and then went back to old murder books with Joe Clarke in mind.

Another hit. A Joe Clarke was on record for the mutilation killing of a 22-year-old woman, Theresa Verity Crowe, at Prahran in June 1980. Joe Clarke had known Crowe, who was a regular at prominent Melbourne discos. Her friends remembered him as a loner, on the fringe of their group, who drank too much and who seemed to be pitied by Theresa. He had been to her flat, in a loft above busy Chapel Street, several times before the night of her murder. His actual conviction was manslaughter. He claimed she died accidentally, smothered by his bulk during consensual sex.

The mutilation, slashing her body from the throat to the groin, he said, was his attempt to put the police off his trail. He succeeded. For days after her body was found the papers were full of talk of a satanic ritual killing.

As Day delved deeper into Joe Clarke's record, Mal and Joe began to look like one man. Day went back to Kylie Ward with a photoboard of 12 mugshots. Among them was a picture of Malcolm Clarke, aged 28. Ward readily picked out her 'creepy boarder'.

In between Joe Clarke's 1980 and 1983 priors was the murder of Bonnie Clarke, living with her mother in Northcote. Day's initial excitement cooled. How could this Joe Clarke be responsible for Bonnie's murder in December 1982, if he had been convicted of the Crowe killing 30 months before? There were more questions than answers, but at least his inquiries had somewhere to go. He called up the files on Crowe and the West Brunswick rape.

'It's then I find he was never caught for Crowe until he was caught for the rape in August 1983,' Day says. That put Clarke firmly in the frame.

Bonnie was killed some time after 12.30 am on 21 December 1982. She was digitally raped and suffocated. There was no semen present and her body appeared to have been wiped down. When found, Bonnie's bedclothes were pulled over her naked body and there was a stab wound in her chest. Her bloodied pyjamas were stuffed between her bed and the wall.

There was no sign of forced entry. Police noted that, while the back door was unlocked to allow two dogs in the house access to the rear yard, the house was a minefield for unwary intruders who, to enter through the back door, would have to negotiate hanging baskets and a beaded curtain, which was noisy when disturbed. Also, the dogs, one of which was habitually noisy with strangers, had not barked.

Day spent some time analysing the Joe Clarke and Bonnie Clarke crime scenes. Joe or Mal Clarke as he was variously known, had known all three victims as either a friend, a neighbour or as a member of the same household. He was familiar with their homes. Each victim had been sexually assaulted. While Crowe and the rape victim each had bite marks on their bodies and Bonnie Clarke did not, all three victims suffered some form of knife wound.

And each crime scene was cleaned up in some way afterwards. In the case of the West Brunswick rape, Joe Clarke wiped the floorboards where he had crept on all fours into his victim's bedroom. Inside Theresa Crowe's loft, he wiped clean the coffee cups they had used. And Bonnie Clarke's body was wiped down.

Greater Union cinema's timesheets showed Mal Clarke worked day shift on the day of Bonnie's death. It was now late April 2001, a couple of months into the reinvestigation. Day now knew the mystery boarder Mal Clarke was capable of killing, and he factored in also that he had not only the ability to have committed the murder, but the opportunity.

Forensic science failed the first police inquiry that could have led detectives to the serial offender who was Malcolm Joseph Thomas Clarke. A medical examiner found Theresa Crowe had been dead for 12 to 15 hours before she was found, on 25 June 1980.

As he was known to Crowe's friends, Clarke was interviewed by police, but he had an alibi for the period in which the investigators were told she was killed. There was no need to put any pressure on him. Satanic ritual or not, he was out of the frame.

But Theresa Crowe had in fact been dead for five days before she was found, not 15 hours.

The bitter winter cold combined with her unheated apartment acted like a refrigerator, slowing her body's decomposition, confusing the pathologist and derailing the investigation. The truth was that Clarke's alibi counted for nothing.

Two-and-a-half years later two cops from Brunswick Criminal Investigation Bureau persisted in trying to rouse Clarke from his flat in South Daly Street. At first, it was a routine call. Constables Wayne McDonald and Mark Harris were responding to the rape of a woman in her home.

Clarke was not home the first few times they visited, but they kept going back, doing the sort of laborious checking that is so much of police work.

Wayne McDonald recalled that the rapist had subjected the woman to great degradation over hours, but she talked to him and cajoled him in order to stay alive and to protect her daughter, whom Clarke had threatened to kill.

'It's pitch-black. She can't see him … she is actually feeling his hair; coarse and sandy was how she described it,' McDonald said.

Finally, on one of several return visits, Clarke responded to the knock on the door. The moment McDonald and Harris saw him they both felt strongly suspicious. It was his hair, for a start, and then his awkward manner, that alerted them, McDonald recalled.

That first visit, they just talked, but McDonald and Harris were soon back once more, with a search warrant. If Clarke had been worried by their first questioning of him, he had not acted on his fears. In a laundry basket they found his still-bloodstained clothing from the rape next door.

He admitted the rape once he was confronted with the evidence against him. But there was much more.

While searching the flat, McDonald and Harris found a scrapbook that prompted them to notify homicide to take a look at their rapist. In the scrapbook the searchers had found press clippings about the then three-year-old murder of Theresa Crowe. It was all there. The stark black headlines about satanic killers, the stories about the bright, young woman who danced all night at Chasers and lived in an exotic loft apartment.

Grilled by the crew that investigated her murder, Clarke also gave himself up on the killing of Theresa Crowe, although he claimed it was accidental and he dismissed the mutilation as a device to put police off the track. He was convicted of manslaughter and for that, and the Brunswick assault and rape, sentenced to 11 years' jail. He was, however, paroled in 1992.

But the Brunswick cops had found more odd things in Clarke's flat. There was children's clothing for a start. Out of place in the home of a young single man. Most telling of all, McDonald and Harris found a greeting card addressed to Bonnie Clarke, the little girl killed seven months earlier and one suburb away.

There was only so much the Brunswick officers could do. They had alerted homicide to the evidence about Theresa Crowe, and they did the same with the link to Bonnie Clarke. For now it would come to nothing.

'So back we went to the original crew on Bonnie Clarke. We pushed it and pushed it. We got the opinion back [that] they had formed the view of the mum being involved,' McDonald said.

The original Bonnie Clarke inquiry foundered on the lead investigator's belief, formed early on, that Bonnie's mother was responsible for her death.

Detective Senior Sergeant Eric Lilley, who had worked on the case originally, was struck by the likelihood that the killer was very familiar with the house, and perhaps most significantly, that neither dog had barked when the killing was done.

When Lilley looked at Marion Clarke he saw a woman recently separated from the father of her child. He saw a single mother living in a single-fronted weatherboard in a working-class suburb that had been on the decline for decades. He saw a woman alone who had been phoning a parents' helpline. He saw a woman under pressure.

He accused her of being mentally unstable, of being violent towards Bonnie and, finally, of murdering her. 'He made me feel: there's no sperm, so there's no male involved. You are it,' Marion recalled.

Lilley did interview Clarke, in September 1983, after he had been picked up for the rape and manslaughter, but this time Clarke did not roll over.

The view that Marion was responsible was formed long before that interview. A journalist inquiring about the case in February 1983 – less than two months after Bonnie's murder – was told there was no need for publicity because by then police knew who was responsible.

The greeting card to Bonnie meant nothing in 1983, but in 2001 it mattered greatly to Tim Day.

He was convinced Clarke was the offender. McDonald, who was still in the job, agreed. And Day had found nothing to implicate Marion. He decided to talk to her, but she was wary and untrusting. He looked to her like just another cop sniffing around an old case that had brought her nothing but pain and suspicion.

Marion was technically still a suspect, but she was formally eliminated when she passed a polygraph test in September 2001.

Mal Clarke, or Joe as he preferred to be known, only ever gave away as much as he needed to. Interviewed by a psychologist who was preparing a report for his defence lawyer at the Crowe prosecution, Clarke hid the fact that he had moved out from home in early 1982 and lived with Marion Clarke and her daughter Bonnie in Westbourne Grove, Northcote, for nine months. Clarke claimed he lived at home until he moved into the West Brunswick flat from which he had observed the woman he raped.

He was the eldest of five children. He had learning problems and attended a special school for several years. His father regarded him as uncontrollable, but his parents had other problems to deal with. One of Clarke's sisters was physically handicapped, another had Down's syndrome.

When he was not working he would wander the streets on his own. The psychologist's report to the Supreme Court described him as of dull-to-normal intelligence, socially inept and isolated, and severely and chronically maladjusted.

He was unable to form and maintain 'appropriate relationships', it said. He had difficulty with sexual relationships and was immature. While physically able, it concluded Clarke had a personality disorder that prevented him forming any real attachments.

He had no close friends and by his late 20s had yet to have a girlfriend. He was severely and chronically maladjusted. For recreation, he had a model train set.

By 2001 his interest in the model train sets had turned into an obsession with the tourist steam train, Puffing Billy, which ran through the Dandenong Ranges east of Melbourne. Almost 10 years out of jail, he had held a series of jobs as a carer in homes for the elderly, and had become a volunteer guard for Puffing Billy's runs through the dripping fern gullies and eucalypt-scented forests of the Ranges.

His fascination with trains had led to his first criminal conviction back in June 1972, when as an 18-year-old he illegally shunted a train through the railyards. His passion for trains never left him, but he kept away from alcohol which, he had learnt, always drew him into trouble. And he had a girlfriend, Lyn, a grey-haired woman whose mother he had nursed for a time. They were planning to marry. His mates – acquaintances really, for Clarke had retained his social awkwardness – were fellow train buffs.

After Kylie Ward's phone call to Iddles, and Day's probing of the case, a new man came into Clarke's circle and befriended him. Over time they did become close mates in a way that was unusual for Clarke, and they spent a bit of time together. This bloke did not look or speak the least bit like you might imagine an undercover cop would.

Which showed how good he was.

Slowly, the undercover cop worked around to topics like sex and children, the cleaning of bodies – which Clarke had done as an aged care worker – testing out his man. Clarke had no idea he was dealing with a police officer.

One night when Clarke returned home Lyn told him that a Detective Senior Sergeant Ron Iddles had dropped by, left his card and said something about coming back and wanting a DNA sample from Clarke.

It was to do with the murder of Bonnie Clarke, back in 1982, and Iddles was checking up on everyone who had boarded at the Westbourne Grove house. Clarke was not to know he was the first and last boarder that Marion Clarke took in.

Lyn handed him Iddles' card and he wondered about the mystery of DNA analysis and what it might find. There had been an article in the paper just the other day about how old murders could be solved with new scientific techniques. He hardly gave it a thought at the time.

Had this moment arrived even four months ago, Malcolm Clarke would not have had the first notion of how to respond. Iddles he had never heard of, but this could not be good news. Now at least, Clarke was connected, hooked up with someone who could help him. His new mate would have an idea.

His new mate already had introduced Clarke to a new world of friends and money. 'Tel', which was what he called himself, was a crook and, he and Clarke had done a few jobs. Nothing very dangerous, and nothing that Clarke was much good at either, but it was clear Tel knew people in crime.

As far as Clarke could see, Tel was into blackmail and standover tactics. Together they picked up takings from a few brothels, and one time, with some other mates of Tel's, they had burgled a factory, hauling out a safe. Clarke just had to stand lookout. It was not difficult, but the lifelong loner felt he was accepted by these blokes, and some real and easy money was in the offing.

It had seemed too good to be true. Now, this Iddles was on about a 20-year-old murder. Tel had often said that when he was in trouble he just had to tell his boss, and it would be fixed. Everything Tel had said so far had worked out, and he had often said if Clarke found trouble then he would have to come clean for it to be sorted out. Give the problem to Tel's boss, and have it out of the way.

Now at least, if he was going to panic he had someone to go to. And when he panicked, the undercover cop was ready. And so was a hidden video camera to capture the conversation.

Just as Clarke had withheld as much as he could from the psychologist who interviewed him over the death of Theresa Crowe, so he skirted around Bonnie's death. Finally though, in talk punctuated by long silences, he gave himself up to a confession.

'I was pissed … As drunk as a skunk,' he offered as the past ran screaming towards him.

'I went through the back lane. Over the fence. Back door was unlocked. Through the door. Through the kitchen into Bonnie's room. Bonnie's [night] light was on. She had a small dog [that] was up on her bed.

'I don't know what killed her, probably shock.

'She was just a beautiful little girl. A little girl that [sic] was really lovely.'

In the back pocket of his pants, he had a Staysharp knife in its plastic sharpening scabbard.

Later, he made another start to put it all together, while the video camera secretly and silently captured his confession. 'Fucking 20 years I have lived with this,' he said. 'It was an accident that she died. I had a fair bit to drink that night, and um, I think I went in and, um, played with Bonnie … I was quite pissed … I think she wanted to scream or something and I covered her head. And I probably had a knife with me. I don't know. I was that fucking drunk. There was no struggle, which I thought someone … would struggle, but she did not struggle. One hand came up when I put [the pillow] over her face. Her hand came up, then it just dropped.' Horribly, he mimes this last gesture of the little girl's hand falling by her bed.

There was much more to his confession, about how he licked his finger before assaulting Bonnie, and this had played on his mind as a possible DNA source that Iddles might be on about, because he also told his listener that he did not 'blow' that night.

But in any event, he had crossed a line that could not be uncrossed. And with the undercover admissions complete, he was told there was another interview straight after. The formal one, with Tim Day.

Before this, he rang his de facto wife. He was for the moment mentally broken and resigned to his fate. 'I will not be home … That's right, I said I won't be home … I am at St Kilda Road. I am being charged with the murder of Bonnie … would you mind packing up my belongings for Puffing Billy?'

Tim Day said the case would not have been solved without the extraordinary bravery of some of the people whose lives were fractured by Clarke. While the key to connecting him to the crime were the words 'assistant projectionist', it was the resilience and bravery of the 1983 rape victim who contrived to survive the attack that enabled her attacker's prosecution, said Day.

'Without Wayne McDonald and Mark Harris' arrest of him in relation to the rape, the Crowe matter may have gone unsolved forever, and likewise Bonnie Clarke,' he said.

Day praised Bonnie's mother. 'Marion Wishart showed a lot of faith in us. She had to go back into the abyss even after living with the burden and stigma of accusation. That took a lot of courage.'

In June 2004, when Clarke's jury came back with a guilty verdict, Wayne McDonald was not there to see it happen. He was out in the eastern suburbs on booze bus duty. He still wonders what the card to Bonnie Clarke was about: 'Maybe it was remorse. Maybe it was done prior to the murder,' he said. 'It was just something that was there that led to a very strong conviction that he was involved.'

Mal Clarke took it badly. As the judge thanked the jury for their efforts, Clarke sat in the dock silently mouthing angry abuse at Day and his undercover companion. It was probably the undercover who was the real target of Clarke's mute diatribe.

The last anyone in court noticed of Clarke was his face contorted with scorn, or bitterness, or maybe betrayal.

Marion Wishart was there to see justice for her little girl, but the trial had taken an enormous toll. She had appeared to grow perceptibly older by the day, never more so than when the videotaped confession was replayed.

Now, she was drained. Emotionally wrung out. There was nothing to celebrate, just the possibility of a life without suspicion, and the chance to enjoy the memories of her daughter.

LAW OF THE LAND

Bluetongues. That's what they call them up this way, which is the dusty-stubble grain country around Hopetoun in north-west Victoria. Local young bucks, in their late teens and early 20s, sowing their oats and on the tear. Harmless, mostly.

Tim McDonald doesn't know where the name came from but there's a trio of bluetongues in his court this morning and he's about to take a little stick to them.

Nathan, Shane and Andrew are boys out of Berriwillock, a blink-and-miss-it on the Calder Highway, 60-something kilometres to the east. Today they're standing, shuffling their feet and shamefaced, fronting the once-every-two-months sitting of McDonald's Hopetoun Magistrates Court on charges of theft.

Saturday night a few weeks back, the three paid a visit to a young woman's home in Sea Lake. She wasn't there but the door was open, so they decided on a quick rummage through her scanties drawer, souveniring a couple of lacy bras and several G-string panties. They were seen leaving the premises, says police prosecutor Russell 'Bluey' Reid, wearing the aforesaid garments over their own clothes.

Perhaps unnecessarily, he adds that they had all been drinking.

Their excuses, he tells the court, went like this:

Shane: 'Drinking.'

Andrew: 'Just stupid, I suppose. On the piss.'

And Nathan, burly, brown-tanned and gormless-looking: 'I don't remember being there.'

McDonald, in bow tie and dark double-breasted suit, leans forward in his high-backed chair and pulls on the required air of po-faced severity. But behind the wire-rimmed glasses, his eyes are twinkling.

He asks: 'How often do you cross-dress?'

'Not too often,' answers one.

'Hang on. That implies you've done it before.'

'Well, yeah. At football functions and that.'

'Hmmmm,' says the magistrate. 'Do you want to see a psychologist?'

The Kalkee Road runs close to due north and near enough to dead straight out of Horsham through the flat, yellow–brown heart of the Wimmera.

It is a glorious blue and sunny morning with just enough warm breeze to pull the last of the moisture from the wheat. Higher, a stronger wind tugs wispy pony-tails out of the few lonely clouds. Tim McDonald blows an early-summer cold into a succession of tissues and points his department-issue Berlina through the centre of his magisterial patch.

McDonald, 55, is one of 17 circuit magistrates delivering travelling justice to country Victoria. His Worship's is a sprawling jurisdiction, spread over something like 40,000 square kilometres, from Ararat west through the Grampians to the South Australian border; north to the Big Desert; east through Wyperfield and Rainbow to the Calder; and south to Ararat again through St Arnaud.

He also acts as coroner and for the Victorian Civil and Administrative Tribunal and alternates courtrooms between Edenhope, Stawell, Horsham, Hopetoun, St Arnaud, Ararat and Nhill, burning up about 60,000 kilometres of bitumen and gravel track every year.

But he and his circuit magistrate colleagues now run their roadshow to a mere remnant of the state's historic network of country courthouses.

Until 1963, there were 230 courts statewide. A decade later there were 211. Now, following rationalisation under the Courts Management Change Program in the mid-1980s, there are only 54.

State Attorney-General Rob Hulls, who as a solicitor in Queensland for the Aboriginal Legal Service used to do similar court runs through the Gulf of Carpentaria, has given a commitment that there will be no more closures. Regional and rural communities, he says, need to see justice in their midst and working in their communities.

'The courthouse is not only a place where justice is dispensed when the court is physically sitting, but it's a place where in the past people have been able to go to get advice and often can be seen as a meeting place. And it's a symbol. It's a symbol that justice will be delivered for and on behalf of that local community. Our justice system belongs to the people so it's vitally important that our justice system goes out to the people.'

So today, justice in the form of Tim McDonald is going, via the Kalkee Road back route, to the 800 people of Hopetoun, at the bottom edge of the Mallee, 390 kilometres from Melbourne.

And, in a sense, the magistrate is going home. He was born there in 1947 at the Hopetoun Bush Nursing Hospital. His grandfather ran the Commonwealth Oil Refinery depot and a skin store at Beulah, 25 kilometres south, and his mother's people had a wheat and sheep property at Rosebery East.

Young Tim might have been a bluetongue too, but for the nomadic nature of his father's job with the State Savings Bank. When he was six months old the family moved to a branch at Terang and 12 years later to Warrnambool. Three years later, they went back to Hopetoun but Tim was sent to board at Monivae College, half the state away in Hamilton. And from there to Melbourne where he followed his father into the SSB.

But the local connection remained and smoothed his way when he returned as a newly-appointed magistrate in 1988.

'It's what made it a lot easier for me,' he says. 'People knew I came from hereabouts so I was accepted. In the bush, if you're not born there you're a bloody ring-in. I might have been gone 40-odd years, but I was still classified as a local.'

So today he runs the last 60 kilometres up the Henty Highway from Warracknabeal on cruise control, pointing out the local sights: Batchica, Lah and Galaquil, railway siding silos passing for towns; the tree line marking Yarriambiack Creek to the left; the old swimming hole at Brim; a memorial plaque that's about all that's left of the hamlet of Goyura.

But then, nothing lasts forever. 'Aw, hell,' he groans, indicating a mound of grey weatherboards and roofing tin in the weeds by the side of the road in Beulah. 'That's where me dad used to live.'

In the eight weeks since he last passed through, someone has knocked over the old family home.

Some days you just can't get respect. The magistrate's chair in Horsham court is a huge, mattress-fat, swivelling monster, jammed between the lip of his desk and a rear wall of off-white tiles that are like something from a railway station toilet. Each sitting, His Worship must carefully shoe-horn his admittedly comfortable frame into the thing.

Luckily, he doesn't take himself too seriously. On his office wall next door, he keeps a photograph of graffiti from the police cells in which a local recalcitrant laments the amount of time he's been locked inside. Worse, the crook complains, he now has to front 'that fat cunt Tim McDonald'.

(It wasn't always this way, Mr McDonald says later. Back in the early 1980s, when he was an investigating solicitor with the Costigan Royal Commission into the painters and dockers union, he took up jogging and eventually was fit enough to run from his home in Nunawading to work in South Melbourne. 'Now I couldn't run a tap,' he laughs. 'Couldn't, as they say, run water downhill.')

The courtroom is in utilitarian milk-chocolate brick, with grey carpet and four rows of uncomfortable grey, moulded-plastic seats for the public. The bench is veneer, fronted by a bar table and a confusion of microphones, printers and computer gear. The clerk's desk is decorated with a couple of A3 calendars, colour-coded to the courts of the circuit: orange for Edenhope, yellow for Stawell, purple for Nhill.

It is another adjournment and the room is empty but for a couple of bored local paper reporters. One complains how the day is dragging: 'I wish he'd move it along. I was hoping to get in some golf this arvo.'

Outside, a client, fined earlier, pursues a similar theme but from the opposite direction. 'Bloody McDonald. He's trying to whip through it all before lunch so he can piss off and play golf.'

It's been one of those days. Family law orders and breaches; exceed blood-alcohol counts; drunk and disorderly; speeding offences; contest mentions; an application for a firearms permit; driving an unregistered vehicle. A husband who breached an intervention order three times – on the same day it was granted. A young bloke picked up for drink-driving in his own driveway. A Murtoa barmaid done for exceeding .05 who says she only had the one drink – 'I always have a can on the way home from shopping.'

'You must have had a bellyful the night before,' says McDonald.

'Well yeah,' she admits. 'A bottle of wine and 10 cans.'

A young couple front on a family matter. She wears a long purple, hippie-ish dress and he is in tight black jeans, black T-shirt with the sleeves rolled up and motorbike boots. They carry a couple of squirming, barefooted toddlers. 'You can put the kids down,' says McDonald. 'Just let them play, they'll be right.'

The mum raises a doubting eyebrow. 'Are you serious?'

And now there's Jeremy, who took a few too many drinks, broke a shop window and is pleading guilty to charges of D&D and drinking in a public place. He is big, burly and boofheaded, probably in his late teens, but with the vacant face of a sulky 14-year-old. The few answers he gives are in grunts and monosyllables.

Says he drinks most weekends. Could probably handle a slab without getting legless. He's unemployed but can afford the grog because his mum gives him an allowance of about $80 a week.

The magistrate is incredulous: 'Eighty!!?'

A local solicitor rises to assist. He knows Jeremy, and explains that he is the beneficiary of a trust on behalf of his late father, a successful farmer and property owner, and as such is ineligible for the dole.

Mr McDonald is less than impressed: 'People before you have slaved and worked their guts out to get this property and to build it up into a good farm, and what are you doing with it?'

'I dunno.'

'Well, I do and other people do. It's … it's going up against a wall.'

The magistrate is 'a spade's a spade sort of bloke', a copper notes a few days later. 'People around here appreciate that sort of thing.'

If there is such a thing, Tim McDonald could perhaps best be described as an easy-going enthusiast. At the lower end of average height, with a neatly clipped near-white moustache and well-salted, rapidly thinning hair, he is earthy, with a robust sense of humour and a concussive, hair-trigger laugh. There's a tendency to take the mickey, but balanced with self-deprecation.

His job, he says one night, is hardly rocket science. 'Common sense. That's really all magistrating is … It's about having a sense of common sense.'

Despite the rising and the bowing and Your Worship-ing, 'I've never felt important. I know it's an important job, but I've never felt important in myself.'

Deep down, he suspects, what a good magistrate most needs is a fair bit of been there, done that. 'I'm a person who's been through life with, um, what can I say, "considerable experiences". It's an asset. I think it would be very difficult to do my job if you'd been whiter than white all your life.

'I think I bring living experiences and a work history which has given me some knowledge about how people ought to be dealt with. Thirty-five years in the courts, that gives you a bit of experience. I mean, if you've been chopping trees for 35 years you ought to know which way to chop a bloody tree and not have it fall on you.'

It was a circuitous route to get there. About 1966, after a couple of years at the bank, he met some blokes in a pub one lunchtime. They said they worked in the courts. When he went back that afternoon they were still there. 'I said, "Jeez, you blokes have got a good job." And about a month later I'm working as a clerk of courts.'

He started at the old gothic City Court in Russell Street and went from there to the County Court as a bench clerk for the sessions judges and then, after a year or two, to Warrnambool. Never a great student – it took two attempts to get his leaving certificate, although he made the First 18 – he says he staggered for years through his Clerk of Courts exams and a Stipendiary Magistrates course at Melbourne University, before eventually getting his law degree.

He became a solicitor in 1982 and joined the Costigan Royal Commission, worked in the Coroner's Court and Crimes Compensation Tribunal and in 1985 became the first registrar with the new Administrative Appeals Tribunal. In early 1988 he was appointed a magistrate and, with his wife Kate and two children, moved to Horsham.

For him, it was a return home, but Kate, a librarian at Horsham College, found it harder at first. 'Here, people in the street, total strangers, would say hello and I found that very unusual. I wasn't used to it, you just didn't do that in the city,' she says. 'But it all sort of fell into place. Now I do it myself.'

Being a magistrate – like a policeman or politician – in a small town can also mean living in a fishbowl. The McDonalds' retreat is a sprawling home they are renovating on a couple of hectares in the relative seclusion of Halls Gap in the Grampians, but even there they keep pretty much to themselves. 'We're not in the social circle,' says Kate. 'But you do feel people watching you at times, when you're out, to see how much you drink or whatever.'

'It's important to keep yourself as clean as you can,' says her husband, who can also immerse himself in the Mount Difficult golf course he and other locals have carved out of farmland a few kilometres north of town, with its tin shearing-shed clubhouse and series of soft, steamy hazards left by the resident emu troupe.

'You're in the backblocks out here. You've got to go a long, long way to catch a tram.' He says it with utter approval, sweeping an arm across 180 degrees of cinemascopic early-evening horizon.

The Berlina is running dead west and beeline-straight through a grid of three-chain farm tracks. Ahead is the parched bed of Lake Albacutya; to the north the Mallee scrub and heath 'emptiness' of the Big Desert; and to the south the white-topped sandhills surrounding Lake Hindmarsh.

It has been a long, sometimes frustrating, bluetongue-infested day at Hopetoun. The last case, a contest hearing involving five boys charged with theft, criminal damage and driving offences after a late-night escapade through the Wyperfeld National Park, dragged out all afternoon through adjournments, negotiations, argument and no-case submissions. A final testy exchange with an argumentative solicitor closed the hearing on a bad note.

But all this space is a tonic. Ahead is another 250 kilometres through Rainbow, Jeparit, Nhill and the Little Desert, through Edenhope and Wrattonbully to Penola, just across the South Australian border, where he's spending the night.

The drive doesn't faze him; he simply soaks in the scenery as it evolves from wheatfield through scrub cypress and broombrush, bulloak and melaleuca into red gum forest and sweeping Coonawarra vineyards. He points out wedgetails, shinglebacks, wallabies, grass parrots and black cockatoos. He is an evangelist for the big country and everything in it.

It's a standing gag among his staff – 'Did he have you bird-watching?' asks his clerk – but a cause of some concern to his wife.

'I do worry about all the driving,' says Kate. 'I know there are times when Tim will be out there looking at trees or tractors or birds. You can be distracted out there.'

McDonald downplays any risk. He might average 1000 or 1200 kilometres a working week, but rationalises it as only a couple of hundred a day. The philosophy behind the provision of country courts is that no-one should be more than 100 kilometres from the nearest courtroom – and in his patch few would be further than 50 kilometres away.

'So it's not as bad as it seems,' he says. 'Those people who live in those small towns, all they have to do is travel for half an hour and they're in court. There are not many people in the city who spend less than half an hour getting to court. It's distance but not time. It's pretty much the same story for me. And put it this way, it's easy driving. You're not stopping for traffic lights, dodging trams and pedestrians. It's pleasant driving. And it's through all this beautiful bush. You've got to love it.'

Michael is waiting for his ride. He sits at the back of the Edenhope shire offices with his skinny legs stretched out in front of him, softly whispering to his sister and a mate. He's going away for a while, but seems remarkably sanguine about it. Another tough break in a life of them.

And he's the only one the magistrate has slotted all week.

He is 33, small, bird-thin, with long, greasy hair pulled back in a pony-tail; spidery tattoos run down his arms to his bony wrists. A vineyard labourer, he wears a brown suede vest, black jeans with a fat silver chain running from belt to back pocket and filthy work boots.

A few weeks back the local coppers found him at the wheel of his car, obviously intoxicated. Asked to take a breath test, he said something along the lines of 'I'm not taking no fuckin' breath test'. Asked why, he said: "Cos I don't fuckin' haffta.'

It was his sixth offence involving drink-driving, so his licence is gone for eight years, he's off to jail for two months and he's waiting for a policeman to drive him there.

Every eight weeks the shire offices' council room doubles as Edenhope Court. It is modern and airy, with the new shire crest of dancing brolgas pressed in brass into one wall. The participants sit, like dinner guests, around the long oval of an impressive 12-seater red gum table. As in many small towns the original courthouse has been given up to other uses.

Three days ago McDonald sat at Stawell Court, 160 kilometres and an era away. The courthouse there is an imposing gold era edifice in sandstone: balconied, arched and surrounded in red wrought iron. Its bench sits beneath an ornate, carved wooden canopy. Edenhope's only connection with history is an Australiana-themed plaque honouring the brave men of Kowree Shire who 'answered their country's call in the Great European War' of 1914–18.

What they do have in common is that at least 80 per cent of offences involve alcohol. Of the eight cases at Edenhope today, all but one are due to drinking.

On the long drive home, Mr McDonald ponders whether crime patterns are different in the country from the city and whether the nature of crime has changed in the 13 years he has been driving the circuit. 'Crime hasn't changed,' he decides. 'Kids will get into trouble. So-called adults will get into trouble. It's what causes them to get into trouble now. It's the base cause, that's all. Now, it's more often to do with gambling, more often to do with drugs. But most of all it's still alcohol.'

And poverty? 'I don't know about that. Why are they broke? They're on the punt, they're buying drugs, buying alcohol. That's why. They're too often pissed, doing dope and they can't get a job. Or if they've got one, they're punting it all. That's poverty, yeah I accept that.'

And it's a vicious cycle, he says. In his Family Court he sees the Department of Human Services bringing protection applications on behalf of children. Years later in his Children's Court he sees the same children facing criminal charges.

'Is it the kid's fault? I don't know. But you have to ask, what hope have some of them got?'

Not far up the road Michael is behind the cage in the back of a police car, heading for a cell.

The bloke who sent him there says sentencing, and especially jailing, people is the most important and difficult part of his job 'because you are dealing with people's lives and in many cases not just their lives, but their families' lives'.

'If you ask if it weighs on me, yes it does. But I've got a bad memory, I can walk out of that court and remember everything that's gone on. But in two days' time it'll be gone. I think subconsciously you do that. You get on with it.

'A great magistrate and a great mate, Brian Cosgriff, once told me: "When you retire, you'll feel a great weight come off your shoulders." It might be true.

'But at the moment I don't know that I even feel a weight there.'

CHASIN' - STORIES FROM THE HEROIN PLAGUE

3: The high life

This is the score at Box Hill. You step straight off the train and go up into the shopping centre just past Maccas. If you're really hanging out – which is most times – you'll do a hard left out through the automatic doors and into the plaza.

Less often you might take a more circuitous route, wandering round past Pete And Rosie's, Cheesecake Heaven and the Nutshack then out through the next set of doors near Healthy Appetite. Heading out to feed your own unhealthy one.

You catch the eye of the Asian guys by the fountain or squatting by Timezone. (You don't trust the skip dealers, because, like you, they're junkies supporting a habit, and half the time you'll get ripped off.)

Anyway, one of them will give you a look, maybe a little whistle. So you turn around and follow them – not too close – and they'll go out the other end of the plaza near the needle exchange. You might want to duck through the supermarket, dive into a shop, because that's where you'll lose the UCs: the undercover coppers.

Come out, and jump into a car for a quick run around the block, or perhaps they'll do the deal right there and disappear. And so do you: back on the train or off to a mate's flat that doubles as a shooting gallery. If you're really hanging you'll nick down the Box Hill gardens to whack up under a tree. And you're sweet, for one more day.

Frank and Tiana, 18- and 19-year-olds going nowhere, work the Ringwood line nearly every day, scoring just enough heroin to get by and then a little bit more to deal and make their money back. They boast they've been off the stuff for four days: 'Except we had a little tiny taste yesterday, like a real small one.'

This afternoon, in return for a freebie, they've helped Adam and Emily buy a quarter-gram down by Nunawading station. Only took five or 10 minutes to do the business, but it's just a little too fraught out there in the open. They'd much rather be at Box Hill, where you can blend in and out of the crowd – and where there's both the supply and the demand.

For decades Melbourne's Box Hill has suffered the reputation of the sober-sided suburb. Epicentre of the inner-eastern dry belt, it has remained prim, parched and prohibitionist since the Local Option vote of 1920 banned licensed premises from operating within its borders. Alcoholically at least, it is a place of happy abstention.

But down in the suburb's CBD, in a brick strip between the Box Hill Central and Whitehorse Plaza shopping centres, you can buy a cap of heroin for $20. If you are known to the dealer you might haggle him down to $15. And, if you're just starting out, a likely prospect, you might even pick up a hit for next to nothing.

Recently a young man was taken to Box Hill Hospital, comatose and diagnosed as brain dead after a massive overdose. 'His partner told us that they'd bought that heroin supply that put him down for $5 a cap,' says local ambulance paramedic Steve Wood. 'Five lousy bucks.'

Local youth and drug workers say that despite the suburb's genteel image, Box Hill ranks alongside Springvale, Fitzroy, Footscray and Dandenong as one of the four or five biggest heroin-dealing centres in Melbourne.

'It's a major battle all the time to convince people that there's a heroin problem over this side,' says Peter Nixon, youth worker with Open Family. 'In the east we've got just as many hassles as Broadmeadows or Footscray or whatever.'

Box Hill police Senior Sergeant Laurie Wilkes disputes the picture of the suburb as a heroin hot spot. 'I asked the drug taskforce people last year how we rated against those other places and they said we were well down the scale,' he says. But he admits the area around Box Hill Central has a long-standing problem with dealing and may now be going through another upsurge.

In November 1996, in response to a rash of street-level drug offences, a Victoria Police taskforce launched a 12-month crackdown on dealers and users in the area. 'By and large, that special operation was a success and really stood on that area for some time,' says Senior Sergeant Wilkes. 'But I have noticed that some of the people who were charged originally now seem to be drifting back again.'

Rachel Burns, co-ordinator of the Youth Adult Bureau in Nunawading, says the main effect of the crackdown was simply to move the problem elsewhere: 'What the police and all the workers in the area realise is it just gets moved up the train line. As Box Hill was getting cleaned up and the drugs pushed out, suddenly there was a problem in Mitcham, in Ringwood or Nunawading.'

Ironically, the things that make Box Hill Central work so well as a transport and shopping hub are the same things that make it hard to control drug trafficking there.

A big suburban shopping mall sandwiched between a railway station and a bus interchange, it is Melbourne's second biggest transport hub after Flinders Street Station. About 47,000 people live in the suburb but up to 30,000 pass through the complex every day.

'It's quite unique,' says Peter Nixon. 'Trains underneath, buses on top, transport in and out. Two different modes of easy access and people hanging around to do deals. You can be in and out of the centre in 10 minutes and have scored or dealt in the meantime.'

The plaza between the complex was designed as a meeting place, somewhere to soak up the sun between shopping trips. But with easy access – and escape – from three directions and the anonymity offered by the crowds, it has attractions for street-level heroin dealer and buyer.

There is also a large Asian population trading on Maroondah Highway, Station Street and Carrington Road, leading to talk of triad and Vietnamese dominance of the heroin trade. But figures from last year's crackdown showed that well over half of heroin-related arrests were of non-Asians.

Box Hill's experience shows heroin is making its way into the homes and veins of middle-class Melbourne, maybe because it is fashionable but more likely because it is cheap and plentiful right now.

'People don't believe it happens in the so-called better suburbs and they've got to be woken up to the fact that it does, and that it's a universal problem right across Melbourne,' says paramedic Steve Wood.

Two weeks ago, says Wood, he and his partner had to revive an overdose victim who passed out at the wheel of his car in the middle of Riversdale Road, Camberwell – the very heart of conservative Melbourne.

'There are lots of nice young yuppie people in very nice Victorian cottages, using socially and overdoing it and being caught out,' says fellow paramedic Tony Armour.

'They're out there – initially at least – using recreationally. They'll all sit around, have a glass of wine and a hit of heroin,' Armour says.

Senior Sergeant Wilkes doesn't know about that. 'Our drug offenders around here could hardly be described as middle-class or yuppies,' he says.

It doesn't mean they didn't start out that way. Take Frank and Tiana, Emily and Adam here, sitting out in the sun having their ritual post-hit smoke. They're all from good, if fractured, families.

Frank's mum and dad are ex-police, he says. Now divorced, his father's a manager with a communications firm, his mother a church-going social worker. Tiana's mum has a property in Gippsland and her dad's a mechanical engineer. He shot through from home when she was 15, she left at 16.

Tiana got into the smack while living in a house full of users. 'It was really intriguing,' she says. 'They'd all go down the end of the house when their hit got there and they'd go, like: "Wicked." And they'd come back stoned, noddin' off in this dream. And they'd all go, "Don't touch it, it's bad shit" and of course you'd really want to.' She gave Frank his first taste: 'I knew if she put it in front of me I'd say, "Gimme some." And she did and I did and that's why I'm here. That quick.'

Adam and Emily, in their early 20s, began using last August after their daughter, born three months prematurely, died. 'We'd used a little bit before, but we got flat out into it after she died,' says Adam. 'Just to stop the grieving,' says Emily.

Now they've each got a $100-a-day habit and are dealing around Box Hill and Ringwood to support it. Adam is out on bail pending burglary charges. Their families have disowned them.

None of them is under any illusions about the future; most likely they'll wind up dead. 'But it's everywhere,' says Frank. 'If you're a junkie you can't hide from this stuff, you'll run into it wherever you go.

'It's amazing how different it'll change your life. When I met Tiana, I had a full-time job and everything was sweet. All of a sudden I was living in some dump in Healesville, I lost my job, all these people were just coming in and shooting up all over the house. We were sleepin' on our wallets and cigarettes 'cos people are just scumballs, they were just rippin' us off. But that's heroin. It's the drug you love to hate.

'I love the stuff personally, I reckon it's great. I mean you're freezing cold if you don't have it, then you go and have this whack and you feel so normal, so good.

'But then, shit, on the other hand it'll kill you.'

JUST ANOTHER NIGHT
IN THE 'BURBS

I t was night time, mid-winter. He was lying face-down in an unlit section of parkland and someone had a knee lodged in his back and his right arm in an armlock, but drug squad Detective Sergeant Malcolm Rosenes could still see.

He could see his whole life falling away. His family. His career. The house in the suburbs. He was 48 years old and he could see 15 years, maybe more, in jail. He could see his three boys, young adolescents now, growing into adults without him.

Just minutes earlier he was a shadow among the trees in Caulfield Park, waiting to clinch a deal involving thousands of ecstasy tablets. Across the way, in Park Crescent, the houses were shut up against the bitter cold, blind to the drama about to unfold at their doorsteps.

Rosenes was edgy. He didn't like Caulfield. It had a sprawling new police station down on Hawthorn Road, and he reckoned the cops there did not have enough going on to distract them.

But it was not the Caulfield cops he needed to worry about. Rosenes, a drug squad detective, had been running an informant; a convicted drug dealer who realised Rosenes was bent.

About a month earlier, Rosenes had taken leave of absence using holiday and sick leave. About the same time Rosenes' informant had begun co-operating with the Victoria Police Ethical Standards Department. He did not see that.

It was about 7.30 on Sunday evening, 29 July 2001. Caught in torchlight and told to drop, Rosenes did as he was told and lay with his arms straight out from his body, his face against the chilled grass. The knee that pinned Rosenes' back belonged to Detective Senior Sergeant Neville Taylor of ESD's corruption investigation division.

Taylor arrested him on charges of drug trafficking and of conspiracy to traffick. Rosenes was unresponsive. When first arrested he had groaned an indecipherable reply.

As his hands were cuffed and his pockets emptied of mobile phones and keys, he was limp and mute and kept his eyes closed. His mind was racing.

Taylor lifted him to his feet and walked him over to an unmarked car in a roadside car park, and sat next to him in the back seat. The front seats were occupied by ESD corruption investigators, Inspector Naylor and Senior Sergeant McWhirter. They drove the car out of the immediate area and parked about a kilometre away. As far as ESD was concerned, Rosenes had unfinished business back at the park.

Taylor wanted Rosenes to complete the drug deal, to get the pills off the street.

'Malcolm, listen to me,' began Taylor, who recorded the conversation. 'We've been working on you for two-and-a-half months ... listen, this is it, you are done, OK?

'You cannot ask for … there are no deals. I want to get those tablets now. You have about no time to decide if you want to stand up and say that you actually helped us get the drugs back. Do you understand that? Do you understand me? It's your choice. You could do it right now.'

By now Rosenes' eyes were open, but he refused to speak. Told he had a choice, and about five seconds to decide whether to co-operate, he broke a little. Rosenes said: 'What's in it for me?'

'No deals,' Taylor answered. 'No deals, Malcolm. What's in it for you is what you are going to say.'

Taylor then played Rosenes a tape recorded the day before, of Rosenes and his informant setting up the deal in Caulfield Park. Briefly, Rosenes tried a bluff, tried to pass off the episode as his own, personal operation. Some sort of wildcat undercover bust. 'You don't know what [quantity of drugs] there is … I know what there is, all right,' Rosenes said.

'All right, you jump down my throat, you make me threats … I'm going to fight, you know, in my time this was going to lead to a man who was possibly a South African who manufactures and imports ecstasy, all right, that's where it was going … Now, so far I know that … the street where the contact is, I know where and approximately … all right, now that's what I have learnt. Now that's my part of it.'

Taylor had heard too much on the surveillance recordings to believe that Rosenes was trying to run down some dealer. 'Come on, Malcolm, don't …' Taylor said. 'Do you understand that we've been on you all day, all right? We've been on you for the last two-and-a-half months.'

Taylor urged him to make the phone call to close the deal, to get the drugs, but Rosenes claimed the deal would be put off.

Taylor: 'Well, we're going to get one step closer to another bloke, someone ...'

Rosenes: ' ... they'll just shut it down and it won't go any further and you'll never get past fucking ...'

Taylor: 'Well, we're wasting time now.'

Rosenes: 'No, we're not wasting time. We're fucking talking about my fucking life. All right, well take the handcuffs off.'

Taylor: 'No I won't take them off. They're not coming off, we're not doing anything. Look, are you going to do this or not? Mal, we've got to, we're running out ...'

Rosenes: 'I want to do whatever I can do to save my soul, all right.'

But first, to help save his soul, Rosenes wants to know what they know, and what that knowledge means for him.

Rosenes: 'What's fucking happening with me, then I'll fucking think about it and everything and I'll do what you want, but I won't ...'

Taylor: 'What do you want?'

Rosenes: 'Where am I going, what's happening with me ... what have you got, what have you got?'

He is told that as well as tonight's deal, he is known to have sold 2800 tablets and collected $50,000 two weeks earlier. Taylor told him the best thing he could do is start helping right now, so it can be used to his advantage later. Rosenes answered: 'I won't be here for the trial ... they'll fucking take me out.'

Taylor told him: 'Mal, I can't cut you a deal, all right. Mal, listen to me. I can't cut you deals but if you do nothing there's no possibility of anything.'

They are sitting in a parked car in a dark suburban street in Caulfield, weighing the future. This moment has been coming for Rosenes as if it were fated, the pieces of it locking together irreversibly.

They were onto him before the informant came with his offer of information on Rosenes back on 20 June. They knew, two weeks ago, when he sold the 2800 tablets to his informant. And five days after that, they knew when he showed the informant a substance he said was amphetamines.

Just three days ago Taylor was at Melbourne Magistrates Court securing a search warrant for Rosenes' house. The corruption investigation division briefing followed the next day.

And seven hours before he was picked up in the park, around lunchtime on Sunday, the ESD cops gathered at Caulfield Racecourse in readiness for busting Rosenes. The sole hitch was that the drug deal was running a few hours behind schedule and the arrest was made in darkness.

Rosenes is close to making the phone call, but first he wants to know his likely sentence – the 'quote'.

'All I'm worried about is little old me, right,' Rosenes tells Taylor.

'The policeman from the drug squad that's fucking … they'll want to bring back the death penalty for me … I don't want it to look as if it was that fucking bad because it wasn't …

'Well, you've weighed it up in your mind. You've spoken to the [Director of Public Prosecutions] … I want to know what the quote was for Rosenes … tell me what they would have told you. You would have put the brief together. You would have got a quote off them.'

He wonders: Will he spend 15 years in the same cell as his informant, the man who helped do him in?

'I'm fucking not going to be there for my kids growing up,'

Rosenes says. 'How am I going to tell them that? I've got to fucking look people in the eye.'

But, he is told, there is no quote. And no comfort either. Rosenes worries aloud that his co-offenders will give him up. Do a deal and leave him hanging. A copper has to be worth more than anyone else.

Taylor spells it out for him: 'What happens is you make the call, everything's sweet. [The drug contact is] going to go and meet you. No-one's going anywhere. All we're going to do is we'll follow him to the meeting place and then our people are going to move in and arrest him.'

From the back of the car Rosenes makes the phone call, arranging to take the money to a meeting place at the corner of Bambra Road and Balaclava Road, on the park's southern boundary. The ESD police and Rosenes remain parked where they are, a kilometre away, waiting for word that Rosenes' contact has been arrested.

Several times the man rings Rosenes on the appointed mobile phone, puzzled because he cannot see Rosenes' car which is still parked in Park Crescent, some distance away from the meeting point.

Rosenes says he will be there soon. By now, Rosenes has been under arrest for more than an hour.

Another hour passes before they drive back to Park Crescent, where Rosenes' car is searched by police and a sniffer dog. They search his clothes. They search his shoes. For Malcolm Rosenes, career cop, life has turned full circle.

From there they travel to Alma Road to search a flat that had belonged to Rosenes' father, which was spoken of on the surveillance tapes. Rosenes sits in the kitchen while police comb the flat.

It is approaching midnight by the time that search is finished. The only thing of interest found there is a receipt for a safety deposit box.

What he does not know is that his Israeli drug syndicate contact has been busted and that 40,000 ecstasy tablets have been found in the contact's motel room. It will not count against Rosenes, whose involvement tonight centred on 12,500 tablets he was to pick up in return for $225,000, but together with the haul from the motel it is now the biggest ecstasy bust in Victoria's history.

The longest night of Mal Rosenes' life grows longer still as they detour on the way to his home to check the deposit box, which is empty.

He has already told them there is nothing at his home of interest to them – 'It's just a fucking ordinary house' – but even as he says it he must know his words count for nothing.

It is almost 1 am when they enter the house, a modest, low, single-storey place of pale brick and glass. The children are asleep. Rosenes' wife is seated on their bed. He locks the family dogs away in the laundry so the drug dog can work undisturbed.

Taylor, Rosenes, his wife and other ESD police wait in the lounge room while the search continues, which it does until about 2.30 am.

Rosenes' rights to contact a friend or relative and a lawyer were suspended earlier for fear communication could result in the destruction of evidence. Now he is told the other suspects are in custody and the evidence has been seized, so he may try to contact a lawyer, which he does later from the ESD office.

Rosenes is not left alone for the rest of the morning.

From the time he was arrested almost every word he spoke was tape recorded but for a brief period during the search of his father's flat. The recordings revealed, in the words of County Court Judge McInerny, Rosenes as a cold, calculating and self-interested criminal. His belligerent 'what's in it for me' attitude was the real measure of the man, the judge said.

While there, sitting at the kitchen table in his dad's flat, Rosenes mused without prompting, Taylor recalled.

Rosenes spoke about having been sick and contemplating suicide, and how he probably would not last long enough to be tried in court. He would kill himself.

He spoke about having been a fool, about his own stupidity and how he thought his informant had been badly treated. How he was just trying to help him. He spoke about how people did not understand just how easy it is to go bad overnight.

Malcolm Rosenes did not commit suicide, and he did survive to stand trial, to plead guilty and agree to testify against his co-accused.

Two years later and a lifetime away from that night, Malcolm Rosenes pleaded guilty to seven counts of drug offences, including the Caulfield Park bust: trafficking in a commercial quantity of ecstasy, an offence with a maximum penalty of 25 years jail.

He received credits in sentencing for the fact of the guilty plea and the fact he helped internal investigators with revelations about drug squad corruption, and also that he would be a prosecution witness in other cases.

On 24 October 2003, he was sentenced to a total of six years and three months jail, with a minimum three years six months before becoming eligible for parole.

DARK PLACES

Always, during the jailhouse introductions, he carries within himself a kernel of fear, or, at least, a lingering sense of unease. It is driven by the violence he knows his clients carry within themselves, and the fact he may need to push them to reveal it. Usually, that edginess stays with forensic psychologist Ian Joblin for entire meetings but, sometimes, it becomes something else.

Like the first time he met Martin Bryant, less than two weeks after Bryant shot dead 35 people at Port Arthur.

Bryant is heavily bandaged, and shackled by his ankles and one wrist to a hospital bed. His lawyer is there, medical staff and prison officers. He giggles a lot. Joblin begins with some innocuous questions.

'What sort of music do you like?'

'ABBA.'

'What do you like to drink?'

'Guinness, Baileys, Sambuca.'

He asks about Bryant's mother: 'She would be upset if she saw me like this.'

And his father, prompting an odd leap of thought: 'Dad

died a couple of years ago. I was very sad about that. Dad used to drink Cascade.'

Bryant is tall, but his pale complexion, fair hair and slim build make him appear insubstantial. His gestures are effeminate and, when he denies some detail about the shootings, he grins and giggles behind his hand.

Unease shifts to incongruity.

'My original charter was to check out his IQ, but it's more than that. His [deficient] IQ doesn't explain the offences,' Joblin says. 'Here's this pathetic, immature, stupid, fatuous creature handcuffed to the side of his bed, charged with one of the worst crimes this century. I wanted to find out what's going on with this guy and how this person in front of me could possibly have committed these crimes.'

Bryant told him he had planned to travel to Austria that winter to be reunited with an Austrian woman he had met: 'But this got in the way.'

And he would break the flow of Joblin's questions to him with his childlike attempts at conversation. How long was the plane ride from Melbourne? Were many people on board? Did you get airsick? What sort of car do you drive?

'I was over-awed,' Joblin says of their first meeting. 'It didn't jell: that this poor, pathetic character had been out doing what he did. Anyone is capable of anything in my book, if you get a guy like Bryant capable of doing what he did.'

In that sense, Bryant sits alongside Frankston serial killer Paul Denyer and rapist and double murderer Raymond 'Mr Stinky' Edmunds: others whose unthreatening manner jarred with their crimes.

Those charged with the most serious offences Joblin meets in jail, on his 'house calls'. But most come to his office, dispatched by their lawyers and introduced by a summary of the case against them. They can be anything: a vigilante kneecapper, a flasher, a middle-aged matron who has taken to thieving from shops. Or a psychopath, although they don't use that word in court much any more – too emotionally loaded. Comparatively few of Joblin's clients are return visitors. He interviews them, writes his report and, if they are convicted and imprisoned, that is the end of it.

In the case of convicted child murderer Robert Arthur Selby Lowe, it did not proceed that far. Lowe was so full of evasions, half-truths and outright lies that, Joblin says, he could do nothing with him and refused the case.

He may spend as little as one hour with them, or many hours over several visits. Of the few who do return to Joblin, it is usually after five, six, maybe 14 years; sometimes with different names.

'Typically, I go through their history to see if there is anything of significance, but also to observe them, to see how they are functioning: whether they're boozed or stoned, unintelligent or mad. Whatever,' he says. 'But, rather than talk about the offence, I talk about their history: their education, employment, who cares about them or what they do. That'll take half an hour and, at the same time, I can make an assessment.

'Then we'll talk about the offence and go through it. When you are talking about a sex offence, or a bashing, or a murder, or even a person who's had no trouble with the police who is up for a .05, for them, it's a catastrophe that's upset their whole life. If you get heavy in an interview, you'll lose them.

'I'm basically here to get hold of what's going on and why they offended. And that's it. I don't view myself as a sentencing option for ongoing treatment.'

Joblin prides himself on knowing more about the psychology of criminal behaviour than almost anyone in this country. There is a book in him, but he has no time to write it while he continues to produce between a dozen and 20 reports of varying complexity for the legal system, each week.

He works mostly for defence lawyers – not out of any philosophical bent, but because the prosecution has access to its own people. He insists working for the prosecution or the defence has no effect on his work. On occasions, he has discovered his reports were not produced in court, presumably because they were not considered 'helpful'.

'In my opinion, it's important courts understand why an offender offends. Now, the courts, or the police, or the guy's solicitor may not agree with that but, in my opinion, it's important,' he says. 'There will be courts that want to know about the guy before he is sentenced and that is a role I can play.'

Today, a young woman he has seen before and whom he calls Margaret Julia has brought her poetry. Whenever he addresses her it is by both Christian names, a gesture of formality to disguise the awfulness that has brought her here.

In the poems are the things Margaret Julia cannot tell her family. Some days, she sits and begins writing and the words come tumbling out before they have formed in her head. There they are on the page, stark and brittle and bleak, as new to her as to any first-time reader. Poems of loss and foreboding, of death and suicide. Poems about going to jail.

Margaret Julia is 22, tall, slim, unaffected, giggly when she is self-conscious. A kid from a country town planning to resume her studies. But she expects it will need to be by correspondence. She is dismissive of her writing. 'It's all crap.'

Across the desk, Joblin leafs through her poems. 'It's all morbid,' he says. 'It's all sadness.'

Margaret Julia suggests she may redraft one of the poems. He tells her: 'Don't change it. The truth is in the spontaneity.'

'That's about prison, that one,' she says.

And he says: 'It's all good stuff. Does it make you feel better?'

She says: 'I don't know if I am getting rid of the past, or preparing to be locked up.'

Later, he will prepare a psychological report for her lawyer. Margaret Julia enjoys drinking. Once too often she got very drunk, drove through a stop sign and took out another car. Both drivers survived, but a little girl in the other car was killed. That is the dreadful, irretrievable truth of what she has done. Margaret Julia's blood-alcohol reading was four times the legal limit.

'Would you put her in prison for two years?' Joblin says. 'Would you?'

The hum of the city drifts in through the open office window. Traffic noise, a car horn, a jackhammer. Life goes on, but here, and for a grieving family, it has paused. Who knows for how long?

There is nothing fancy about Joblin's office. None of that modern glass and steel surface look. It is in a 1930s office building. The decor appears to be mid-70s. White walls lined with timber veneer bookcases, their shelves bowed with age. Picture rails in mission brown. A potted plant has sent a creeper along one wall. Something with broad variegated leaves lives in the opposite corner alongside a beige-coloured modular lounge. The windows are metal-framed casements. Like the picture rails, they are dark brown. Clients sit facing him across the desk from a timber-framed armchair, also dark brown. No-one comes here to be impressed or overawed.

Joblin does not judge. There is no moralising in his approach. It appears to rely heavily on the client's account, but he says he cross checks their stories with medical and legal records, and with other family members. He spent hours talking to Bryant's mother. Margaret Julia's mother has been asked to write a family memoir.

His retreat is a hobby farm north-east of Melbourne. Only publicity and inquiry prompts recollection of individual cases. He sheds the memory of each case as he signs off his report. To do this job, he says, you need a very effective mental 'delete' button.

'It's very easy to say I know this guy's problem, just give him to me, [but] I don't know how to counsel and it's not my area of expertise. I don't have anything to do with treatment. I'm not in the business of solving crime or excusing crime. I'm not saying: "Poor little dears commit offences." I see my role as investigative – to try to find out what's happened and to be firm enough in that opinion to stand up in court and be tested by cross-examination.'

Joblin was born 53 years ago, the third of five children, and had a thoroughly conventional upbringing. His father was an Anglican minister, vicar to a succession of villages on New Zealand's North Island. Because of his father's occupation, Joblin was able to attend the best boarding schools in the country, so, after primary school, he begged his parents to enrol him at the upper-crust Wanganui Collegiate, and then hated every minute of the place. Hated its rules and restrictions. Hated its conformity and enduring its contrived rigors. Cold showers were compulsory. So was an early-morning run and so was 40 minutes of homework before breakfast in a cavernous dining room where talking was prohibited. Then he made the mistake of not liking sport.

'I failed everything. Failed miserably. I didn't like sport, I was unpopular,' he recalls. 'I used to look at it and think: "This is just like a damned prison".'

And he was punished.

'I got caned and caned,' he says. Caned for being late, or using the wrong door of the dormitory, or not having a shower or not hanging his towel properly.

'We got regular canings. It had no effect, no deterrent value at all, except to push me further away from conforming to the supposedly sophisticated values of the school.'

He was not entirely friendless, and, although on reflection he says the school taught him valuable lessons about respect for others, it was a miserable time, compounded by his total failure in the matriculation exams.

At one point, he confided in his mother that he had no interests and few friends. She suggested he develop an interest in sport, which he did, contriving to follow a Springbok rugby tour of New Zealand. It succeeded to the extent that when he repeated matriculation, at the local high school, he played in the school rugby side. He also discovered girls but, while he enjoyed himself a bit more, his academic results were not much improved.

In New Zealand, he says, there were three career paths for school leavers: banks, insurance and oil. He joined Shell; left after a couple of years and tried to join the police; was refused entry either because he failed the medical or his matric, he can't recall which – although it may have been both – and became a parole officer.

He thinks now that he was an experiment for the parole service.

'I was sort of a junior assistant probation officer. For the next two or three years, they posted me around the North Island.'

While on a posting he saw an advertisement calling for applicants for a Rotary exchange program with South America. He applied, was successful, sold his Sunbeam Alpine sports car for the fare and sailed to Panama.

'You have got to bear in mind that what I am is the son of an Anglican minister in dinky little towns in New Zealand. Pretty naive.'

He was supposed to be gone 12 months, but 12 months stretched into three-and-a-half years. On reflection, he thinks that period of self-reliance may be what enabled him to break out of his mould.

He taught English in Santiago, managed a dairy farm, picked apples and went looking for Che Guevara, but the revolutionary was killed before the vicar's son – who wanted to hear his ideas of agrarian reform – caught up with him.

He had a fixed notion of travelling overland to Hudson's Bay in Canada before crossing to Vancouver and shipping home. By foot and local bus he worked his way through Peru, Ecuador and Colombia. But the Hudson's Bay run he did in style: in a Pontiac convertible driven by a Southern belle called Leigh Wilson whom he met at a party in Atlanta. Some years later, they married.

Back in New Zealand he entered university as a mature-age student, studying psychology with the intention of returning to parole work. As a junior assistant parole officer, there had always been someone in court who seemed better equipped than he – the mental health professional. But, instead of returning to parole work, he started lecturing and pursuing post-graduate studies. In 1976, he and his family moved to Melbourne in order for him to teach the psychology of criminal behaviour, a diploma course for prison and police officers.

That continued until 1981 but, having been pressed by several solicitors to prepare court reports for their clients and having lost interest in teaching the course, he became, in his words, a 'gun for hire'.

His has been a journey into the mind's darker side. His travelling companions have been killers, rapists and pedophile priests, violent thugs, career criminals and thousands of lesser offenders caught in the legal system by ill fortune and circumstance.

So, is there such a thing as evil, and where does it come from?

'I think badness is learnt. It might be that an evil – whatever that might be – person has learnt his evil behaviour, but he is not born evil. It's a development. He's learnt it at home or on the streets or he has learnt that his jolly in life, his only satisfaction, is by being bad … and, if that's the case, he's going to be anti-social.

'Denyer. I don't know where it came from with him. He must have learnt it. At some point, I think he felt rejected enough or bad enough to want to take that badness out on animals and, at that point, the first of those incidents, he's gone. In a situation like that, it's always important to find out why the first occurred because the rest follow. There's gratification in it.

'Denyer's motive was to get his kicks out of killing. For no reason. He indicated that the last unfortunate victim pleaded with him to come back and "Dad'll give you money" and he killed her in any case. Extraordinary stuff. But that's the motive; that's the basis of Denyer's crime.'

Psychologically, Joblin says, it is often the mischief offences that are most interesting: the uniformed cop who parks his marked car in order to expose himself to passers-by, or the affluent shoplifter. These, he says, are message crimes.

'It's expressing in an anti-social way what can't be expressed in a positive way. The middle-aged woman who takes up shoplifting is trying to say something which she can't say or which she feels no-one will listen to.

'The guy who gets his gratification from an early age from snowdropping or flashing, and typically behaves that way through life, has a disorder and that can be worked on. The message flasher does not necessarily have a psycho-sexual disorder. The interesting thing is to find out why he chooses that behaviour as a response to stress.'

There is always a reason. Like the young woman in her 30s who, raised by her father from the age of eight, went out one morning to her local McEwans store, bought an axe, returned home and caved in the side of her father's head. She resisted revealing her background until it was suggested her father was sexually abusing her, which he had done almost from the time her mother had left.

The woman, now in her early 40s, refused to have the abuse disclosed in open court, so it was hidden in the psychological report handed up to the judge.

Joblin says parents often have a great degree of responsibility for the wrecked lives of their children.

'The people I see now as adults had a shocking upbringing with a lot of physical or emotional or sexual abuse from those who should have cared: their parents. They're rejected. They can't live at home because of the abuse and they go. If they're on the streets, they're lost.'

But Bryant? Not so. His parents worked hard to help the son they realised had enormous problems.

Bryant had many difficulties, but one problem typical of young people that he did not have was a lack of money. Bryant was made wealthy when an eccentric woman for whom he became a close companion died, leaving him her entire estate.

Helen Harvey died in a road smash, aged 59, leaving Bryant properties and investments totalling $649,000. Bryant's father was the executor of the estate, but when he died Bryant was rudderless and rich.

'He had dinner with his mother the night before Port Arthur. Whatever Mrs Bryant did was not going to solve the problem. He's a misfit for a whole lot of reasons. You talk of feelings of rejection, feelings of alienation, feelings of isolation, but he also had feelings of immunity through the money he inherited and all the power that is associated with that. That sense of power, for that personality with that immaturity, and those feelings of rejection was a disastrous combination.'

There is a practised casualness about Joblin's speech: no hint at the significance of the question to a man with a record of violence. 'Do you trust yourself?'

Not everybody can answer yes.

Margaret Julia has left. Now Joblin is looking for the reason a client bashed his way into a house and took an iron bar to the occupants, a man in his 40s, his teenage son and a friend. Had the bar he used as a javelin shifted direction slightly, it could have been a murder charge. As it is, the man is explaining that he feared his teenage daughter was being used for sex in the house. Already, he has detailed a moderately chaotic personal life – from his father's aggressive belittling of his mother, to his own fractured relationships and his inability to control his daughter. She had been sent down from the country by her mother, from whom he is estranged.

'She came down to go to school and it just got tossed by the wayside … She got mixed up with those friggin' idiots … I thought everyone was laughing at me … Basically, I have ruined part of my life,' he is saying.

Joblin tells him: 'It is your perception that you act on … What you acted on is what you thought it was.'

Later, they talk footy. Heavy them and you lose them.

'If people can't tell me [why they offend], I'm going to go through a lot of possibilities,' he says. 'Most people know what they are doing is wrong. There's a kick factor. There's a kick in the risk-take. There's a kick in guys doing a burglary, not necessarily to obtain the goods … Now my point about that is what is wrong with their life that they need the buzz out of doing something that is over the line? I would look at their life and consider what can be done about that lack.'

What keeps him going is exploring the infinite paths that lead to crossing the line.

'Often, with personality disorders you get a consistent pattern of early rejection; of never having the experience of anyone caring about them, of meeting up with others of similar experience in their teenage years and together they are stronger than they are on their own.

'Or you get the feeling of normlessness; that there's no more values in society. We've done everything, what else is there? We've got a car, we've got a good house, a pool, we've got booze, we've got drugs. There's nothing else in life for me except one thing, and that's to cross the line into anti-social behaviour.

'Or they may feel they are down the bottom of the pit. Nobody likes them. They've been told 100 times that they are of no value to anyone, so they behave according to that: self-fulfilling prophecy.

'There are cases where you can predict that whatever you do for that particular bloke, he is going to be back. He is going to carry on using drugs and living on the line. But it's very important that one continues investigating why a person has committed a crime, and not put them in a pigeon hole.

'I don't suppose I'm surprised any more by the nature of crime because, after a while, there's nothing new in the actual act. What is new is why that person has done it and that must remain always a mystery to solve.

'The day I cease to be mystified is the day I take down my shingle.'

THE BATSMAN AND
THE BOUNCER

There's one thing on which everyone agrees: it was a devastating punch. A knockout. A sudden, single left hook, cocked and thrown a short distance to collide against David Hookes' right cheek.

It stopped him in his tracks and probably mid-sentence. The light went out of his eyes and he went down, not buckling but, according to one, as rigid as a plank of wood. Like a felled tree, said another. When the back of his head hit the bitumen it made a sickening sound.

The rest is confusion.

There is a thing called the Rashomon effect. Named for the Japanese film, it describes how subjective perception affects recollection – how different observers can see the same event yet recall it in very different, often contradictory, but plausible ways. Hidden somewhere is the truth.

There is a little of that in every criminal proceeding. But during the 13 days of Zdravko Micevic's trial, for the manslaughter of cricketer David Hookes, in September 2005, Rashomon inhabited Victoria's Supreme Court Two like an obfuscating, confusing presence.

In one view there is a punch thrown in desperate, reflexive self-defence. In another it is delivered as accurate and forceful payback. Defendant, participants and even bystanders, leaning over balconies or behind gates, from metres away or several storeys above, recounted very different memories of that night.

A quagmire of contradictions, counsel for the defence Terry Forrest, QC, called it 'a stop-start slideshow of recollections'. It might have to do with self-interest or self-protection; the effects of stress or selective amnesia. A 'rose-coloured version' or 'mischievous revisionist history'. It may have been the chaos and the noise.

Or it might just have to do with how quickly it happened, how everything so suddenly and stupidly went bad.

On Sunday 18 January 2004, David Hookes was 48 and coach of the Victorian Bushrangers cricket side. Hookes was also part of Australian cricket folklore for the five successive fours he had belted off England bowler Tony Greig during the 1977 Centenary Test.

Zdravko Micevic was 21 and on the security staff at the Beaconsfield Hotel in St Kilda. He had been something of an accomplished sportsman himself, having won an Australian junior welterweight title in boxing.

Neither had heard of each other, in fact Micevic was not even born when Hookes launched his extraordinary assault on the South African-born Greig's medium pacers. And though their paths would cross at the Beaconsfield that night, there was nothing to make them intersect except bad behaviour.

That afternoon, at the MCG, the Bushrangers had snatched a six-run victory over South Australia's Redbacks in a one-day ING Cup match. Darren Lehmann, then an international batsman, made 44 and took two wickets in the Redback's narrow loss.

He couldn't have been pleased with the result, but an honourable cricket tradition is to have a few drinks with your conquerors, so when 'Boof' got a phone call from his old friend Hookes, he was happy to accept the invitation to join him at the Beaconsfield. Wayne Phillips, the SA coach, and team physiotherapist Jonathan Porter went with him.

When they arrived, the Victorian contingent – including Hookes and his girlfriend Christine Padfield, Tania Plumpton, a friend of Christine, Shaun Graf, Greg Shipperd, Darren Berry, Robert Cassell and fast bowler Michael Lewis and his girlfriend Sue-Anne Hunter – was waiting. Together they spent the next few hours in a corner of the bar, chatting and watching Australia play out a close loss to India in a one-day international in Brisbane.

There is no evidence they were misbehaving.

The only drama of the evening had been an argument between Lewis and Hunter. The bowler left the pub and waited in his car across the road. An upset Hunter had a conversation with Hookes in the smoke room, a glassed-in alcove away from the bar. About 11.30 pm, while they were talking there, the security staff flicked the bar lights on and off and called last drinks.

It is here that the various stories dramatically diverge.

In one account Hookes tells Micevic they'll leave when Hunter finishes her 'chardy' and is told 'Tell the bitch to skol her drink'. According to Hunter, Hookes replied something like: 'That's no way to speak to a lady and you shouldn't be asking such a young girl to skol her drink.'

In Micevic's version, he would never have behaved so unprofessionally. And Hookes, he says, spoke to him in far less gallant terms: 'Fuck you!' And for emphasis, he claimed, the cricketer added: 'You heard me, fuck you. How many times do I have to repeat myself? Fuck you.'

Whatever the words used, they were enough for Hookes to find himself in a headlock – or perhaps a half-nelson, or a bear hug – and being ejected from the hotel: pushed out the door, in one telling, thrown down the stairs in another.

According to bar staff, two of the women were trying to pull security away from Hookes. 'Some of the ladies were trying to get at Strav [Micevic], trying to rip at him,' Willie Niumata said.

One small area of agreement is the colour of the language that filled the summer air in Cowderoy Street, outside the hotel. It was crude and aggressive with, depending on who's doing the telling, the bouncers suggesting the cricketing group 'Fuck off and go home' or the patrons, led by a belligerent Hookes, saying something like 'You're fucked, your mob'.

This, Forrest suggested, cross-examining Phillips, was part of a threat by Hookes to use his 3AW radio show to close the hotel business down. The South Australian, while noting that Hookes wanted to argue the toss, said he didn't hear those words but agreed that, in effect, he was promising to 'give the hotel a spray on the radio'.

Tania Plumpton said a security officer leaned over her to threaten Hookes. 'He said David was a smart-arse and he was going to effing well kill him,' she told the court. When asked about Hookes' response, she replied: 'He said something along the lines of, "Oh, you're a tough boy".'

The security staff began to force the cricket group away from the hotel. Forrest chose a football term, suggesting to Phillips that they were trying to shepherd the group down Cowderoy Street, ushering them away from the hotel. 'I think push, rather than usher would be a more appropriate term,' Phillips replied.

'… this was a sort of move from Australian rules to rugby. This was a rolling maul?' Forrest asked.

'I think I referred to it as a kerfuffle,' Phillips answered. 'But, yes, rolling maul is a good one.'

Whatever the description, it was enough to bring neighbours to their windows and balconies. A couple called 000, one suggesting there was a punch-up beginning. One, Craig Ravells, gave evidence he saw arms swinging and a man trying to pull loose, as if he were being held. He heard women screaming, begging and shouting: 'Let us go' or 'Let him go'.

Christine Padfield had gone to get her car, hoping, she said, to get Hookes away. While she was gone, Graf said the group was heading away from the pub. He had his arm around Hookes 'and we thought we were out of harm's way … [but] the security continued to follow us and were verballing, loud and abusive'.

When the car arrived, he said the security tried to stop Hookes getting in. 'I turned around and saw one of the bouncers had tried to pull him to the ground. He lifted his hands up and said, "Hey, I'm out of your pub, I'm out of your pub." And that's when he got hit.'

Micevic told it differently. Giving evidence, he said staff simply wanted the group to leave but they would start to walk away, then come back again. He said the two groups had pushed, shoved and wrestled as they moved along Cowderoy Street.

He claimed that during the scuffle, Hookes hit him twice in the stomach, grabbed him by the shirt and pulled him down, so his head was near Hookes' chest. He said he could not break Hookes' grip and was scared that he would not be able to protect himself, or that he would be kicked. 'I was worried of getting pulled down to the ground and I threw a punch back,' he said.

Other witnesses didn't see it that way. Leesa Rogerson was waiting for a taxi and remembers a man facing a group near the centre of the road when 'a guy sort of jogged from the group towards this guy and punched him in the face'.

Robert Cassell said he was about five metres away and 'probably saw the bouncer's last two or three steps and then he punched him'. Another witness, Anthony Perks, said: 'He loaded up and it was a big hit.'

Paul Chow, watching from his townhouse, said Hookes' arms were by his side when he was hit. Another neighbour, Joseph Robilotta, said he had heard yelling and screaming and the words: 'You want to be smart … now it's time to face the music.' A man in a white shirt turned around, and a bouncer in a long-sleeved white top hit him. 'Mr Hookes was just standing by, no clenched fists, no aggressive nature whatsoever.'

However it happened, the punch instantly knocked Hookes unconscious. 'David was completely out,' Graf recalled. 'I was close enough to see his eyes, he was completely cold as he hit the deck.'

Rogerson said Hookes 'fell backwards and fell flat like a tree'. Perks said 'he fell as if he wasn't understanding anything and he hit the road hard. He didn't try to stop or break his fall at all. He fell like a plank.' Paul Chow said Hookes hit the road with 'an audible splat'. Jonathan Porter heard 'a sound like fist hitting flesh and the sound of a breaking bone'.

When the back of Hookes' skull hit the roadway it cracked like the shell of a hard-boiled egg. He suffered a depressed, shattering fracture.

Jonathan Porter, the SA physiotherapist, ran to him. Hookes was flat on his back, unconscious, unresponsive, with blood coming from his nose and mouth. His pulse was already thready and weak. By the time paramedics arrived he was already in cardiopulmonary arrest. He died in the Alfred Hospital the next day.

By then, Forrest suggested in his opening, the Rashomon effect was already beginning. 'That young man [Zdravko Micevic] has been demonised by some sections of the press. David Hookes has been sanctified by them. Neither of those images are real.'

Nor he contended were the accounts given by Hookes' friends. By and large, he said, their evidence was selective, 'the writing of history, we say, to preserve reputations and honour, rather than what really happened'.

Probably 20 times in the past month, he told the jury, he had been asked how his client could get a fair trial. 'He can and he will, because the system guarantees it. You guarantee it. You guarantee him your decency, your fairness, your experience of life, your capacity to evaluate what you see and hear before you …

'You will give him a balanced, sane, rigidly, intellectually honest appraisal of the evidence.'

There are lots of stories told in almost every criminal court case. Different versions, recollections, interpretations and memories. Juries don't have to choose which story is true. They don't necessarily have to *believe* any of them. But if they choose to accept the one put to them by the prosecution, they must do so beyond reasonable doubt.

The 13 men and women spent days rigidly, intellectually and honestly weighing up all they had been told. Then they found Zdravko Micevic not guilty.

With Peter Gregory

WHAT'S A NICE GIRL
LIKE YOU ...?

The sound of a cane striking bare buttocks is a sharp, somehow wettish, crack.

'Thank you, mistress,' whispers George.

George is naked, pale, hairless and small, and seems to diminish further with each echoing *thwack*. He has a wobbly, round belly and kneels on skinny, bowed legs. His shoulders slump, his eyes are downcast and his little penis is in total retreat. His backside is striped pink and the droopy ears of his leather dog mask sweep the floor with every flinch at every stroke.

'Thank you, mistress.'

The room is old-blood red, lit by a single, struggling globe. In one corner is a massive polished-wood St Andrew's cross, padded at its centre in thick black leather; in another, a thicket of switches and canes. A pulley and chain hang from the ceiling. From pegs on one wall dangle lengths of rope, cuffs and gags; on another, a strait-jacket, a rubber full-body suit and a breath-control mask; on the next, cats-of-nine-tails, floggers, straps, paddles and a plaited bullwhip.

George sees none of them. His eyes stay on the floor or, if he can sneak a glimpse, on Mistress Saskia's ankles above her high stilettos. George has a thing for feet.

Thwack!

'Thank you, mistress.'

Mistress Saskia is tall and willowy, lightly freckled, with dark eyes under arching brows, high cheekbones and a short, black Betty Boop bob. She has a lavish, Gothic tattoo on her right shoulder and a series of designs above those ankles. She is compressed into a two-piece mauve latex catsuit: a strangling bodice that flattens her breasts and a long tube of skirt, cross-laced down the back to show a little of her trim, bare bottom. Her voice is scornful and commanding.

Five minutes ago she had the submissive George suspended upside down from the ceiling, disciplining him with pinched nipples and flicks and slaps of a leather cat. Now she is finishing him with six from the cane. He must not cry out or they will start again. 'Take it!' she tells him.

'Unhh!'

'Right, start again then! That's six. Don't think I'm joking, slave! If I have to tie you down to get through these and gag you, I will. Understand me? Try again …'

She snaps her wrist and lays the cane across his poor, purpling arse. Pauses, then gives him another.

'Thank you, mistress,' responds George, his voice ascending the register with every strike.

'There's one to go, slave, isn't there. It's not going to be very nice. Don't think it's over. GET DOWN!'

She peppers his rump with open-handed slaps. Four, a pause, four more, and finally a full-force, thunder-crack smack. 'Now crawl out,' she orders. 'Go on, get out. Get out of my room! Go. Go!'

George, head bowed, arms limp, pauses momentarily at the door and whispers.

'Thank you, mistress.'

Mistress Saskia, dominatrix, works at a nether end of Melbourne's euphemistically titled adult industry. She is part of a thriving and, apparently, increasingly accepted – or at least tolerated – workforce.

Sex sells. And in what once was the world's most liveable city, it sells very well.

Melbourne's Yellow Pages has 218 listings and 87 display ads, across 21 pages, for escort workers and agencies, and 35 for striptease artists and their booking companies. There are 93 licensed brothels and 1909 people registered under the Prostitution Control Act as licence-exempt prostitution service providers. Sex workers doing shifts at brothels or working for other 'service providers' do not need licences, so no-one knows exactly how many there are, nor how many work the streets – but it's in the thousands.

Then there are topless waitresses; nude models; bondage and discipline dungeons; lingerie showgirls and sexy-wear salespeople; lap dancers; jelly-wrestlers and fetish website models; and Bunnings-like chains of sex shops. Long lines of after-work suits queue outside lap-dance men's clubs. There are double shows, libido stimulants, hot vibes and blonde-on-blondes. They advertise in newspapers and on late night TV, on billboards and mobile hoardings pulled around the CBD behind motor scooters, and these, suggests one operator, have 'desensitised' Melbourne into a blase consensual relationship with a once underground industry.

It is a trade overwhelmingly staffed by women. Which invites the old question: What's a nice girl like you doing in a job like this?

Dominica squirms in Ronaldo's lap. She is wearing a theatrical pout and nothing else. Ronaldo is wearing a dopey half-smile that sits somewhere between guilty pleasure and humiliation. Exactly a week from now he'll be married to someone else.

Dominica has already pulled down his jeans, lashed his bum with his belt, and used it as a bridle while she rode him like a horse. Now she guides his hands as they massage bubble bath suds around her breasts and 18 of his best mates hoot and cackle at his discomfort.

It is 10.30 Saturday night and they are under a party light-strung carport in outer west suburban Delahey. There's a karaoke machine beside the fridge and a couple of tables laden with chips, dips, snags and sushi, bourbon, scotch and beer. This is the second of Dom's three private strips of the evening. The next, around midnight, will be a double act for a couple of dozen aggressively crowding footballers at Bundoora. It's always a risk with privates so late in the night: by the time you arrive the guys are well-pissed and playing up. The grog goes in and the brains go out.

But this one is just fun. The blokes are Filipinos with ocker accents and sensibilities, laughing, joking and applauding. They are friendly, solicitous and, within the context, respectful.

There are two schools of thought among strippers about doing privates, says Dom. One is to put on a sexy performance, the other is to give a more 'comic' show. She leans to the latter. 'You're not going to, like, *turn on* this room full of 30 guys,' she says. 'They're not into this stuff all the time … they're embarrassed.

'It's like a social ritual. You throw a buck's night and you're obliged to get strippers. The best man, it's his job to get the stripper along, and so I see it that I'm really there to give them a bit of a laugh and, you know, humiliate the buck basically.'

Dominica has just turned 21. She is an elfin figure with long, straight brown hair, a pretty, open face and a smile that says she's in on the joke. She's been stripping for a year, mainly weekends and some lunch shows, but when she pulled up tonight in her battered sedan, wearing brown hipster cords, T-shirt and rimless glasses for her short-sightedness, she looked exactly what she is the rest of the time: a university student.

A straight A student at her ladies college, she won an Enter score in the high 90s and is now majoring in history/politics at uni. She came to striptease after a couple of 'crap' part-time jobs: 'You've only got so much time on this planet. I wanted a job that will bring in the most pay for the least possible hours. And stripping was it.'

Coming from a hippie family where everyone was unselfconscious about wandering the house naked, she says: 'I've always been comfortable with nudity and I thought, "Well, it sounds like easy money, I'll give it a go."' Doing her books the other day, she found she had cleared $22,000 in the past six months.

But she says, almost apologetically, she still hasn't told her parents – which is why Dominica is not her real name. 'Not because I thought they'd crack the shits or throw me out of home, but mainly because I think they'd really worry about me.

'Maybe one day. I do think about it. We've always had a really open relationship and I've always been totally truthful about everything else, so it does conflict within me. There are times I want to tell them and there are times I'd rather let sleeping dogs lie.'

She has no illusions about society's attitudes to what she does. Recently she told an old school friend, whose reaction was 'Oh, Dom, I thought you were a feminist.'

And she is. But there's something about the job she finds empowering. 'I don't think it needs rationalising. If it works for you, that's cool. I don't think there's anything immoral about it, certainly. It's not hurting anyone. It's me and it's my decision.'

Even the double shows and hot vibes don't make her uncomfortable. 'It's not something I've agonised over. I guess I'm a very intellectual person, so what I think of as myself is up in my head, so I'm not really being violated.

'It's really a lifestyle. The only thing with me is that it's different from 95 per cent of the other girls out there. But I'm having fun and it's a good way to make good money very quickly … and the money is important. You wouldn't do this stuff for peanuts.'

Crystal stops and waits a few seconds before tapping on the hotel suite door. She concentrates, head back a little as if sniffing the wind. She is just a bit psychic, able to pick up on unseen signals. In 19 years of knocking on strange doors, never quite knowing what's on the other side, that's been a valuable gift.

Crystal has become attuned to her senses, able to feel if there's someone else in there who shouldn't be. She works each job to ensure she is always in control. Does the booking, and does it her way: listening carefully on the phone, getting a feel for the other's voice or if there's someone else in the background. Inside, she does a quick sensory recon, checking if anyone's hiding in a closet, say.

She never lets the men behind her. She's always focused on them, always looking at them, even in the sexual position, because you never know if they've got a weapon somewhere. She's only been wrong once, in Warrandyte in 1990. Somehow didn't notice the bars on the windows and was raped. But tonight nothing seems amiss. She puts on her best smile, knocks, and meets another very nice gentleman.

When she was 16, Crystal shocked a teacher by telling her that she wanted to be a call-girl. She was joking – in fact she'd considered becoming a nun – but looking back, suspects it must have been her *forte* all along. She has been an escort, on and off, since 1990, after getting into prostitution four years earlier to pay off a business debt.

She is 45 now and winding back – 'you have to look at the age limitations in this job' – and has diversified into a straight business as a masseuse, but still sees a few clients each week. Business is through word of mouth or her newspaper ad: 'A lady of quality. Private escort'. When gentlemen call she quotes them $160 an hour, asks what they're looking for, and provides an accurate description: 'I'm a tall, elegant blonde; five foot eight; size 10; 38-inch bust; blue eyes and middle 40s.'

When she began doing this, she says she sat down and worked out what men *really* wanted. 'Most – and I emphasise *most* – do prefer a nice lady, who smells good, looks good, talks nice, isn't drug-fucked, and has a genuine smile on her face.

'I'll always spend 15 minutes having a chat, making you feel comfortable, finding out what you do for work, whether you're tactile. I might put my hand on your knee, get you a coffee, might sit on a couch holding you. And then I'll say, "Would you like to go up for a massage?" It's more personal, more ladylike.'

But she always advises girls to stay out of the game. 'It does consume your life and there's a price you pay for everything you do. But it has its benefits too. If you're legit, pay your tax, you can give yourself a good education, raise your children well, buy a home. But too many girls don't have a goal or a time to get out. A lot shoot it up their arm, live with hoons and give it all to them.

'I've made my money work for me,' she says, sweeping an arm around the living room of her new $600,000 eastern suburbs home.

Crystal says she likes both the job and what she gets out of it. She meets a lot of interesting people and rubs shoulders with some powerful ones. She gets taken out to nice places and pampered. It's a bit of a buzz.

And then she has sex with a total stranger. Yes, she says, but you need to be able to switch off, to separate yourself from *doing the job*. 'I never do anything I don't want to, it's my choice, my body. I mean I know what I'm there for, but the actual sex act is really only a small period of the time. The rest of the job, whether it's two hours or five, I do a lot of talking. And I'm a good talker.

'Young girls today think they don't have to do anything for the dollar because they've got the looks, the nice figure, but they don't give themselves. That's my bread and butter. I give myself.'

The Beret Man wraps another layer of Gladwrap around Steffanie's naked, immobile body. He steps back, checking the effect, nods and takes another photo. Dressed all in black, grey pony-tail falling from beneath the beret, he moves back in, adds strips of duct tape. Takes another photo. Then another and another.

Mummified in cling-film, Steffanie keeps her eyes tightly shut. This isn't so bad. Later, when he gets the knife and fake blood or when he dresses in his military uniform and starts filming her, will be much worse. That's when she finds it so hard not to laugh.

This is Stef's part-time gig. Three or four hours every Monday afternoon, playing out women-in-peril scenarios for a series of fetish and bondage websites. She has been doing it for eight months, at $100 an hour, and though it was a little freaky at first, she's come to trust Beret Man. 'Now I don't really think about it much. I tell some of my friends about the stuff I see and they're like "What?" They're shocked, but nothing really shocks me any more. Not too much.'

She is 20, tall, big-breasted and bottle-blonde with perfect teeth displayed behind a ready smile. After school she tried a year at graphic design then another as a dental nurse, but hated it and quit. After she was laid off from her next job, part-time at Coles, she saw an ad for nude models and thought she'd give it a go, mainly for a stir. But the money was so good she kept going back. Now she works topless waitressing, even did her first strip the other week. She plans to start her own website, 'just fluffy stuff'.

'My family all know what I do and are fine with it,' she says. 'When I start my site, Mum sews, so she's going to help with the costumes, and Dad's an accountant, so he'll look after the money. My younger sister, she's like: it's fine, just don't tell her the details.

'It's just something that happened, but now I couldn't do a nine-to-five job, I'd be bored to death. Not after this stuff. It's too much fun, always something interesting going on.'

And the aficionados of her website adventures? 'I wouldn't want to meet any of the people who are looking at this, over in Germany or wherever, wouldn't want to know them. But I'll take their money.'

Mistress Saskia lets a long sigh escape as her slave disappears through the dungeon door. 'That,' she says, 'was bloody hopeless.'

It hadn't gone the way she wanted. She'd forgotten poor George was hard of hearing and the mask had only added to his deafness. So he couldn't follow her commands, lying on his back instead of his belly; not putting his wrists together to be tied; giving her that blank stare when he was forbidden to look at her at all. Worse, she'd had to yell.

She hates having to raise her voice at them. Much better to keep it soft, monotone and pleasant, which gets that really nice control thing happening: 'It's really quite evil, but niiiice. You can say the most evil things to them, tell them what terrible things you're going to do to them – but with a lot of love in your voice.'

Mistress Saskia loves her job, harshly ministering to a clientele of submissives, masochists, fetishists and bondage devotees at the Correction Centre in St David Street, Fitzroy, at $140 per half hour and $240 for the hour. 'But you can't be in this industry specifically for the money,' she says, 'or you'd go completely mad.'

She came to it after leaving her country town about 10 years ago and briefly drifting into brothel work. She'd been sexually abused as a girl and, though she didn't realise it at the time, thinks the work gave her back her 'sexual power'. But she didn't enjoy it and someone suggested she try BDSM – bondage, discipline and sado-masochism.

'I was just really natural at it, I think because I'm a creative person.' She trained under a dominatrix for eight months, has worked in chambers in New York and London, and is now one of the Correction Centre's most popular doms, with glowing customer testimonials – 'so caring throughout, yet so devilish at the same time!' – on its website.

There's a growing trend lately where people want to experience 'a different sexual lifestyle', erotic sessions with a bit of kink. But Mistress Saskia is old-school. 'I don't do sex. They don't touch me, I don't take my clothes off. It's very strict.'

She specialises in humiliation, discipline, torture and bondage with esoteric sub-specialties including fluid play, breath-training and equestrian and puppy training. 'I'm really interested with playing with people on this level. It's dark. Sometimes I'm the only person they tell their secrets to, their fantasies and fetishes, and I get to play with that.

'You're constantly thinking of ways to torture people. Everything's about power. You go to Bunnings or

Officeworks and suddenly everything's there. You know: paper clips! I can't walk into a supermarket kitchen section without thinking, "Hmm, what would that be good for?" And a hardware shop, wooo, it's heaven.'

But she knows what other people think. She's had them turn away, call her a prostitute, seen old girlfriends turn insecure when their partners are around 'as if I'm this sexual monster'. In fact she's in a 'vanilla relationship' – straight, no whips – and works part-time in a bar for 'balance'. Her mother knows what she does and, despite taking a year to get used to it, is now 'fine with the details'.

And, while she might be a sadist, don't think she's cruel. 'No, I'm soft,' she insists, a feline glint in her eyes. 'I'm a kitten.'

'Who wants to see tits?' A fingernails-on-blackboard voice chainsaws through the chatter in the chintz-decorated dining room above Swan Street, Richmond. 'C'mon, guys! Who … Wants … TITS!?'

The Irishmen on table 11 do. And the four suits-and-ties – manufacturer, management consultant and two accountants – certainly do. They're already blowing approval through their party hooters and digging in their wallets for twenties. When Maxine Fensom collects enough, her two waitresses will peel down their lace teddies and work the rest of the lunch topless.

It is an unusually quiet Friday at one of Maxine's Naughty Lunches, but Max works the room in her usual ringmistress mode: teasing, cajoling, gleefully abusive. Her patter is a mix of double entendre and flat-out crudity. She wears a black Chanel dress, cut low to display her pneumatic figure and a pair of black hoop earrings engraved with a diamantine boast: 'Sexy'. She has a mischievous face, waist length hair and the mouth of a dockworker – every third word an economical four letters. But it's all part of her *schtick*.

Since 1988, Maxine, 46, has managed to parlay experiences gained in a short, failed stint at psychiatric nursing, dance trouping and lingerie lunches and a flair for self-promotion into an impressive X-rated empire. She is Melbourne's most indefatigable entrepreneur of sex, running not only her lunches, but Maxine's Elite Strippers; Maxine's Escorts; Miss Nude Australia contests; Hookers and Deviates balls as well as importing a range of lingerie. All from an ever-ringing clutter of five mobile phones.

Max describes herself as a pornographer – 'just for a joke' – then says she wants to be accepted like anyone else. 'I'm just a nice, normal girl running a business and providing naked talent.'

Still, she has a clear eye for the realities of the skin trade. 'Sure, I think Melbourne people are adventurous and sexy,' she says. 'You can see they're obviously interested by the numbers who go to Sexpo or men's clubs. But I also think what they're offering is not sexy. The clubs aren't sexy at all – it's solitary, it's not fun and it's a bit sad.'

And a career span for strippers and escorts? 'Realistically, I think within five years you should be able to get in, be smart, make a stack of money and get out.'

Financial advisors offer to talk to her girls and she laughs. 'They're not interested, no way. They just want to buy a new dress.' They want to create a lifestyle, and it's a lifestyle that requires upkeep: porcelain teeth and breast implants that need to be redone in 10 years.

'And they do it. But, really, after you hit 30 or 35, what happens? Are you still going to have the pink talons and the peroxide hair, pumped-up lips and the big tits and look like a stereotype of Pammy Anderson?'

Deb Osmond totters on one high heel in Inkerman Street, St Kilda. Her other shoe is in her left hand because it's given her a nasty blister, which is one more thing you don't need in her game. She's pinked her hair with lipstick, and squeezed into a sensational black op-shop frock which reveals most of the big bright tattoo on her left boob. The bag slung over her other shoulder is bulging, a couple of beer bottles poking out. She's just finished a $100 job and the client, a regular, always likes a drink afterwards.

Now she's looking for a lift to Brunswick to score some speed.

Deb is 43 and turned her first trick not far from here, in a car outside the Gatwick Hotel, 30 years ago. She was a 13-year-old runaway who'd fallen in with some bad sorts and they forced her into it. Literally put a gun to her head. She still remembers the fella she did it with. He was a musician and kept his trumpet on the back seat of his car. 'God, I hated him, he was gross. And he was old, as old then as I am now.

'I didn't know a great deal about sex. I didn't know whether you got paid for it or if it was something you only did with your husband, because it wasn't talked about in our home.'

She'd been a pretty good kid until then, she says. 'I had an extremely good upbringing. Grew up in Middle Brighton and went to a ladies' college. No violence at home.' But her parents had separated and she couldn't cope, so she ran away.

The crims who turned her out were soon arrested, but she kept selling herself. 'I was still on the run and I thought I've got to survive, so I'm gunna keep working. But I'm not going to work for any other arsehole, and I never have.'

Deb still works the streets of St Kilda, still servicing clients in cars or hotel rooms, but has wound back, making just enough money to get by. 'That's the beauty of the street, you don't clock in, you don't clock out, you work when you want to and on who you want.'

It wasn't like that in the beginning. She got into the pills and then the smack and most of those days are a blur. But she was making thousands for a while. 'I got big tips 'cos I was so young – there's a lot of sick bastards out there.'

She gave up both heroin and the game when she had the first of her four kids and took a series of square jobs. She worked in a fish and chip shop, did spot welding, worked in supermarkets, assembled medical equipment and classified as a professional knitter, but came back when the family was struggling for money.

'I don't feel bad about it,' she says, 'because I don't think it's a degrading job. It's a job I enjoy. Most of my clients, regular clients, are also friends; I don't have a problem having sex with them. What I don't enjoy is other people's low opinions. A lot of upstanding citizens are two-faced, very nasty people. It's made me very bitter towards society as a whole.

'You get car loads of people driving past and calling us a slut. Obviously they didn't learn anything at school: we're whores, not sluts.'

These days, Deb pretty much sticks to herself. She doesn't have a circle of friends but doesn't have time to get lonely. She goes op-shopping, does arts and craft or just reads a book. She doesn't save her money. 'To what purpose? Because society says you save up and buy a house? I don't think so.'

She can't see retiring either. 'I could be 80 and still have clients. There might be someone out there who fancies old fanny.'

And to the old question, 'What's a nice girl like you ...' she quickly answers: 'Being as naughty as possible.'

And smiles, almost as if she really believes it.

Acknowledgments

Thanks are owed again to those who let us peep and pry into their lives of crime and justice, especially John Smallwood and Liz Gaynor; Tim and Kate McDonald; the members of the Alternate Jury; Ian Joblin; coppers like Brian Rix, Ron Iddles, Greg Hough; Robbo Robertson and Keg Keating and other members of the Newport Community Police; Mick the helpful burglar; and the revealing working girls, strippers and whip-crackers of 'What's a Nice Girl …?' Also to those who understood when we intruded on their grief, especially Lorraine Russell and Marion Wishart.

To our fellow journalists: Steve Butcher for his work on 'The War Within'; John Silvester for his help on 'The Police Killers' and 'Prime Suspect'; Peter Gregory for his input on 'The Police Killers' and 'The Batsman and The Bouncer'. Also to the other members of the *Age* Law and Justice team, Andrea Petrie, Stephen Moynihan, Julia Medew, Selma Milovanovic and Dan Oakes, and to Andrew Rule for his encouragement.

To our photographer colleagues, particularly Craig 'Wombat' Abraham, Craig 'the Toe' Sillitoe, Simon Schluter and Jason South.

To our pain-free editor Ali Orman and senior editor Patrick Mangan.

And, of course, to Jeni, Mick and H; Anne, Erin and Gemma.